American Headway 5

THE WORLD'S MOST TRUSTED ENGLISH COURSE

SECOND EDITION

Liz and John Soars

OXFORD
UNIVERSITY PRESS

Scope and Sequence

SKILLS DEVELOPMENT

LISTENING	SPEAKING	EVERYDAY ENGLISH	WRITING
The American Dream – an interview with Jeong Kim p. 10 National stereotypes p. 11	Discussion – immigrants and emigration p. 7 Discussion – nationality stereotypes p. 11	British and American English *We've got a small **flat**.* *We **have** a small **apartment**.* p. 12	Formal and informal letters p. 113
"The Importance of Being Earnest" – a scene from Oscar Wilde's play p. 19	Information gap – finding out about Iris Murdoch p. 14 Acting out a scene from a play p. 19	Sounds and spelling – a poem about pronunciation *tough, bought, cough, dough* p. 22 Homophones *through, threw* p. 22	Storytelling p. 114
An interview with Anita Roddick, founder of *The Body Shop* p. 30	Simulation – planning an advertising campaign p. 31 Discussion – the role of advertising p. 31	Word linking and intrusive sounds *English is an international language* *blue eyes* /w/ *my office* p. 32 /y/	A business report p. 116
An interview with Hollywood star Drew Barrymore p. 40	Maze – how to become a celebrity p. 40	Tags and replies *"I love your movies." "Oh, you do, do you?"* *You haven't seen my car keys, have you?* p. 42	Expressing a personal opinion p. 118
A romantic meeting – another couple tells the story of how they met p. 44 When love lasts forever – an interview with 102-year-old Olive Hodges p. 49	Discussion – do you believe in fate? p. 44	Getting emotional Sounding anxious, grateful, etc. *Get this heap of old metal out of my driveway! Now!* *You mean more to me than words could ever say.* p. 50	Discussing pros and cons p. 119
An interview with foreign correspondent Simon Winchester p. 57	Discussion – how television reports the news p. 57	Responding to news *"Guess what! I won $5 million."* *"You're kidding!"* p. 58 Sounding sarcastic *"Pete. I wrecked your car. Sorry."* *"Great. That's all I needed. Thank you very much."* p. 58	A letter to a newspaper p. 120

SKILLS DEVELOPMENT

LISTENING	SPEAKING	EVERYDAY ENGLISH	WRITING
Words of wisdom – ten people talk about advice they have been given in their lives p. 64	Prediction game – Dilemma! How well do you know your classmates? p. 63 Discussion – words of wisdom p. 64	Breaking the rules of English *"Ending a sentence with a preposition is something up with which I will not put."* p. 66	Describing a personal experience p. 122
An interview with American painter Joe Downing p. 68	Discussion – appreciating art p. 67 Discussion – my favorite work of art p. 69	Softening the message *Can you help me? I was wondering if you could possibly help me?* p. 76	Reviewing a movie or book p. 123
An eyewitness account – Justin Baines p. 80 Peace and goodwill – the Christmas truce of 1914 p. 83	Discussion – an important event in your life p. 81 Discussion – can enemies become friends in wartime? p. 83	Telling jokes *"Why is an archaeologist never successful?" "Because his career lies in ruins."* p. 86	Personal profile p. 124
The cycler and the gymnast – jigsaw conversations about Nastia Liukin and Lance Armstrong p. 92	Discussion – are we obsessed by sports? p. 88 Quiz – how healthy and fit are you? p. 93	Clichés *Easier said than done. At the end of the day, it's your decision.* p. 94	Entering a competition p. 125
Far-flung spots – people talk about places they have visited p. 100 A meeting in the desert – an unusual story about a train trip in the far west of China p. 101	Which island would you like to visit? p. 96 Retelling a story p. 101	What on earth! *earth, ground, soil* p. 104 Everyday expressions *I had to move heaven and earth to get here.* p. 104	Describing a trip p. 126
Do you believe in miracles? – a radio program about a visit to Lourdes p. 110	Discussion – talking about time p. 107 Discussion – can miracles exist in the age of science? p. 110	Euphemisms *a disadvantaged senior citizen, pass away* p. 112	Bringing a biography to life p. 127

OXFORD
UNIVERSITY PRESS

198 Madison Avenue
New York, NY 10016 USA

Great Clarendon Street, Oxford ox2 6dp UK

Oxford University Press is a department of the
University of Oxford. It furthers the University's
objective of excellence in research, scholarship,
and education by publishing worldwide in

Oxford New York

Auckland Cape Town Dar es Salaam
Hong Kong Karachi Kuala Lumpur Madrid
Melbourne Mexico City Nairobi New Delhi
Shanghai Taipei Toronto

With offices in

Argentina Austria Brazil Chile Czech Republic
France Greece Guatemala Hungary Italy Japan
Poland Portugal Singapore South Korea
Switzerland Thailand Turkey Ukraine Vietnam

OXFORD and OXFORD ENGLISH are registered
trademarks of Oxford University Press in
certain countries.

© Oxford University Press 2010

Database right Oxford University Press (maker)

Editorial Director: Laura Pearson
Publishing Manager: Erik Gundersen
Managing Editor: Louisa van Houten
Development Editor: Jonathan Bucchino
Design Director: Susan Sanguily
Design Manager: Maj-Britt Hagsted
Associate Design Manager: Michael Steinhofer
Senior Image Editor: Trisha Masterson
Image Editor: Robin Fadool
Design Production Manager: Stephen White
Senior Manufacturing Controller: Eve Wong
Production Coordinator: Hila Ratzabi

ISBN 978-0-19-472921-5 STUDENT BOOK
WITH MULTI-ROM (PACK)

ISBN 978-0-19-472922-2 STUDENT BOOK
(PACK COMPONENT)

ISBN 978-0-19-472885-0 MULTI-ROM
(PACK COMPONENT)

Printed in China

This book is printed on paper from certified
and well-managed sources.

10 9 8 7 6 5 4 3 2 1

ACKNOWLEDGEMENTS

*The authors and publisher are grateful to those who have given permission
to reproduce the following extracts and adaptations of copyright material:*

Illustrations by:

p8 c 2003 Frank Cotham (All rights reserved)/The Cartoon Bank; p9
Fran/www.CartoonStock.com (synonyms); p26 Harley Schwadron/
www.CartoonStock.com (meeting); p29 Arnaldo Almeida/www.
CartoonStock.com (The Boss); p31 Rose Hardy; p32 Geoff
Waterhouse/Just For Laffs (leaving); p37 Leo Cullum/The Cartoon

Bank; p39 Ali Pellatt (couple); p39 Ali Pellatt (background); p48/49
Mike Moran; p53 Barb Bastian (article); p54 Barb Bastian (article);
p56 John Morris/www.CartoonStock.com; p58 Geoff Waterhouse/Just
For Laffs (sarcasm); p60 Oxford Designers & Illustrators (pig); p62
Mike Twohy/The Cartoon Bank; p65 Lewis Carroll Alice's Adventures
in Wonderland images created by Sir John Tenniel and coloured by
Diz Wallis/Macmillan Publishers Ltd.; p76 Geoff Waterhouse/Just
For Laffs (lion); p76 Geoff Waterhouse/Just For Laffs (monk); p76
Geoff Waterhouse/Just For Laffs (wedding); p76 Geoff Waterhouse/
Just For Laffs (dog); p82 Geoff Waterhouse/Just For Laffs ; p84 Mike
Baldwin/www.CartoonStock.com; p85 Alan De la Nougerede/www.
CartoonStock.com; p86 Geoff Waterhouse/Just For Laffs (knights); p86
Geoff Waterhouse/Just For Laffs (thief); p86 Geoff Waterhouse/Just
For Laffs (heading); p86 Geoff Waterhouse/Just For Laffs (lawyers); p86
Geoff Waterhouse/Just For Laffs (artist); p90 Kes/www.CartoonStock.
com; p91 Darren Hopes; p93 Carroll Zahn/www.CartoonStock.com;
p94 Geoff Waterhouse/Just For Laffs (therapy); p94 Geoff Waterhouse/
Just For Laffs (wanted); p94 Geoff Waterhouse/Just For Laffs (leaving);
p101 Jamel Akib (conductor); p101 Jamel Akib (train); p101 Jamel
Akib (dreaming); p111 Stan Waling/www.CartoonStock.com; p112
Aaron Bacall/The Cartoon Bank (dehired); p112 Bernard Shoenbaum/
The Cartoon Bank (stimulus); p117 Mark Duffin.

Commissioned photography:

p13 MM Studios (books); p14 MM Studios (books); p21 MM Studios
(book); p33 MM Studios (sunglasses, camera).

Cover Stock Photography:

Pixtal/AGE Fotostock: (top left); Photo Alto/Jupiter Images: James
Hardy (top center); dbimages/Alamy: Roy Johnson (top right);
PhotoAlto/AGE Fotostock/: Vincent Hazat (left center); Masterfile:
(right center); Masterfile: (bottom right); ASP/Getty Images: Kirstin
Scholtz (bottom left).

Stock Photography:

p3 Hulton/APA/Archive Photos/Getty Images (Capone); p3 Rex Features
(Mother Teresa); p3 Archivo Iconigrafico, S.A./Corbis UK Ltd. (Van Gogh);
p3 Bettmann/Corbis UK Ltd. (Marx); p3 Qi Heng/Xinhua Press/Corbis UK
Ltd. (Yao Ming); p3 Lyn Goldsmith/Corbis UK Ltd. (Marley); p3 ABACA
Press/Press Association Images (Kidman); p3 Rich Pedroncelli/Associated
Press/Press Association Images (Schwarzenegger); p4 Andy Caulfield/Getty
Images; p5 Corbis UK Ltd. (medical); p5 Bettmann/Corbis UK Ltd. (queue);
p5 Bettmann/Corbis UK Ltd. (Ellis Island); p6 New York Public Library ID
801540/Art Resource (girl); p6 Corbis UK Ltd. (family); p7 Hulton Archive/
Getty Images; p9 Sean Sullivan/Getty Images (snowboarding); p10 Scott
Lituchy/Star Ledger/Corbis UK Ltd.; p11 Hiroshi Kutomi/Axiom (Japanese);
p11 Imagestate Media Partners Limited/Impact Photos/Alamy (map); p11
Chris Caldicott/Axiom (women); p11 David Constantine/Axiom (drinking);
p11 Atlantide S.N.C./Powerstock Superstock (men); p11 Yadid Levy/
Powerstock Superstock (game); p12 Daimler Chrysler UK Limited
(Chrysler); p12 BMW (Mini); p13 J.R.R.Tolkien, The Lord of the Rings, Part
I, The Fellowship of the Ring, 2002/Harper Collins Publishers (Tolkien); p13
Laurie Lee, Cider with Rosie , Vintage Classics, 2002/Harper Collins
Publishers (Lee); p13 John Grisham, A Time to Kill , Arrow, 1992/Harper
Collins Publishers (Grisham); p13 The Lost Continent:Travels in Small-town
America. Bill Bryson , Black Swan, 1999/Transworld Publishers Ltd (Bryson);
p14 Iris Murdoch, Under the Net, Vintage Classics, 2202; The Sea The Sea,
Vintage Classics, 1999/Harper Collins Publishers (Under the Net); p14
Archives du 7eme Art/Photo12.com (Kate Winslet); p15 Peter Nicholls/News
International Syndication; p16 Nina Rangoy/Camera Press; p18 Bettmann/
Corbis UK Ltd. (photo); p18 Bettmann/Corbis UK Ltd. (sketch); p19 Donald
Cooper/Photostage; p20 Paramount Collection/Kobal Collection; p21
PhotoDisc/Oxford University Press (woman); p23 McDonald's Restaurants
Ltd (logo); p23 Nike UK Ltd (logo); p23 Singapore Air (logo); p23 Toyota
(GB) PLC (logo); p23 "Shell" emblem reproduced with the permission of
Shell International Petroleum Company Limited (Shell Property only)/"The
trademarks used in these materials are reproduced with the permission of the
trademark owners."/Shell (logo); p23 Apple Computer Inc. (logo); p23 The
Body Shop (logo); p23 Mercedes-Benz (UK Ltd. (logo); p23 ADIDAS AG
(logo); p24 Ron Giling/Still Pictures; p25 Stock Connection Inc/Alamy
(port); p25 David Hoffman Photo Library/Alamy (landfill); p25 Ian
Mckinnell/Getty Images (supermarket); p25 Howard Kingsnorth/Getty
Images (girl); p26 Ted Russell/Getty Images (press); p27 David Sacks/Getty
Images (John); p27 John Lamb/Getty Images (David); p29 Oxford University
Press (interview); p30 The Body Shop (shop, products); p30 Johnny Green/
Press Association Images (Roddick); p32 Romilly Lockyer/Getty Images
(telephone); p33 Laforet Vincent/Sygma/Corbis UK Ltd. (Oscar); p33
PhotoDisc/Oxford University Press (dollars); p33 Thinkstock/Getty Images
(limousine); p33 Rex Features (shoe); p33 Rubberball Productions/Getty
Images (bouncer); p33 Zooid Pictures (magazines); p33 PhotoDisc/Oxford
University Press (stars); p34 Scott Barbour/Getty Images (stars); p35 John Lamb/
Getty Images; p36 ABACA Press/Press Association Images (Cher); p36
Reents/Siemoneit/Sygma/Corbis UK Ltd. (DiCaprio); p36 Ian Daniels/Rex
Features (Barrymore); p36 Jonathan Blair/Corbis UK Ltd. (Redford); p36
Dave Pickoff/Associated Press/Press Association Images (Kissinger); p36
Masatoshi Okauchi/Rex Features (Depp); p38 Deutsche Press-Argentur/Press
Association Images; p41 Associated Press/Press Association Images (family);
p41 John Spellman/Retna Ltd./Corbis UK Ltd. (premier); p41 Everett
Collection/Rex Features (Spielberg); p41 Archives du 7eme Art/Photo12.com
(helmet); p41 Ronald Grant Archive (couple); p42 Oxford University Press
(late); p42 Pablo Corral V/Corbis UK Ltd. (restaurant); p42 Oxford
University Press (driving); p43 Steve Joester/Getty Images (mirror); p43
Patrick Molnar/Getty Images (father); p43 Photodisc/Barbara Penoyar/
Oxford University Press (twins); p43 Microzoa/Getty Images (cat); p43

Yellow Dog Productions/Getty Images (fans); p43 PhotoDisc/Oxford
University Press (wedding); p43 Blend Images/Alamy (couple); p43 Sean
Murphy/Getty Images (older); p43 Amy Harris/iStockphoto (Buddha); p45
Elle Magazine; p46 Elle Magazine; p47 Craig Lovell/Eagle Visions
Photography/Alamy; p49 Professor John Hodges (couple); p49 Professor
John Hodges (girl); p50 Stuart McClymont/Getty Images; p52 From The
New York Times, © 16th Juanary 2009. The New York Times All rights
reserved. Used by permission and protected by the Copyright Laws of the
United States. The printing, copying, redistribution, or retransmission of
Material without express written permission is prohibited (Times); p53 Eric
Thayer/Reuters/Corbis UK Ltd. (plane); p54 Gary Hershorn/Reuters/Corbis
UK Ltd. (plane); p57 Gamma Presse Images © Enrico Dagnino/Black Star/
Katz Pictures (desert); p57 EPA/Press Association Images (interview); p58
Greg Ceo/Getty Images (laughing); p59 Popperfoto/Alamy (Confucius); p59
Chris Bland/Eye Ubiquitous/Corbis UK Ltd. (Buddha); p59 Bettmann/
Corbis UK Ltd. (Parker); p59 Gianni Dagli Orti/Corbis UK Ltd. (Socrates);
p59 Bettmann/Corbis UK Ltd. (King); p59 Bettmann/Corbis UK Ltd.
(Austen); p59 Francis G. Mayer/Corbis UK Ltd. (Washington); p60 Mike
Robinson/BBC Photograph Library (Keane); p64 Cornell Capa/Magnum
Photos; p67 Georges Seurat, French 1859-1891, A Sunday on La Grande
Jatte, 1884, 1884-86, oil on canvas, 207.6 x 308 cm, Helen Bartlett Memorial
Collection, 1926.224/Art Institute of Chicago (Seurat); p67 Kobal Collection
(Casablanca); p67 Steve McCurry/Magnum Photos (Afghan girl); p67
Draped Reclining Mother and Baby 1983 (LH822) The Henry Moore
Foundation. Bronze, length 265.5 cm/Harper Collins Publishers (Moore);
p67 Rafal Tomasik (station); p67 Ace Gallery Institute of Contemporary Art
(Donovan); p68 Joe Downing; p68/69 Photo Gallas/Le Thor/Joe Downing;
p69 Private Collection/Andre Morain Collection/Vidonne Mauhamadamy
Paris/Joe Downing (orange); p69 Private Colllection/Joe Downing (blue);
p70 Jim Cornfield/Corbis UK Ltd. (hand); p70 Charly Franklin/Getty Images
(crossroads); p70 Ralph H Wetmore II/Getty Images (lightning); p70 John
Wilkes/Getty Images (waterfall); p71 Rex Features; p72 Walt Disney
Attractions; p73 Bettmann/Corbis UK Ltd. (wife); p73 Walt Disney
Attractions (desk); p73 Camera Press (Disneyland); p75 Richard Levine/
Alamy; p77 Keren Su/Corbis UK Ltd. (China); p77 Gianni Dagli Orti/Corbis
UK Ltd. (Mona Lisa); p77 Hulton Archive/Getty Images (bomb); p77 Chris
Collins/Corbis UK Ltd. (New York); p77 Mary Evans Picture Library
(Darwin); p77 Rex Features (Berlin); p77 Photo Scala, Florence (Greece); p77
Rex Features (Panama); p78/79 Bridgeman Art Library (Vesuvius); p78/79
Bettmann/Corbis UK Ltd. (figures); p79 Bridgeman Art Library (Vesuvius);
p79 Schenectady Museum; Hall of Electrical History Foundation/Corbis UK
Ltd. (Marconi); p79 Corbis UK Ltd. (sea); p79 Bettmann/Corbis UK Ltd.
(Titanic); p80 Bettmann/Corbis UK Ltd. (Titanic); p80 Oxford University
Press (sea); p80/81 NASA/Neil Armstrong/Corbis UK Ltd. (Aldrin); p80/81
John Sandford/Science Photo Library (moon); p81 fStop/Alamy; p83
Bettmann/Corbis UK Ltd. (trenches); p83 Imperial War Museum (soldiers);
p87 Clive Brunskill/Getty Images (canoeing); p87 Glyn Kirk/Action Plus
(racing); p87 Ryan McVay/Getty Images (rockclimbing); p87 Billy Stickland/
Getty Images (wrestling); p87 Jeff Hunter/Getty Images (scuba); p87 EPA/
Powerstock Superstock (skateboarding); p87 David Wilkinson/Getty Images
(football); p87 Glyn Kirk/Action Plus (javelin); p87 John Lamb/Getty Images
(yoga); p88 Mario Tama/Getty Images; p89 Mario Tama/Getty Images
(marathon); p89 Paul Grover/Rex Features (crowd); p92 Peter Dejong/
Associated Press/Press Association Images (trophy); p92 Giuliano Bevilacqua/
Rex Features (Liukin); p92 Chris Wallis/Rex Features (bicycle); p92 Sipa
Press/Rex Features (jumping); p95 G. Schuster/Zefa; p96 Bryan & Cherry
Alexander (Greenland); p96 Richard Wareham/Zefa (Zanzibar); p96 Manuel
Bauer/Rex Features (Tristan da Cunha); p97 Bryan & Cherry Alexander
(woman); p97 Bryan & Cherry Alexander (plane); p97 Bryan & Cherry
Alexander (town); p98 Stanley Gibbons (stamps); p98 Manuel Bauer/Rex
Features (man); p98 David Robinson (aerial); p98 Manuel Bauer/Rex
Features (house); p99 Dave G. Houser/Corbis UK Ltd. (beach); p99 Michael
S. Lewis/Corbis UK Ltd. (child); p99 Bojan Brecelj/Corbis UK Ltd. (man);
p100 PhotoDisc/Oxford University Press; p101 Simon Wichester
(Winchester); p102 Bettmann/Corbis UK Ltd.; p102/103 Jon Arnold Images
Ltd/Alamy; p104 Joe McBride/Getty Images; p105 Musees Royaux des
Beaux-Arts, Brussels/akg-images; p106 Gary Buss/Taxi/Getty Images
(spring); p106 Gary Buss/Taxi/Getty Images (summer); p106 Gary Buss/
Taxi/Getty Images (winter); p106 Gary Buss/Taxi/Getty Images (autumn);
p108 Oxford University Press; p109 J.Bryson/Sygma/Corbis UK Ltd. (Dali);
p109 The Persistence of Memory, 1931, The Museum of Modern Art, New
York. c Salvador Dali, Gala-Salvador Dali Foundation, DACS, London 2003/
Photo Scala, Florence (painting); p109 Bettmann/Corbis UK Ltd. (Gala);
p109 Bettmann/Corbis UK Ltd. (easel); p110 Hulton Archive/Getty Images
(painting); p110 Hulton Archive/Getty Images (St Bernadette); p110 Rex
Features (grotto); p110 Rex Features (pilgrims); p115 PhotoDisc/Oxford
University Press; p116 Tina Rencelj/iStockphoto; p118 Oxford University
Press; p121 iStockphoto; p122 Frank Vetere/Alamy; p123 Archives du 7eme
Art/Photo12.com; p124 Oxford University Press; p125 PhotoDisc/Oxford
University Press; p126 Cesar Lucas Abreu/Getty Images;

1 This land is your land!

STARTER

1 Why are these people famous? What do they have in common? Discuss with a partner, then with the class.

1 Al Capone

2 Mother Teresa

3 Van Gogh

4 Karl Marx

5 Yao Ming

6 Bob Marley

7 Nicole Kidman

8 Arnold Schwarzenegger

2 Match each person with their country of birth and the country they died in or live in now.

Australia   Austria   **China**   England   **France**   Germany

India   **Italy**   Jamaica   **Macedonia**   the Netherlands   the United States

3 Do you know why any of these people emigrated?

Unit 1 · This land is your land!   3

1 Look at the photo. What things can you identify? What is their significance?

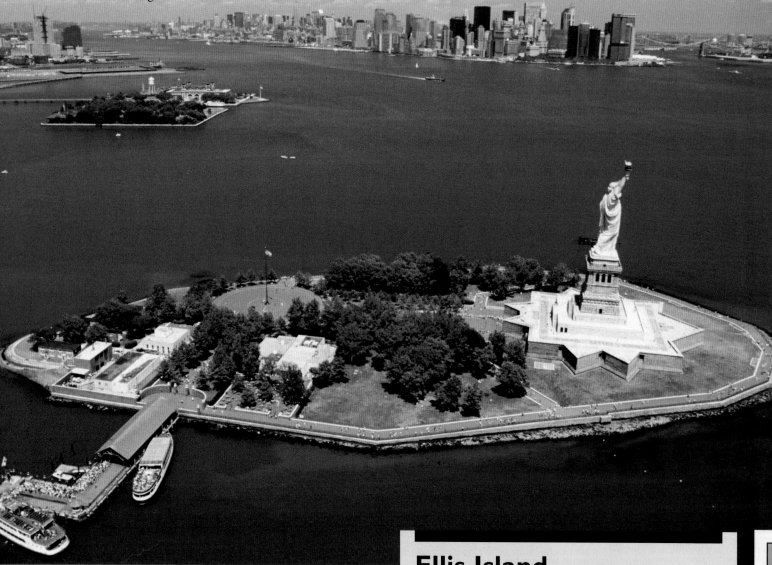

2 Read the introduction to Ellis Island. Choose the numbers you think are correct. Then answer the questions.

   1. Check the numbers with your teacher. Do any surprise you?

   2. Which countries do you think the immigrants came from?

   3. Why is Ellis Island a symbol of "the American dream"?

Ellis Island is a symbol of the U.S.'s immigrant heritage. For more than six decades – 1892 to 1954 – this island, about one mile southwest of New York City, saw an estimated (1) 5 / 7 / 12 million immigrants pass through it. Today their descendants account for almost (2) 10 / 20 / 40 percent of the population of the United States. During peak periods, as many as (3) 500 / 2,000 / 5,000 people each day were checked and questioned. Ellis Island, like its neighbor the Statue of Liberty, is a symbol of the American dream of freedom and opportunity. (background: Ellis Island; foreground: Liberty Island)

3 Read an excerpt from the British writer and journalist H.G. Wells. Use a dictionary if necessary.

Answer the questions.

1. Why does Wells call Ellis Island "this filter of immigrant humanity"?
2. What words and images does Wells use to illustrate the huge numbers of people?
3. What do you learn about the way the people were processed?
4. How would you answer Wells' final question? What has it all amounted to?

Medical Examination, Ellis Island 1910

TALES FROM ELLIS ISLAND

H.G. Wells 1907

I VISITED ELLIS ISLAND YESTERDAY. It chanced to be a good day for my purpose. For the first time in its history this filter of immigrant humanity has this week proved inadequate to the demand upon it. It was choked with twenty thousand or so from Ireland, and Poland, and Italy, and Syria, and Finland, and Albania. Men, women, children, dirt, and bags together. All day long, the long procession files, step by step, bearing bundles and trunks and boxes, past this examiner and that, past the quick, alert medical officers, and the clerks. It is a daily procession that would stretch over three miles, that in any week in the year could put a cordon of close-marching people round London or New York, that could populate a new Boston. What in a century will it all amount to?

Ellis Island 1917

4 Read about some individual immigrants. Work in three groups.

Group A Read about the Russian girl on page 6.
Group B Read about the German boy on page 6.
Group C Read about the Polish baby on page 7.

Answer the questions.

1. Who is telling the story?
2. What is the problem?
3. What is the role of the commissioners? How do they treat the immigrants?
4. What do you learn about the families and background of the immigrants?
5. Is there a happy ending?

5 Find partners from the other two groups. Compare the three stories, using your answers to Exercise 4.

A RUSSIAN GIRL

AGE 20

A HANDSOME, CLEAR-EYED RUSSIAN GIRL of about twenty-years, the daughter of a farmer comes in and sits down before us. She is clean and intelligent looking. She nervously clasps and unclasps her hands and the tears are welling in her eyes.

"That girl," says one commissioner, "is an interesting and puzzling case. Her father is a farmer in moderate circumstances. A young man with whom she grew up, the son of a neighbor, came here two years ago, and last year wrote to her father that the girl could come over and he would marry her. So she came, alone. But the prospective bridegroom didn't show up. I wrote to him – he lives somewhere in New Jersey – and last week he appeared and looked her over. Finally he said he'd changed his mind. He wasn't sure whether he wanted to marry her or not. Naturally her pride was somewhat wounded. She says she doesn't want to go back to be laughed at by her family, and I can't let her land. So everything is at a standstill. She could work, look at her strong arms! A nice girl, too. Well, I don't know what to do. You don't know any lady who wants a servant, do you? No? Well, I just don't know what to do with her."

He turns again to the girl.

"Are you willing to marry Peter if he comes again?"

The girl nods and says, "I am," the tears brimming over.

"Well, I'll write to the fellow again and tell him he's a fool. He'll never have such a chance again."

William Williams Papers, Ellis Island Commissioner, March 1910

B GERMAN BOY

AGE 13

THEY ALSO QUESTIONED PEOPLE ON literacy. My uncle called me aside.

He said, "Your mother doesn't know how to read." I said, "That's all right."

For the reading you faced what they called the commissioners – like judges on a bench. I was surrounded by my aunt and uncle and this other uncle who's a pharmacist – my mother was in the center. They said she would have to take a test of reading.

So one uncle said, "She can't speak English."

A commissioner said, "We know that. We will give her a prayer book."

The night they said this, I knew that she couldn't do that and we would be in trouble. Well, they opened up a prayer book. There was a certain passage there they had you read. I looked at it and I saw right away what it was. I quickly studied it – I knew the whole paragraph. Then I got underneath the two of them there – I was very small – and I told her the words in Yiddish very softly. I had memorized the lines and I said them quietly and she said them louder so the commissioner could hear it. And that served the purpose. She looked at it and it sounded as if she was reading it, but I was doing the talking underneath.

Arnold Weiss, 1921

POLISH BABY
AGE 0

THE POLISH WIFE OF A Pennsylvania coal miner, both admitted a year before, had gone back suddenly to Poland to visit her old father, who had taken sick and might soon die. The visit over, she returned to America. She would be admitted at once, for little visits do not count against quotas. Her husband was at Ellis Island, waiting for her. We told him everything would be all right, but he still looked extremely nervous. Then the ship came in, the *Lapland* of the Red Star line, from Antwerp, and we found out why he was so nervous. On the day before the ship made port, out on the high seas, a baby had been born to the returning mother. Mother and child were both doing well in the Ellis Island hospital, everyone was delighted, until the inspector admitted the mother, but excluded the baby.

"Why?" asked the father, trembling.

"Polish quota exhausted," pronounced the helpless inspector.

They brought the case to me. Deport the baby? I couldn't. But somebody had to act quickly, for the mother was not doing well under the idea that her baby would soon be taken from her.

"The baby was not born in Poland," I ruled, "but on a British ship. She is chargeable to the British quota. The deck of a British ship is British soil."

"British quota was exhausted yesterday," replied the inspector. That was a blow. But I had another shot.

"Come to think of it," I remarked, "the *Lapland* hails from Antwerp. That's in Belgium.

The baby is Belgian. Use the Belgian quota."

"Belgian quota ran out a week ago," said the inspector. I was stumped.

"Oh, look here," I began again. "I've got it! It is clear to me that the mother was hurrying back, so the baby would be born here and be a native-born American citizen. No immigrant business at all. This baby had the intention to be born in America, only the ship was a day late and that upset everything. And – under the law – the baby, by intention, was born in America. It is an American baby – no baby Pole at all, no British, no Belgian – just a good American baby. That's the way I rule!"

Henry Curran, Ellis Island Commissioner, 1922–26

Vocabulary work

6 Find the words or phrases in your text that have similar meanings to these phrases. Explain them to your partners from the other groups.

Text A
1. plays nervously with her hands
2. her eyes are filling with tears
3. her pride was hurt
4. no progress can be made
5. she finally starts to cry

Text B
1. took me away from the group
2. stood in front of
3. particular
4. learned … by heart
5. worked well

Text C
1. shaking slightly
2. a big disappointment
3. I made another attempt
4. comes from
5. unable to think of any answer at all

What do you think?

• Read and comment on these quotes.

1. *"No country has received a more diverse variety of immigrants than the United States."*
   Do you think this is true? What other countries have received great numbers of immigrants? From where?

2. *"Each successive group of arrivals, however, is viewed as less desirable than their predecessors."*
   How do people generally react to immigrants? Why do you think they react like this?

• What's the difference between … ?

a refugee   an undocumented worker

an asylum seeker   an immigrant

Are any of these groups in the news at the moment?

• Do you have many immigrants in your country? Which countries do they come from? Do you know of any that have become famous and/or successful?

• What causes people to emigrate? Is there any country you would like to emigrate to? Why?

LANGUAGE FOCUS
Avoiding repetition

There are several ways to avoid repeating words or phrases.

1 Leaving words out
The girl nods and says "I am . . ." (= I am willing to marry Peter.)

What words have been omitted in these sentences?
She told me to clean up, but I already had.
Frank won the match. I didn't think he would.
A present for me? How nice. You shouldn't have.

2 Reduced infinitives
Just *to* can be used instead of the whole infinitive when the meaning is clear from the context. Which words are omitted after *to* at the end of these sentences?
"Your mother doesn't know how to read." I said, "That's right. She never learned to."

They said she had to take a test for reading. So one uncle said, "Does she have to?"

3 Synonyms in context
bags . . . bundles . . . trunks . . . boxes
told her softly . . . said quietly

Think of another word for these words.

| huge | rich | kill | injure | argument |

▶▶▶ **Grammar Reference p. 143**

Leaving words out

1 Complete the sentences with an auxiliary verb or a modal verb. Make the verb form negative where necessary.

1. I tried to fix my car, but I __couldn't__ . I didn't have the right tools.

2. "You look awful. Why don't you see a doctor?"
   "I _____. He just told me to take it easy."

3. "It's a long trip. Be careful driving."
   "Don't worry. We _____."

4. I met your sister last night. She thought we'd met before, but we _____.

5. "Have you read this report?"
   "No, I _____, but I _____."

6. The weather forecast said that it might rain this afternoon. If it _____, we'll have to cancel our tennis match.

7. My car's being repaired at the moment. If it _____, I'd give you a ride. Sorry.

8. I'm so glad you told Sue exactly what you thought of her, because if you _____, I certainly _____!

9. I got that job I applied for, so I was thrilled. I really didn't think I _____.

10. "Come on, John! It's time to get up!"
    "I _____! I'll be down in a second."

11. "I think I'll give Bob a phone call."
    "You _____. You haven't been in touch with him for ages."

12. I went to a party last night, but I wish I _____. It was awful.

13. My husband insists on doing all the cooking, but I wish he *didn't* – it's inedible!

14. "Aren't you going to Colorado for your vacation?"
    "Well, we *will*, but we're still not sure."

15. "Andy got upset at the baseball game and started insulting everyone."
    "He _____! That's so typical. He's always doing that."

CD1 2 Listen and check. Practice with a partner.

2 Ask questions and try to find things that you have in common with other students in the class.

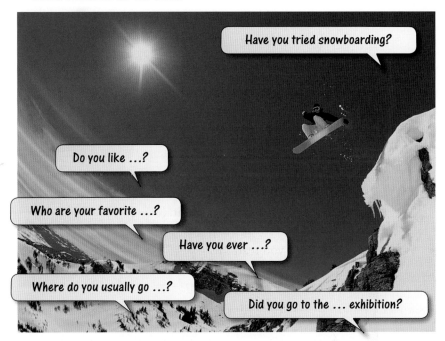

Have you tried snowboarding?

Do you like ...?

Who are your favorite ...?

Have you ever ...?

Where do you usually go ...?

Did you go to the ... exhibition?

3 Tell the class what you found out, using some of these expressions.

Things in common	Things different
Juan's been to Brazil, and **so have I.**	He's tried snowboarding, **but I haven't.**
He likes jazz, and **I do, too.**	He comes from a big family, **but I don't.**
He doesn't eat meat, and **neither do I.**	He didn't see the movie, **but I did.**
He isn't married, **nor am I.**	He hasn't been to Paris. **I have, though.**
He can't drive, and **I can't, either.**	

Reduced infinitives

4 Write the responses, using the verb in parentheses and a reduced infinitive.

1. **A** Can you come over for dinner tonight?
   B _Thanks very much. I'd love to._ (love)

2. **A** Did you mail my letter?
   B _____ (forget)

3. **A** I can't take you to the airport after all. Sorry.
   B _____ (agree)

4. **A** Was John surprised when he won?
   B _____ (not expect)

5. **A** Why did you slam the door in my face?
   B _____ (not mean)

6. **A** You'll be able to enjoy yourself when you're finished with your exams.
   B _____ (intend)

CD1 3 Listen and compare your answers.

Synonyms in context

5 Complete the sentences with a synonym of the word in *italics*. Change the part of speech where necessary, as in the first example.

1. I don't *trust* this government. I have no ___faith___ in them whatsoever.

2. She is not only a *skilled* painter, she is also a(n) _____ piano player.

3. You've managed to *persuade* me. Your argument is very _____.

4. Advertisements are not allowed to *lie*, but they _____ us in subtle ways.

5. Chess is a game of *tactics*. You have to plan your _____ well in advance.

6. The doctor read my notes *carefully*, then gave me a(n) _____ examination.

7. He has an *annoying* habit of always being late. It really _____ me.

8. It's *very important* that you don't tell anyone. In fact, it's _____.

9. Skiing can be *dangerous*, but I like to take a few _____.

10. She wasn't *scared* at all by the dog, but I was _____.

6 Find synonyms, or near synonyms, for these words. Write sentences to illustrate their differences in meaning.

- enemy
- love
- talk
- friend
- hate
- laugh

An enemy is who you're fighting against in a war.
A business wants to do better than its competitors.
We are rivals in love, but opponents in games.

"Sometimes, from time to time, now and again, occasionally, at times I wish I'd never been given this Thesaurus."

LISTENING AND SPEAKING
The American dream

1 What does the title *The American dream* mean to you? Can you think of any people for whom the dream has come true?

2 Read the excerpt from a newspaper article about Jeong Kim.

From Rags to Riches
Korean immigrant who came to the U.S. with nothing sells his business for $1.1 billion

AT THE AGE of 16, Jeong Kim found himself abandoned and living alone in a strange land. He was desperate, but he had a dream. Through hard work and determination, he built himself a career, and twenty years later, he sold his business for $1.1 billion.

Jeong Kim, one of America's richest Koreans

3 Read the questions from the first part of an interview with Jeong Kim. Work in a group. Discuss what you think his answers might be.
1. What were your early years in the States like?
2. How did you adapt to your new surroundings?
3. Were you close to your siblings when you were growing up?
4. Did you find (your parents' divorce) hard to take?
5. How did this difficult childhood affect you?
6. You were 16 years old. You were on your own. What did you do?
7. How did you earn money to pay rent?

4 **CD1 4** Listen to part one of the interview. Compare Jeong's answers with your ideas in Exercise 3.

5 **CD1 5** Listen to part two. Answer the questions.
1. How did Jeong decide which career to pursue?
2. Why wasn't age a problem when he became a partner in a business?
3. What are the three ingredients that Jeong gives for success? Which does *he* have?
4. What was his big idea?
5. Why couldn't he find other people to back him?
6. Why is he so positive about taking risks?
7. How does he compare himself with Steve Jobs?

6 **CD1 6** Listen to part three. Are the statements true or false? Correct the false ones.
1. Smart people always have an advantage over other people.
2. Jeong achieved his success with the help of other people.
3. Now he wants to give something back to society.
4. In America, failure is the worst thing that can happen.

Language work

Complete the sentences from the interview with words from the box.

inferiority complex	aggression	major player	wing
rock bottom	custody	handicap	track record
let me down	realize your potential		

1. My brother took his _____ out on me.
2. The mother normally gets _____ of the children.
3. I felt that my parents had _____.
4. There was a moment in my life when I hit _____.
5. He and his wife were kind enough to take me under their _____.
6. You have to concentrate on the things where you don't have a _____.
7. I had no _____ of running a business.
8. Why not push to the limit and _____?
9. I've always wanted to be a _____.
10. I've always had an _____.

What do you think?

• Which factors in Jeong's life have led to his success?
• Why does he keep working so hard?
• What is his attitude toward the United States?
• "Once you have food to eat and clothes to wear, everything else is extra." Do you share this opinion?
• "Failure is an excellent experience." Do you agree?

VOCABULARY AND SPEAKING
Describing nationalities

1 Complete the chart. Use a dictionary if necessary. Add two more countries of your choice.

Country	Adjective	Person	People	Language(s)
the United States	U.S. or American	an American	(the) Americans	English
Brazil				
France				
Mexico				
China				
Denmark				
Japan				
Korea				
Turkey				
Spain				
Switzerland				
Argentina				
Peru				
Thailand				
Ecuador				
Afghanistan				
Russia				
Hawaiian				

2 **CD1 7** Listen to six people of different nationalities speaking English and try to identify where they come from. What do they say about their country and/or nationality?

3 Work in small groups. Choose a few nationalities that you know. First describe them in stereotypical fashion, then discuss how much your experience of them fits the stereotype.

> Americans have a reputation for being loud and obnoxious, and they're always talking about how great and powerful the U.S. is.

> Actually most of my American friends are very polite, and they ...

> I've been told that the first thing an American asks you is how much money you make.

> Well, what I found when I was in the U.S. was ...

4 What is your nationality's stereotype? Are you like that?

EVERYDAY ENGLISH
British and American English

1 [CD1] [8] Read and listen to the conversations with a partner. Which is British English? Which is American English? What are the differences?

1. A Where do you live?
 B We've got a small flat. It's on the ground floor of a block of flats in the centre of town.
 A Have you got a garden?
 B No, we haven't, just a car park at the back.

2. A Where do you live?
 B We have a small apartment. It's on the first floor of an apartment building downtown.
 A Do you have a yard?
 B No, we don't, just a parking lot in the back.

2 [CD1] [9] Read and listen to these conversations in British English. Try to convert them into American English.

1. **A** Have you got the time?
 B Yeah, it's five to four.
 A Did you say five past?
 B No, five *to* four.

2. **A** What are you going to do at the weekend?
 B The usual. Play football with my kids, and do a bit of gardening.

3. **A** Did you enjoy the match?
 B Yeah, it was great, but we had to queue for half an hour to get tickets.

4. **A** Did you have a good holiday?
 B Yeah, really good.
 A How long were you away?
 B Five days altogether. From Monday to Friday.

5. **A** Can you post this letter and parcel for me?
 B Of course.
 A And can you call at the supermarket and buy some crisps?
 B Is that all?

6. **A** Did you watch *The Birds* on telly last night?
 B I did, even though I've seen it twice before.
 A My third time. Isn't it just a terrific film?
 B It certainly is. One of my favourites.

7. **A** Have they brought the bill yet?
 B Yeah. They just have. But I can't read a thing. The lighting is so bad in here.

8. **A** Do we need to stop for petrol?
 B Yes, why not? I need to go to the loo, anyway.

3 [CD1] [10] Listen and compare your ideas.

4 What is the American English for these words? Use a dictionary if necessary.

mobile phone	dressing gown	chemist's	lorry	autumn	windscreen
rubbish	biscuit	wardrobe	pavement	lift	trousers

Do you know any more British English words or expressions?

▶▶▶ **Writing** Formal and informal letters **p. 113**

2 Never at a loss for words!

Grammar: Phrasal verbs
Vocabulary: Tense review
Everyday English: Sounds and spelling

STARTER

1 Read the excerpts. Match them with a cover and type of book. What helped you to identify them?

| a modern romance* | an autobiography | a fantasy | a classic drama | a thriller | a travel story |

*This is also known as "chick lit." = literature for "chicks"/modern young women

1 Nothing prepares you for the Grand Canyon. No matter how many times you read about it or see it pictured, it still takes your breath away. Your mind, unable to deal with anything on this scale, just shuts down.

2 To be, or not to be – that is the question. Whether 'tis nobler in the mind to suffer the slings and arrows of outrageous fortune, or to take arms against a sea of troubles …

3 I never set out to swipe anyone's boyfriend, much less Nina's. The day it all started, picking up a guy was the last thing on my mind. Even I don't go out on the prowl in grubby old boots and a sweater that's seen better days.

4 The group stood silently, mesmerized by the two bodies, which, though dead, continued to spew blood. The thick smell of gunfire hung over the stairway.

5 As for Bilbo Baggins, even while he was making his speech, he had been fingering the golden ring in his pocket: his magic ring that he had kept secret for so many years. As he stepped down he slipped it on his finger, and he was never seen by any hobbit in Hobbiton again.

6 The last days of my childhood were also the last days of the village. I belonged to that generation which saw the end of a thousand years' life.

2 What are your favorite types of books? Which books have you read recently? Why? Tell your partner about one of them.

3 Have you read any books in English? Discuss them, and reasons for reading in English, with the class.

READING AND SPEAKING
Losing her words

1 Work with a partner. Ask and answer questions to complete the biography of the novelist Iris Murdoch.

    Student A   Look at this page.
    Student B   Look at the copy from your teacher.

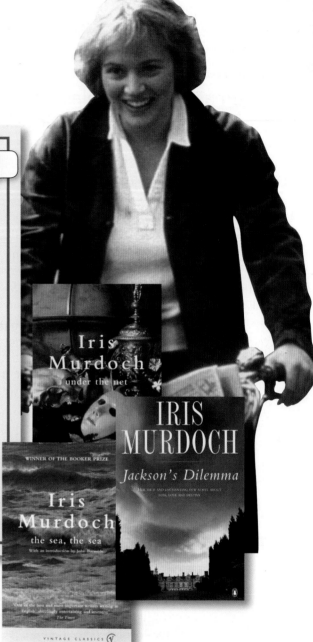

> Where was she born?

> Dublin.

MURDOCH, Iris Jean
1919–1999

She was born in (1) __Dublin__ , the only child of Anglo-Irish parents. She studied (2) <u>classics</u> at Oxford University, then worked for four years in (3)_____. She returned to Oxford to teach philosophy. Her first novel, *Under the Net,* published in (4) <u>1954</u> , was an immediate success. Other titles include *The Sandcastle, The Bell,* and *The Sea, The Sea,* for which she was awarded (5)_____.

She said that in her novels she tried to convey (6) <u>"the unique strangeness of human beings."</u>

In 1956 she married John Bayley, a professor of (7)_____ at Oxford. They had a (8) <u>long, happy—if unusual—</u> marriage, but no children.

Iris was still writing in her late 70s. Her 26th and last novel, *Jackson's Dilemma,* published in 1995, was written while she was suffering from the beginnings of (9)_____. She died in 1999.

The Oscar-winning film, *Iris* (2002), starring (10) <u>Judi Dench and Kate Winslet</u>, tells the story of her love affair with John Bayley and her tragic struggle with the disease.

2 Read these three headings from an article about Iris Murdoch.

- Wild piles of books and papers
- Just a bit of writer's block?
- Utterly at ease with each other

What ideas do you get about Iris's house and its occupants? What is "writer's block"?

3 Read part one of the article and answer the questions.

1. How is Joanna greeted when she arrives?

2. What impression do you get of John and Iris's house? Choose three key words from the text to describe it.

3. What are your first impressions of John and Iris? Likeable or unlikeable? Why?

4. What images do the words in *italics* convey? Use your dictionary.
   a. … the *cheery face* of Professor John Bayley appears at the window, *chewing baked beans* …
   b. … *heaving* tote bags, *spilling* their paper *guts* across the floor …
   c. … Iris Murdoch *spirals gracefully* into the room …
   d. … an *abandoned* glass of red wine *tucked away* under each armchair …

4 Read part two and answer the questions.

1. Why has Joanna requested the interview with Iris?

2. Why is Joanna worried?

3. Both John and Iris try to explain her difficulty with writing.
   How do their explanations differ?
   Who is the most optimistic?

4. How did Iris approach her writing in the past?

5. In what ways does she show that she feels confused?

5 Read part three on page 16.

A VISIT TO IRIS MURDOCH

BY JOANNA COLES

The journalist Joanna Coles interviewed Iris Murdoch at her home in Oxfordshire, England, shortly before the novelist was diagnosed with Alzheimer's Disease.

PART ONE

Wild piles of books and papers

"Bell not working. WE ARE HERE. Knock vigorously." I do, and the cheery face of Professor John Bayley appears in the window, chewing baked beans. "Come in, come in my dears," he exclaims, opening the front door and waving a piece of toast. "I find beans just the thing for lunch, don't you?"

He whisks us through a chaotic hall, past a vast, unsteady pyramid of books and into the most eccentric living room I have ever seen. There are heaving tote bags, spilling their paper guts across the floor, and wild piles of books and papers. The walls are Georgian Green and though it is midday, it's dark, the window impenetrable to the light because of the fig leaves outside.

As we sit down, Iris Murdoch spirals gracefully into the room, and I suddenly notice there's an abandoned glass of red wine tucked away under each armchair, as if perhaps in case of emergency.

PART TWO

Just a bit of writer's block?

"Hello," Iris smiles, her eyes wide and friendly, and although I have already explained on the telephone, I explain again that I'm here because there are rumors she has given up writing for good. It's not the easiest of questions to ask such an intelligent and prolific author, and I am worried she may think me rude for even trying. But can it be true?

To my huge relief she smiles. "Well, I'm trying to do something, but it hasn't, well ..." and then she starts laughing.

"Just a bit of writer's block I think," interrupts Bayley, cheerfully.

"Yes, it's not ... well ... I certainly am trying," she replies.

Iris Murdoch is without question one of the finest writers of her generation, producing 26 novels. Her last book, *Jackson's Dilemma*, was published last fall, but nothing has followed. Has she suffered from this kind of block before?

"I think this is a very bad one," she says absently.

"It has occurred before, darling," says Bayley, leaning towards her reassuringly.

"Perhaps," she says flatly.

And do you still enjoy writing when you can?

"Well, I enjoy it, when I've found a way out, as it were. But, er ... otherwise ..." and she smiles apologetically.

"Otherwise ... I'm in a very, very bad, quiet place."

We are all quiet for a moment before Bayley says to her:

"In the past, because of your philosophical mind perhaps, you've worked the whole novel out in advance, in meticulous detail, haven't you darling?"

He heads off to the kitchen to make coffee.

"I feel gloomy," says Iris. "The books I've written in the past I've done quite quickly. But I'm afraid at the moment that I'm just falling, falling ... falling as it were. But I may get better. I expect something will turn up. I hope so."

PART THREE

Utterly at ease with each other

Bayley returns with a pot of coffee. "You must pour," says Iris patting his arm. "You must pour."

"Pour? Oh, I thought you meant 'paw'!"

And he starts scrabbling in the air as if he's a cat, and we all laugh. Their relationship is not only touching, it's still fresh and young, making sense of what marriage is for. Despite Iris's current problems, they seem utterly at ease with each other.

I wonder if they've regretted not having children?

"Iris has never shown the slightest interest in being a mum," says her husband. "And I'm not sure, but you could say that the best women novelists didn't have children. Jane Austen, George Eliot … I mean the really top notch ones."

As Iris poses obediently for photos, he beckons me over to the kitchen table, where there appear to be two of everything, two honey pots, two mustard pots, two jam pots, and seven jars of coffee.

"We've been to see doctors, you know, and they say the old brain is very crafty. It can come up against a block and for a bit things are a bit strange, but then it finds its way around things again."

6 Answer the questions about part three.

1. How does Iris and John's relationship "make sense of what marriage is for"?

2. How does John explain the fact that they never had children? Does he feel bitter about it?

3. What is John's final note of optimism?

7 Answer these questions about the whole article.

1. In what ways do the house and its occupants reflect each other?

2. What examples are there that show John is proud of his wife's talent?

3. In what ways does he show his love for his wife?

4. Which adjectives would you use for John and which for Iris? Which describe both?

unconventional	loveable	loving
childlike	supportive	bewildered
distracted	gentle	cheerful
encouraging	dispirited	considerate

Vocabulary work

8 Match the words and definitions.

1. to whisk (somebody) away	a. clever in an indirect way
2. rumor (*n*)	b. to gesture to come here
3. prolific (*adj*)	c. information that is possibly not true
4. gloomy (*adj*)	d. to take (somebody) somewhere quickly
5. top-notch (*adj*)	e. likely to fall
6. crafty (*adj*)	f. to use your hands like an animal
7. to beckon (somebody)	g. very productive
8. unsteady (*adj*)	h. dark and sad
9. to scrabble	i. to feel around quickly with the fingers
10. to paw	j. high quality

What do you think?

- Iris always said that she was very lucky to have found John. Why might she have said this? Do you think he felt the same about meeting her?

- How would John Bayley's role in her life differ before and after the onset of her illness?

- Alzheimer's Disease is a tragedy in any family. Why was it a particular tragedy for Iris Murdoch?

VOCABULARY
Phrasal verbs

> **1** A phrasal verb can have more than one meaning. Some meanings are literal, some are metaphorical. In which of these sentences is *take in* used literally? Is it separable or inseparable?
>
> 1. My sister is always taking in stray cats.
> 2. These pants are too big. I need to take them in.
> 3. She was completely taken in by his lies.
> 4. She likes to take in a Broadway show when she's in New York.
> 5. They had so much news that I couldn't take it all in.
>
> **2** Complete the phrasal verbs from the article about Iris Murdoch on pages 15–16.
>
> 1. There's a glass tucked _____ under each armchair.
> 2. There are rumors she has given _____ writing.
> 3. In the past you've _____ the novel out in advance.
> 4. He heads _____ to the kitchen to make coffee.
> 5. I may get better. I expect something will turn _____ .
> 6. (The brain) can come _____ against a block.
>
> ▶▶ **Grammar Reference p. 143**

1 Complete the four sentences, using each phrasal verb twice in an appropriate form.

give away	give up

1. "Guess how old I am." "I _____. You'll have to tell me."
2. They _____ a free CD with next month's magazine.
3. He tried to disguise himself, but I knew it was him. His voice _____ him _____.
4. I played the violin for 10 years, but I _____ it _____.

work out	work up

5. After a huge fight, they ended their 15-year friendship. They just couldn't _____ it _____.
6. She _____ herself _____ into a terrible state of mind about the exam next week.
7. All this physical activity makes you _____ an appetite.
8. I stay in shape by _____ regularly at the gym.

put down	put up

9. Visit us in California. We can easily _____ you _____.
10. _____ the date _____ on your calendar or you'll forget it.
11. Well, we lost the game, but we sure did _____ a good fight.
12. He is always _____ me _____, and I feel so stupid.

get around	get at

13. I think I know what you're _____, but I'm not 100 percent sure.
14. My back itches in a place I just can't quite _____.
15. "I'm getting married!" "I know, Carla told me." "Wow, word _____ fast."
16. Can you _____ New York City easily on a bike?

come down on	come out with

17. Wow, she really _____ you hard. What did you do?
18. They're _____ a new version of this phone next week. I can't wait!
19. He _____ some serious accusations in his speech.
20. I asked if he could _____ his price, and he did.

2 Compare the pairs of sentences. What effect does the particle have?

1. I wrote a letter.   I wrote down his address.
2. I saw her at the station.   I saw her off at the station.
3. You used my toothpaste.   You've used up all the toothpaste.

3 Complete the sentences with a verb and a particle.

get (x2)	make	wear
work	settle	hand
hold	lie	go
stay		

through	away (x2)	on
into	up	back
around	over	off
in		

1. My son spends the day _____ in front of the TV.
2. _____ from me. I have a cold.
3. You told the teacher I cheated! I'll _____ you _____ for that! Just wait!
4. My tooth started hurting as the effects of the painkiller _____ .
5. We're off! _____ tight!
6. _____ your homework carefully before you _____ it _____.
7. The students were very quiet, _____ on their computers.
8. My son is a total mystery to me. I can't _____ to him at all.
9. You didn't believe what he said, did you? He _____ the whole thing _____.
10. Have you _____ your new apartment yet?

4 **CD1 11** Listen and respond to the lines of conversation, using a phrasal verb from this page.

> What's wrong? Are you sick?

> No, I just feel like lying around today.

CD1 12 Listen and compare your answers.

LISTENING AND SPEAKING
I have nothing to declare but my genius!

1 Read these quotes from Oscar Wilde, a well-known Anglo-Irish writer famous for his sayings. What impression do you get of Oscar from them?

> " To love oneself is the beginning of a lifelong romance. "

> " There is no such thing as an immoral book. Books are well written, or badly written. "

> " There is only one thing in the world worse than being talked about, and that is not being talked about. "

> " I never travel without my diary. One should always have something sensational to read on the train. "

> " I can resist anything but temptation. "

2 Are these statements about Oscar Wilde true or false? Discuss with a partner.

1. He was a famous 20th-century writer.
2. He wrote plays, poetry, and prose.
3. His most successful plays were comedies.
4. He never married.
5. He died in London.

3 Read the biographical information about Oscar Wilde and check your answers from Exercise 2.
Which play is considered to be his masterpiece?
What is the meaning of the words *earnest* and *Ernest*?
What is their pronunciation?

OSCAR WILDE
1854–1900

An Irish-born English poet, novelist, and playwright. His greatest success was in the theater with his shrewd and sparkling comedies, such as *Lady Windermere's Fan* (1892) and *An Ideal Husband* (1895). *The Importance of Being Earnest* (1895) is considered to be his masterpiece. Based on the double meaning of the name Ernest, it is an attack on people who take themselves too seriously. Wilde married in 1884 and had two sons. However, in 1897 he went to live in France. He died in Paris in 1900.

4 **CD1 13** Listen to a scene from *The Importance of Being Earnest*. Lady Bracknell is interviewing a young man, Jack Worthing. Answer the questions.

1. Why is Jack being interviewed?
2. What's his occupation? Where does his money come from? Does he earn it?
3. Who is Gwendolen?
4. What does Lady Bracknell like about Jack? What doesn't she like?
5. What do you learn about Jack's family background?
6. Is his interview successful?
7. What advice does Lady Bracknell give him?
8. Which of these adjectives would you use to describe Lady Bracknell?

reserved	aristocratic	snobbish	overbearing	timid
witty	prejudiced	earnest	inarticulate	arrogant
courteous	haughty	patronizing		

5 **CD1 13** Look at the audio script on pages 129–130. Read and listen to the scene again. Then answer the questions.

1. Give some examples to justify the adjectives you chose to describe Lady Bracknell.
2. How did Jack get the last name Worthing?
3. What do you learn about the lives of the English upper classes in the 19th century? What was important to them? What were their attitudes about marriage, work, and property?
4. How does Oscar Wilde make the scene funny? Give some examples.

Vocabulary work

6 Find words in the scene to replace the words in *italics*.

1. There are far too many *lazy* men.
2. I do not approve of anything that *interferes* with natural ignorance.
3. As far as I can *see*, the *people who hunt animals illegally* are the only people who *earn money from it*.
4. A girl with a simple, *innocent* nature, like Gwendolen could hardly be expected to *live* in the country.
5. The *deceased* Mr. Thomas Cardew, an old gentleman *with* a very *kind and generous personality…*
6. *Where* did this Mr. James, or Thomas, Cardew *find* this ordinary handbag?
7. The line is *not important*.
8. I *admit* I feel somewhat *confused* by what you have just told me.
9. To be born, or at any rate, *reared* in a handbag, seems to me to *show no respect* for the ordinary decencies of family life.
10. Our only daughter – a girl *raised* with the utmost care …

What do you think?

- Discuss these questions with a partner.
  1. How do you think Jack came to be in the handbag? Write down as many ideas as you can think of.
  2. Do you think Jack ultimately discovers his origins and marries Gwendolen?

- Discuss your ideas with the class. Your teacher will give you the answers. Read and compare them. Whose ideas were closest?

- Work with a partner and act out the scene together. Remember, it's a comedy, so make it as funny as possible! Perform the scene in front of the class.

LANGUAGE FOCUS
Tense review

1 Which tenses are used in these sentences? Write the verb forms in the correct place in the charts. Fill any spaces with examples of your own.

1. You*'re being* very productive. *Have* you *been inspired* by the play?
2. Jack *was found* in a handbag while the cloakroom *was being cleaned*.
3. It's the first time I*'ve seen* you in ages. What *have* you *been doing*?
4. As soon as we *have* any news, you*'ll be* the first to know.
5. This room *is being used* for a meeting at the moment.
6. I wish I*'d realized* that he*'d been lying* to me all along.
7. He *didn't recognize* his hometown. It *had been rebuilt* after the war.
8. We*'ll have been living* here for three years this November.

ACTIVE	Simple	Continuous
Present		are being
Past		
Future		
Present Perfect		
Past Perfect		
Future Perfect		

PASSIVE	Simple	Continuous
Present		
Past		
Future		
Present Perfect	have been inspired	
Past Perfect		
Future Perfect		

▶▶ **Grammar Reference p. 144**

Simple and continuous

2 Where possible, change the verb forms in these sentences from simple to continuous or continuous to simple. How do they change in meaning? Why is the change sometimes not possible?

1. Everyone's very nice to me. I don't know why.
2. I'll see Luis later.
3. I've cut my finger. It's really hurting.
4. David always gives Pam expensive presents.
5. What do you do?
6. He hit the wall.
7. She was dying.
8. I've been checking my e-mail.
9. The train leaves in five minutes.
10. That room is used as a study.

Perfect and non-perfect

3 Compare the use of tenses in these pairs of sentences. How are they different in meaning?

1. They've been married for thirty years.
   They were married for thirty years.
2. I live in Mexico City.
   I've lived in Mexico City.
3. When I've talked to him, I'll tell you.
   When I talk to him, I'll tell him.
4. The arrangements will be finalized on Friday.
   The arrangements will have been finalized by Friday.
5. Did you ever meet my grandfather?
   Have you ever met my grandfather?
6. I wish I knew the way.
   I wish I'd known the way.

4 This is what the comedian Groucho Marx said to his host at the end of a party:

> I've had a perfectly wonderful evening, but this wasn't it.

The joke depends on two different uses of the Present Perfect. What are they?

Active and passive

5 Correct these sentences.

1. In the excerpt from *The Importance of Being Earnest*, Jack is interviewing Lady Bracknell.
2. His money invests in stocks and shares.
3. Gwendolen can't expect to live in the country.
4. Jack gave the name Worthing.
5. The bag had found at Victoria Station.

Tenses and verb forms

6 **CD1 14** Close your books and listen to an excerpt from a modern romantic novel. You should recognize the opening lines. The speaker is Harriet Grey, a young woman who lives and works in New York. What problems does she have? What do you learn about her "friend" Nina?

7 **CD1 14** Read the text and put the verb in parentheses into an appropriate tense or verb form. Listen again and check and compare. What do you think happens next in the story?

FAIR GAME   25

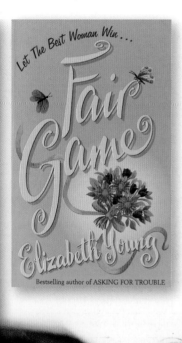

I never (1)_____ (set out) to swipe anyone's boyfriend, much less Nina's. The day it all (2)_____ (start), picking up a guy was the last thing on my mind. Even I (3)_____ (not go out) on the prowl in grubby old boots and a sweater that's (4)_____ (see) better days. All I (5)_____ (think) of, on that drizzly afternoon, was (6)_____ (find) a cab home. (7)_____ (start off) in mist-like fashion, the drizzle (8)_____ (take) it up a notch, as if it (9) _____ (think) about (10)_____ (turn into) actual rain. At this point I was in the Village, with damp hair and a sweater starting (11) _____ (smell) like a wet sheep. That was when I saw Nina (12)_____ (come) out of a chic little restaurant with a guy on her arm.

If I can misquote Jane Austen here, it is a truth universally (13)_____ (acknowledge) that if you are fated (14)_____ (bump into) someone like Nina when you (15)_____ (not see) her for four years, you (16)_____ (look) like death warmed over. While she (17)_____ (look) like a *Vogue* spread in silk and cashmere. Only a few steps away, she (18) _____ (talk and laugh) in her silver-tinkle way to the guy, who (19)_____ (hold) her umbrella up to stop her from (20) _____ (get) wet. The last time I (21)_____ (see) her (at a wedding four years back) she (22)_____ (have) some tall, dark specimen in tow. Although everything about him was theoretically perfect, I (23)_____ (not be) particularly impressed – to me he (24)_____ (seem) just a bit plastic, somehow. I (25)_____ quite _____ (not know) what it was with this one – he wasn't good-looking exactly, but the spark (26)_____ (hit) me at once!

1 Work with a partner. Write down all the English words you know that contain the letters *ough*. Tell the class, paying particular attention to the pronunciation.

2 Read the poem and decide on the pronunciation of the words in *italics*. Use a dictionary if necessary.

Hints on English Pronunciation

I take it you already know
Of *tough* and *bought* and *cough* and *dough*
Others may stumble but not you,
On *thorough*, *plough*, *enough* and *through*
Well done! And now you wish perhaps
To learn of less familiar traps.

Beware of *heard*: a dreadful word
That looks like *beard* and sounds like *bird*.
And *dead*: it's said like *bed* not *bead*
For goodness sake don't call it *deed*.
Watch out for *meat* and *great* and *threat*
(They rhyme with *suite* and *straight* and *debt*).

And *here* is not a match for *there*,
Nor *dear* and *fear*, for *bear* and *pear*.
And then there's *dose* and *rose* and *lose* –
Just look them up – and *goose* and *choose*
And *cork* and *work* and *card* and *ward*
And *font* and *front* and *word* and *sword*
And *do* and *go*, then *thwart* and *cart*,
Come, come! I've hardly made a start.

A dreadful language? Why man alive!
I'd mastered it when I was five.
And yet to write, the more I tried,
I hadn't learned at fifty-five.

3 **CD1 15** Listen and check your pronunciation. Practice reading the poem aloud, taking turns each reading a verse.

4 Write the words from the poem next to their phonetic transcription in column A.

▶▶ **Use the International Phonetic Alphabet (IPA).**

		A	B
1.	/θru/	through	threw
2.	/hərd/		
3.	/mit/		
4.	/swit/		
5.	/hɪr/		
6.	/dɪr/		
7.	/bɛr/		
8.	/pɛr/		
9.	/roʊz/		
10.	/tʃuz/		

CD1 16 Listen to ten sentences with words that sound like those in column A, but have a different spelling and meaning. Write them in column B.

5 The words in Exercise 4 are all **homophones**. These are words with the same pronunciation but different meaning.

Here are some more homophones. Say the word in phonetics, then write the homophones.

		A	B
1.	/bɪn/		
2.	/sɪn/		
3.	/wɛr/		
4.	/wɔr/		
5.	/θroʊn/		
6.	/wɪtʃ/		
7.	/flaʊər/		
8.	/pis/		

▶▶ **Writing** Storytelling **p. 114**

3 Big business

STARTER

1 Work with a partner. Look at the logos of some multinational companies. What is the name of each company? What does it produce or sell?

2 Discuss these questions.
- Are these brand names well known in your country?
- Have you ever bought or used any of their products?
- Do you buy particular brands of food or clothes? Why/Why not?
- What are brands for?

READING AND SPEAKING
The global economy

1 Work with a partner. What do you know about globalization and consumerism? What are their pros and cons?

2 Are these sentences facts (**F**) or opinions (**O**)?

1. There are severe environmental changes taking place in the world.
2. Globalization is synonymous with Americanization.
3. Only 20 percent of the world's population lives in rich countries, but they consume 86 percent of the world's resources.
4. The more people are in debt, the richer the banks become.
5. The United States is a target for the victims of globalization.
6. Debt repayments by developing countries are nine times as much as the aid they receive.
7. The global economy puts no value on morality, only profit.
8. Countries in the industrialized West exploit workers in poorer countries.

What is your reaction to the facts? Do you agree with the opinions? Compare your answers with the class.

3 Look at the title of the article. What do you think it means? Read the article. Which of the topics in Exercise 2 are mentioned?

4 According to the article, are these statements true or false?

1. "The economy" is not the same thing as the economy.
2. People feel optimistic because their lives are so prosperous.
3. The more we spend, the better life is.
4. If people stop spending, the economy collapses.
5. Companies respond to the needs of consumers.
6. It's good that we can buy cheap goods from around the world.
7. Many developing countries export food to pay back their debts.
8. We know how to solve some of these problems, but we don't want to do it.

5 What do you think the words and phrases highlighted in the text mean?

What do you think?

1 What are some of the examples of craziness in the world that Jonathan Rowe mentions? Can you add any more?

2 Is it economic colonialization to sell Kentucky Fried Chicken to the world, or is it just giving people what they want?

3 What do you think is Jonathan Rowe's attitude about the following? What is *your* attitude?

- multinational corporations
- anti-globalization protesters
- economists
- public transportation
- pollution and the environment
- supermarkets
- Western banks
- companies who use cheap labor in poor countries

The writer holds strong views on these issues. Can you present some counter-arguments?

Multinational corporations keep prices down.

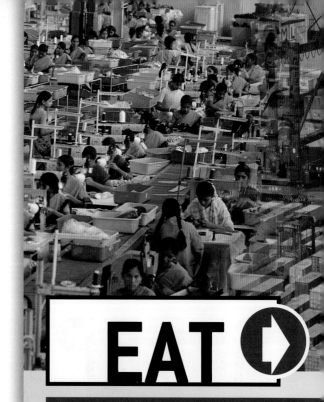

EAT ➡

Economic growth is the route to

I want to talk about the economy. Not "the economy" we hear about endlessly in the news each day and in politicians' speeches. I want to talk about the real economy, the one we live in day by day.

Most people aren't particularly interested in "the economy." "Share prices are flying high, interest rates are at all-time lows. The Dow Jones index closed 63 points down at 10,450.95." We hear this and subconsciously switch off.

Notice that "the economy" is not the same as the economy. "The economy" is what men in suits play with to make vast personal wealth. The economy is where the rest of us live on a daily basis, earning our living, paying our taxes, and purchasing the necessities of life.

Something wrong

We are supposed to be benefiting from all the advantages of a prosperous society. So why do we feel drained and stressed? We have no time for anything other than work, which is ironic given the number of labor-saving devices in our lives. The kids are always hassling for the latest electronic gadgets. Our towns become more and more congested, we poison our air and seas, and our food is full of chemicals.

SLEEP ○ BUY ○ DIE

global prosperity. Or is it? Jonathan Rowe examines the price we pay for this growth

There's something wrong here. If times were truly good, then you'd think we'd all feel optimistic about the future. Yet the majority of us are deeply worried. More than 90 percent of us think we are too concerned about ourselves and not concerned enough about future generations.

Producing and consuming

The term "economic expansion" suggests something desirable and benevolent, but expansion simply means spending more money.

More spending doesn't mean that life is getting better. We all know it often means the opposite - greed, deprivation, crime, poverty, pollution. More spending merely feeds our whole economic system, which is based on production and consumption. Unless money keeps circulating, the economy collapses. Airlines go bust, taking plane manufacturers and travel agents with them. If we don't keep consuming, then manufacturers and retailers go out of business. People don't buy houses, clothes, washing machines, cars. The whole system goes into stalemate.

Creating need

As a leading economist put it, consumer societies are "in need of need." We don't need the things the economy produces as much as the economy needs our sense of need for these things. Why, in our supermarkets, do we have to choose from sixty different kinds of toilet paper and a hundred different breakfast cereals? Need is the miracle that keeps the engines of expansion turning relentlessly. In economics, there is no concept of enough, just a chronic yearning for more. It is a hunger that cannot be satiated.

There is so much craziness in the world. There is an American company that manufactures a range of food with a high fat content. This causes obesity and high blood pressure. By coincidence, the same company also makes products that help people who are trying to diet. Not only that, it even produces pills for those with high blood pressure.

Nearly all of my mail consists of bills (of course), banks trying to lend me money, catalogues trying to make me spend it, and charity appeals for the losers in this ecstasy of consumption – the homeless,

the refugees, the exploited, the starving. Why is it possible to buy strawberries from Ecuador and green beans from Kenya when these countries can hardly feed their own people? It is because these are cash crops, and the countries need the money to service their debts. Notice that servicing a debt does not mean paying it off. It means just paying the interest. Western banks make vast profits from third-world debt.

Making changes

How do we break the cycle? We need to become far more aware of the results of our actions. We buy clothes that are manufactured in sweatshops by virtual slaves in poor parts of the world. We create mountains of waste. We demand cheap food, mindless of the fact that it is totally devoid of taste and is produced using chemicals that poison the land. We insist on our right to drive our own car wherever we want to go.

The evil of the consumption culture is the way it makes us oblivious to the impact of our own behavior. Our main problem is not that we don't know what to do about it. It is mustering the desire to do it.

VOCABULARY AND SPEAKING
Describing trends

1 Look at these newspaper headlines describing trends. Are numbers going up or down?

- P.O. PROFITS PLUMMET
- Inflation soars to 10%
- House prices shoot up
- Microsoft market share tumbles
- Ryanair leap in profits
- Inflation rates plunge to 2%
- Car industry predicts slump
- Consumer spending picks up slightly

"But on the positive side, money can't buy you happiness – so who cares?"

2 Look at the graph about the company *Halico*. Talk about its profits, using the words in the boxes and in Exercise 1.

	Adjective	Noun		Verb	Adverb
a	slight			fall	slightly
	gradual	fall		drop	gradually
	steady	decrease		go down	steadily
	sharp	rise		decrease	sharply
	dramatic	increase		rise	dramatically
	substantial			go up	substantially
				increase	

Halico enjoyed a steady rise in profits in January. Unfortunately, they fell ...

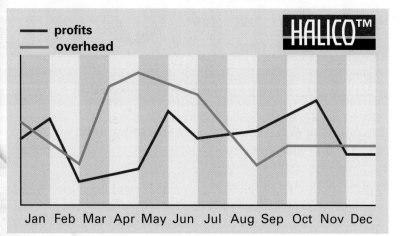

CD1 17 Listen and compare your answers.

3 Talk about *Halico*'s overhead in the same way.

When did overhead peak?
When did it reach its lowest point?
When did it level out?

4 **CD1 18** Listen to information about the sales figures of another company, *Becom*, over a one-year period. Complete the graph.

Comparing statistics

5 Look at the charts of two people's monthly expenditures, and compare them.

> David spends twice / three times as much on ... as John does.
> John doesn't spend anywhere near as much on ... as David does.
>
> John spends 50 percent more / 20 percent less on ... than David does.
> David spends a quarter / 25 percent of his salary on ...

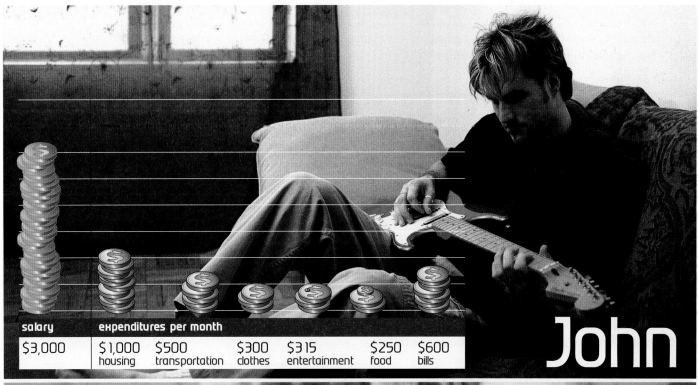

salary	expenditures per month					
$3,000	$1,000 housing	$500 transportation	$300 clothes	$315 entertainment	$250 food	$600 bills

John

salary	expenditures per month					
$8,000	$2,000 housing	$1,400 transportation	$200 clothes	$400 entertainment	$500 food	$2,400 bills

David

6 Your teacher will give you some statistics. In groups, prepare to give a presentation to the rest of the class using some of the vocabulary you have practiced.

LANGUAGE FOCUS
Adverbs

Adverb collocations

> Adverbs often go with certain verbs and adjectives.
> Look at the examples from the article on pages 24–25.
>
> | verb + adverb | adverb + adjective |
> |---|---|
> | hear about **endlessly** | **deeply** worried |
> | turning **relentlessly** | **utterly** destroyed |
>
> ▶▶ **Grammar Reference p. 146**

1 Complete the sentences with an adverb from the box.

severely	deeply	sorely	interminably
eagerly	desperately	highly	perfectly
virtually	distinctly	fatally	diligently

1. I _____ need a vacation. I haven't had a break for three years.
2. The return of the pianist Sara Buechner to the concert stage is _____ awaited.
3. I work with a _____-motivated sales team. We all work hard.
4. It is _____ impossible to get away from cell phones these days.
5. Bad weather has _____ affected the roads this weekend. Driving conditions are treacherous.
6. The politician's speech seemed to go on _____, but in fact it was only thirty minutes long.
7. I hate cold climates. I am _____ tempted to emigrate somewhere warm.
8. I _____ remember your telling me not to call before 2 p.m.
9. Having worked _____ for the same firm for forty years, he was awarded a gold watch.
10. In her anger she yelled at him. Later she _____ regretted this.
11. Two people escaped unhurt in the accident, but unfortunately the third passenger was _____ injured and died on the way to the hospital.
12. Alison made her views on the subject of politicians _____ clear. She dislikes all of them.

2 Match the verbs and adverbs. Make sentences using the adverb collocations.

A	B
scream	passionately
gaze	profusely
love	longingly
break something	hysterically
work	diligently
apologize	deliberately

Adverbs with two forms

> Some adverbs have two forms, one with and one without -ly. Compare these examples.
>
> | flying **high** | **highly** motivated |
> |---|---|
> | doing **fine** | **finely**-chopped onions |
>
> ▶▶ **Grammar Reference p. 146**

3 Complete the sentences with the correct form of the adverb. In which examples is the meaning altered significantly?

hard	hardly

1. We all work extremely _____.
   Some countries can _____ feed their own people.

easy	easily

2. Brazil won the game _____.
   Relax! Take it _____!

late	lately

3. I hate it when people arrive _____.
   What have you been doing _____?

sure	surely

4. "Can you lend me some money?" "_____."
   _____ you can see that your plan just won't work?

wrong	wrongly

5. He was _____ accused of being a spy.
   At first everything was great, but then it all went _____.

free	freely

6. He talked _____ about his criminal past.
   The prisoner walked _____ after twenty years in jail.

most	mostly

7. What do you like _____ about me?
   She worked wherever she could, _____ in restaurants.

wide	widely

8. She has traveled _____ in Europe and Asia.
   When I got home, the door was _____ open.

just

4 The adverb *just* is used in many different ways. What does it mean in these sentences? (Sometimes it doesn't mean very much!)

1. A new pair of socks! That's just what I wanted! Thank you.
2. "Who's there?" "Don't worry. It's just me."
3. You're just as beautiful as your sister.
4. I'm just making some coffee. Would you like a cup?
5. I just caught the train with seconds to spare.
6. "I don't know what to do." "Why don't you just wait and see what happens?"
7. I wish you'd just listen to me for once!
8. We're just about out of sugar.
9. Just look at those children! Aren't they cute?
10. "What's the matter?" "I don't know. It's just ... it's just that I find it difficult to talk to you sometimes."

▶▶ **Grammar Reference p. 146**
Adverbs are also dealt with in Units 10 and 12.

5 Add *just* to these sentences. Match them to the definitions in the Grammar Reference.

1. Thanks for your advice. Listening to you makes me feel better.
2. I've read the most amazing book. You must read it.
3. Hold on a minute. The doorbell is ringing.
4. My vacation was totally relaxing, which was what I needed.
5. My daughter is as hopeless with money as me.
6. I ran as fast as I could and managed to catch the bus before it pulled away.
7. Do what I say. That's all I'm asking you to do.
8. We're about ten minutes or so away from the hotel.

"I would like all of you to think of me as just one of the guys!"

6 **CD1 19** Listen to an interview with the mayor of a major U.S. city.
What is the latest crisis to hit the government? The word *just* is used five times. How many different uses can you remember?

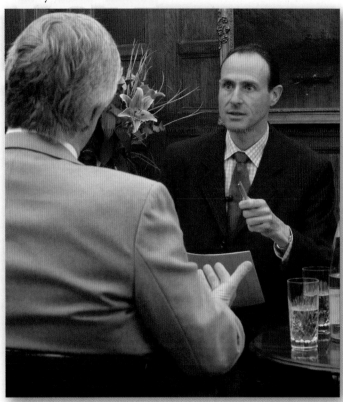

7 **CD1 19** The lines below are similar but not the same as some in the interview. Listen again and identify the differences.

1. We've been hearing at great length in the media about the latest crisis.
2. Polls show very clearly that the vast majority of the population fully support us.
3. My government deserves every penny of their pay raise.
4. I have a lot of respect for our public sector workers, they are very hardworking.
5. Time and time again your advisers have urged workers to accept increases in line with inflation.
6. It seems absolutely clear to me.
7. The effectiveness of our city's caretakers is being greatly hindered by lack of funds.
8. Their salaries are ridiculously small compared to those people working in industry.
9. My own salary is being reviewed independently *and* it will be reviewed impartially.
10. I believe categorically in fair and just compensation for all working people.

Read the audio script on page 130 and check your answers. How many more adverbs can you find?

LISTENING
An interview with Anita Roddick

1 There are over 1,800 Body Shops worldwide. What do you know about the business? Do you know anything about Anita Roddick, who founded The Body Shop in 1976? What do you think she was like?

2 **CD1 20** Listen to an interview with Anita Roddick. Which of these views does she express?

1. Business school teaches sound business practices.
   Business school kills creativity.
2. Successful business people are ruthless.
   They are compassionate.
3. They are ruled by profit.
   Money is just a means to an end.
4. If the environment is damaged, so what?
   It is vital to protect the environment.
5. Think globally.
   Think locally.
6. Amass wealth and count it.
   Amass wealth and give it away.

3 **CD1 20** Listen again and answer the questions.

Part one
1. What can you do at business school? What can't you do?
2. Why do immigrants make good entrepreneurs? What are the characteristics of a successful entrepreneur?
3. What, according to Anita Roddick, is the point of money?
4. What doesn't she want to be? What does she want to be?

Part two
5. What does business control?
6. Why are multinational corporations the big enemy?
7. What are her suggestions for honorable business practices?

Part three
8. What are her children's two reactions to her decision not to leave them any money?
9. What does she consider to be a great legacy?
10. What, for her, is the advantage of wealth?

Language work

4 What do you think the following statements mean?

- I was saved . . . by not doing the traditional route.
- . . . they all dance to a different drumbeat.
- . . . we don't give a darn about money.
- We vomit ideas.
- . . . multinational corporations bow down to nothing . . .

What do you think?

- Do you agree that creative business people "are terribly, terribly bad at managing"?
- What does Anita Roddick see her strengths as?
- Why do you think she has chosen not to leave her great wealth to her children?

SPEAKING
An advertising campaign

1 Work in groups of six. Your teacher will give you roles.

Students A, B, C, and **D** work for a company called *StayWell*.
Student E works for a market research company.
Student F works for an advertising agency.

FEELING GREAT SINCE 1989

StayWell is having financial difficulties. Its most profitable product is a health drink called Sogood. Sales of this vitamin drink have been declining steadily for several years. You need to develop a strategy for the relaunch of the drink.

First look at the chart. It shows how you could structure your answer. It just shows *some* of the reasons for *one* potential strategy. It is not necessarily the right one.

	Who will you target?	What package?	What method of distribution?	Price of drink
	Over 65s	New bottle	Stay with pharmacies	Increase
Reason 1	They already like Sogood so it will be easier to get them to like it.	It will be noticed more easily on the shelf.	It is proven that Sogood sells in pharmacies.	Research has shown they will pay.
Reason 2	The advertising needed to reach them is cheaper.	It will show that it is a new formula.	We have existing relationships with pharmacies.	The new formula justifies the increase.
Reason 3	It is less risky.		It shows that it is a true health drink, not a gimmick.	

Look at your role cards. Discuss what you know, and use your own ideas to plan a campaign.

2 Present your proposals to the rest of the class.

What do you think?

- What is the role of advertising in our lives? Does it inform us of what is available, or does it try to make us buy things we don't need?
- Does the enormous cost of advertising make goods more expensive?
- Think of an advertisement that you like or don't like. Tell the others about it. Why does/doesn't it achieve its goal?

EVERYDAY ENGLISH
Word linking and intrusive sounds

1 When a word begins with a vowel sound, it links with the sound before.

> English‿is‿an‿international language.

Mark the links in these sentences. Practice saying them.

1. We're in class learning English.
2. It's eight o'clock and time for a break.
3. I'm dying for a cup of coffee.
4. We've been in here for over an hour.
5. As a matter of fact, I think our teacher's asleep.
6. She doesn't understand that her English students are about to sneak out.

CD1 21 Listen and check.

2 **CD1 22** When we link two vowel sounds, we add /w/ or /y/ when we speak. These sounds occur naturally.

blue‿eyes	two‿oranges	go‿away
/w/	/w/	/w/

my‿office	the‿economy	three‿apples
/y/	/y/	/y/

Can you figure out the rule? When do we add /w/ and when do we add /y/?

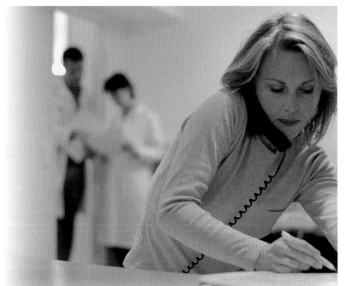

3 **CD1 23** When we spell words out loud, for example our name, there is a lot of linking and intrusive sounds. Why is this?

J O H N	S P E A R S
/dʒeɪ‿oʊ‿eɪtʃ‿ɛn	ɛs‿pi‿i‿eɪ‿ɑr‿ɛs/
/y/ /w/	/y/ /y/ /y/

M A N U E L	G O N Z A L E S
/ɛm‿eɪ‿ɛn‿yu‿i‿ɛl	dʒi‿oʊ‿ɛn‿zi‿eɪ‿ɛl‿i‿ɛs
/y/ /w//y/	/y/ /w/ /y//y/ /y/

Practice spelling your name with speed and rhythm.

4 When we spell names on the telephone, it is easy to confuse various sounds.

S sounds like F.	D sounds like T.
B sounds like P.	M sounds like N.

We can say things like **F as in Freddie, S as in sugar, L as in Laura, V as in Victor.** You can make them up as long as they're clear! You can also use the international alphabet.

A as in Alpha   **J** as in Juliet   **S** as in Sierra
B as in Bravo   **K** as in Kilo   **T** as in Tango
C as in Charlie   **L** as in Lima   **U** as in Uniform
D as in Delta   **M** as in Mike   **V** as in Victor
E as in Echo   **N** as in November   **W** as in Whisky
F as in Foxtrot   **O** as in Oscar   **X** as in X-ray
G as in Golf   **P** as in Papa   **Y** as in Yankee
H as in Hotel   **Q** as in Quebec   **Z** as in Zulu
I as in India   **R** as in Romeo

CD1 24 Listen and write down the names you hear.

5 Think of a new identity and a new job for yourself. Ask other students what their name and company is.

▶▶ **Writing** A business report **p. 116**

4 Celebrity

Grammar: Synonyms and antonyms 1
Vocabulary: Discourse markers
Everyday English: Tags and replies

STARTER

1 Match the lines to make quotations about fame and success.

1 "A celebrity is a person who works hard all his life to become well known,

2 "I don't want to achieve immortality through my work.

3 "There is only one thing worse than being talked about,

4 "What goes up,

5 "Whenever a friend succeeds,

6 "Genius is one percent inspiration,

7 "If at first you don't succeed,

8 "Nothing succeeds

9 "Let me tell you about the rich.

☐ must come down." ANONYMOUS

☐ like success." PROVERB

☐ a little something in me dies." GORE VIDAL

☐ and that is not being talked about." OSCAR WILDE

☐ I want to achieve it through not dying." WOODY ALLEN

☐ and then wears dark glasses to avoid being recognized." FRED ALLEN

☐ try, try again." ROBERT BRUCE

☐ ninety-nine percent perspiration." THOMAS EDISON

☐ They are different from you and me." F. SCOTT FITZGERALD

2 **CD1 25** Listen and check. Do you agree with any of them? What is *your* recipe for success?

READING AND SPEAKING
The cult of celebrity

1 Discuss the questions as a class.

  1. Which celebrities are in the news at the moment? What is the gossip about them? What is their claim to fame? How do they spend their days? Which trendy places do they go to? Where can you find out about them?

  2. *"We cannot avoid becoming entangled in what is called 'the cult of celebrity.' The only question is to what degree we want to pretend to resist."*

  What do you think the term the "cult of celebrity" means? Do you pretend to resist, or do you indulge your fascination with celebrities? Who are you most interested in?

2 Check that you know these words and phrases.

- an icon
- a sitcom
- a talk show
- the afterlife
- to ogle something/one
- fair game for criticism
- to scrutinize something/one
- to bestow fame on somebody
- a fly-on-the-wall documentary
- like a lamb to the slaughter

3 Read the article and put these phrases in the correct place.

  a. this life is our only one
  b. are no more special than the rest of us
  c. an endless supply of human-interest stories
  d. everybody wants to claim a bit of you
  e. I have indulged in small talk
  f. by volunteering to be the subject
  g. sometimes it lasts a lifetime
  h. What can be done
  i. undignified and unflattering
  j. they want to do with their lives

4 Would Jack Delaney agree or disagree with these viewpoints? Find evidence in the article.

- Most fame is undeserved.
- It is possible to survive fame intact.
- The public is consistent in the way it treats celebrities.
- Newspapers used to be more respectful.
- Television subjects ordinary people to humiliation.
- Most people want to be famous.
- The cult of celebrity should make us feel ashamed.

Do *your* views differ?

5 Answer the questions.

  1. Think of celebrities currently in the news who fit the three categories of fame mentioned in the first paragraph.
  2. What two reasons does the writer provide to explain our obsession? Do you agree?
  3. Why does Jay McInerney hate himself in the morning?
  4. What do you think the "viciousness of voyeurism" means? What are the "myths we too readily absorb"?

cult of celebrity

We are fascinated by their every move, and we want to know everything about them. Jack Delaney asks why we are obsessed with the rich and famous.

1 Some are born famous (like royalty), some achieve fame (like movie stars), and some have fame thrust upon them (like crime victims). Sometimes their celebrity is short-lived, (1)____. In some rare cases, for example Diana, Princess of Wales, and Marilyn Monroe, it can be transformed by death into a sort of iconic status. But whatever the causes or circumstances, being a celebrity changes your relationship with the world. From being a private person, you become public property, and (2)____. You are the object of envy as well as admiration, fair game for criticism, interrogation, ridicule, and spite.

We make 'em, we break 'em

2 We treat the famous with a mixture of reverence and brutality. We adore them, praise them, scrutinize them, and destroy them. We make them unable to tell where their real selves end and the PR-manufactured images begin. We have no mercy, we show no shame. It is easy to assume that all aspects of a celebrity life are free to be examined because he or she is on display, which means he or she doesn't have the same reality as everyone else. And it is precisely because many modern celebrities (3)____ that we feel justified in treating them with such contempt. We build them up and knock them down.

So who are the famous?

3 It used to be the case that fame was bestowed only as a consequence of some mighty achievement or gruesome misdeed, when newspapers were filled largely with accounts of such things as earthquakes and wars, and when it was deemed contemptible for journalists to delve into the private lives of famous people, even the very famous.

4 It is now possible for people who are living ordinary private lives to become famous, for at least a short time, through the media – by appearing on game shows or talk shows, for instance, or (4)____ of a fly-on-the-wall documentary. The readiness of people to let program-makers into their homes, to answer the most intimate questions about their lives, and to allow themselves to be filmed in the most (5)____ situations, never ceases to amaze.

5 Given this ghastly invasion of one's life, why is fame so desirable? Ask an average bunch of 10-year-olds what (6)____, and a large proportion of them will say that they would like to be famous. Not for anything in particular. Just famous. Period. In the adult population, otherwise perfectly normal people think nothing of confessing all about their personal tragedies on daytime TV.

Why are we so obsessed?

6 The American writer Norman Mailer said that in an age without religion, celebrities are our new gods. If we have no faith in an afterlife and (7)____, then celebrity is the nearest any of us will get to immortality, and the pursuit of it becomes more urgent. At the pathological extreme of this motivation are murderers like Mark Chapman, who assassinated John Lennon partly, he said, to make himself famous.

7 Another feature of modern society is the power and omnipresence of the mass media. Its explosive expansion in the past couple of decades has created an insatiable need for new material. All the newspapers, magazines, television shows, and blogs require (8)____. These are increasingly delivered in the form of interviews, profiles, gossip columns, photo shoots at gatherings, and soundbites by or about people who are celebrated for something they have done, or for a position they occupy in society, or in some cases for just being a celebrity. There are some totally talentless people who are simply famous for being famous. As Andy Warhol said, "In the future, everyone will be famous for fifteen minutes."

Love it or loathe it?

8 The American writer Jay McInerney commented, "I have enjoyed a little celebrity in my time, and I have ogled any number of models, (9)____ about popular film stars. But at least I hate myself in the morning. I fear as a nation we're losing our sense of shame in this regard."

9 So how do you feel when you read a gossip magazine, or tune into a talk show? Do you love it or loathe it? (10)____ to curb our fascination, particularly when the glittery sacrificial lambs go so willingly to slaughter? Probably not a lot. But perhaps we should be more aware of the viciousness of voyeurism and the myths we too readily absorb.

What do you think?

1 Discuss the questions.

- Why do we want to hear bad news about famous people more than good news? In what ways are celebrities unreal?
- What do you know about "reality TV"? Are there TV shows in your country like the ones described in the article? What are they like?
- What is the mentality of stalkers? What makes someone want to kill the object of their obsession?

2 Read what celebrities themselves say on the subject of fame. What do you think each quote means, and do you agree with it?

It wasn't my choice to be an open book, but when people found out what my life was like when I was 14 or 15, I didn't deny it. I think the more imperfect you are, the more human you are.

Drew Barrymore *actor and director*

For years I've been popular in America – not because of my talent, but because I'm famous.

Cher *singer and actor*

celebrities *on celebrity*

If you were me for a month, you might change it to two weeks.

Robert Redford *actor and director*

People want you to be a crazy, out-of-control teen brat. They want you miserable, just like them.   **Leonardo DiCaprio** *actor*

Fame, celebrity - it's not such a big deal in Europe. People seem to understand that you just have a weird job. It's strange in the States. Most fans here are great, but there's a handful who have seen the movies and feel they know you. They think it's all right to touch you and ask personal questions.   **Johnny Depp** *actor*

The nice thing about being a celebrity is that when you bore people, they think it's their fault.

Henry Kissinger *American diplomat*

3 Do you know …

- any other icons? What do they represent?
- someone who the press has built up and knocked down?
- an ordinary person who has become a celebrity?
- anyone who is famous simply for being famous?
- any children of celebrities who have had problems?

VOCABULARY

Synonyms

1 Find words in the article on page 35 that mean approximately the same as these.

paragraph 1	forced	
	fame	
	respect (noun)	

paragraph 2	great respect and admiration	
	cruelly	
	worship (verb)	
	examine	
	ruin (verb)	
	compassion, sympathy	
	guilt	
	suppose	
	exactly	

paragraph 3	result (noun)	
	mainly	
	considered	

paragraph 6	belief	
	killers	
	killed	

2 Complete the sentences with a synonym of the words in *italics*. Often the part of speech changes. The words appear in the article on page 35 and the paragraph has been given.

1. She *succeeded* in building up a $50 million company. This _____ won her many awards. (*1*)

2. She's always *finding fault with* her kids. She _____ them for their appearance, their laziness, everything. (*1*)

3. He *admitted* murdering his employer. This _____ came after days of interrogation. (*5*)

4. His recovery after the operation was *astonishing*. I was _____ to see him sitting up in bed when I visited him in hospital. (*4*)

5. You simply must *control* your finances better. If you don't _____ your spending, you'll be in serious trouble (*9*).

Antonyms

> Look at these examples of antonyms from the article on page 35.
>
> Sometimes their celebrity is **short-lived**, sometimes it **lasts a lifetime**.
>
> From being a **private** person, you become **public** property.

3 Complete the sentences with a word that has the opposite meaning of the words in *italics*. Sometimes the part of speech changes. The first three words appear in the article on page 35.

1. You thought those stories about her were *real*, but she _____ them all.

2. His ability to make money is *admirable*. However, I have nothing but _____ for the appalling way he deals with his employees.

3. I know most people *love* traveling, but I _____ it. I'd rather stay at home.

4. I've always been *successful* at work, but my private life is a total _____.

5. At first people thought it was a *genuine* Van Gogh, but later it turned out to be a _____.

6. I find it difficult to *relax*. There is so much _____ in my life. So much to do, so little time to do it.

7. I was sure I had seen her before. I *didn't recognize* her face, but her voice was _____.

8. This road is *straight* for a few miles, but then there are a lot of tight _____, so be careful.

9. One of my cats is quite *tame and domesticated*. The other is totally _____.

10. You thought she dropped the vase *accidentally*, but believe me, it was _____.

"It's not enough that we succeed. Cats must also fail."

LANGUAGE FOCUS
Discourse markers

1 **CD1 26** Listen carefully to a woman speaking, and decide what she's talking about. Answer the questions.

1. What was the most important aspect of the occasion for the speaker?
2. What was special about the dresses?
3. How were the people from the press behaving?
4. What *wasn't* so important to the speaker?
5. What was the occasion?

2 **CD1 27** Listen to another version of the monologue. What are the differences? Can you remember any?

> **1** There are many adverbs and expressions that show the speaker's attitude about what he or she is saying.
> ***Honestly***, I think you should quit your job.
> ***Admittedly***, you'd lose a lot of money.
> ***Surely*** job satisfaction is more important than money?
>
> **2** These expressions can also structure and direct a piece of discourse.
> ***As I was saying***, I'm still enjoying the work.
> ***As a matter of fact***, I earn very little in my job.
> ***Anyway***, who cares about money?
> ***By the way***, do you know how much Lara earns now?
>
> ▶▶ **Grammar Reference p. 147**

3 Complete the monologue with expressions from the box.

anyway	apparently	mind you	as I was saying
at least	all in all, though	admittedly	of course
naturally	by the way	to tell you the truth	
still	no doubt	I mean	
obviously	so to speak	quite honestly	
actually	guess what?	as a matter of fact	

❝All the A-list stars were there. That model, Angeline, (1)_____ I think it was Angeline, was there with her boyfriend. (2)_____ they've been going out for months. (3)_____, it was a glittering occasion. Stars everywhere and the crowds outside just begging for autographs. (4)_____, I couldn't believe my eyes. And the dresses! (5)_____, I don't know how much they would have cost – a fortune, I imagine. All designer labels, (6)_____. The photographers were (7)_____ having a field day, and (8)_____ there were reporters everywhere, falling over each other, (9)_____, to interview the biggest names. (10)_____, we didn't have the best seats— (11)_____ we were in the back row. (12)_____, we could still see everything. (13)_____, I was so busy star-watching that I didn't pay attention to the plot. (14)_____ you would've done the same.

(15)_____, I'm not too keen on thrillers, but it must have been good, because at the end the whole audience stood up and clapped. (16)_____, I'm not so sure what the story was about, but you really should go and see it when it comes out.

(17)_____, it was an amazing evening, and to top it off we went to Quaglino's for dinner afterwards, and (18)_____ Sarah Jane Fox and Brad Brat were at the next table! How cool is that? (19)_____, Sarah Jane Fox has terrible skin problems. (20)_____, who cares about that when you have that much money!❞

CD1 27 Listen again and check. Which expressions could be used in more than one place? Where?

4 Complete the conversation, either with a discourse marker from Exercise 3, or with appropriate words.

HAVE YOU HEARD ...?

ANA Have you heard that Jan is thinking of marrying Paul?

BEN (1) _Really?_ I don't know what she sees in him.

ANA I know what you mean. Mind you, (2)_____.

BEN Yes, I suppose having all that money does help.

ANA Where did he get his money from?

BEN Apparently, (3)_____.

ANA He's been married three times before. Did you know that?

BEN (4)_____, it's just once, I think.

ANA They'll have a big wedding.

BEN Of course (5)_____.

ANA Oh, well. Good luck to them.

BEN Absolutely. (6)_____, did you hear that Jenny and Mario had a car accident?

ANA Oh no! What happened?

BEN It wasn't serious. They skidded into a tree, but (7)_____ they weren't going fast. The car's destroyed , but (8)_____ no one was injured.

ANA Thank goodness for that. I should get in touch with them, but I don't have their number.

BEN As a matter of fact, (9)_____. I'll give it to you.

ANA Great. Thanks a lot. (10)_____, I have to get going. I'm meeting Jan for lunch.

BEN OK. See you later. Bye.

CD1 28 Listen and compare your answers.

5 Complete the sentences with your ideas.

1. **A** Excuse me, you look familiar. Have we met before?
   B Actually, _____.

2. **A** Why has your business been so successful?
   B Basically, _____.

3. Why did the CEO award himself a 50 percent pay raise? Surely _____?

4. Have you heard the latest about Mei-lin and Eric? Apparently, _____.

5. I don't think Marco and Linda should get married. I mean, _____.

6. I wish I were famous. All that money, all those parties every night. Mind you, _____.

7. **A** Wasn't that a great play last night!
   B To tell you the truth, _____.

8. I agree, it was a great game, and they deserved to win it. By the way, _____.

9. Why doesn't James ever call me? Why is it always me who calls him? After all, _____.

10. I don't have a clue what to do about all these problems. Anyway, _____.

SPEAKING
How to become a celebrity

1 Work in small groups. You have decided that it is your destiny in life to be famous. You want to get on the list of celebrities who are invited to all the best parties, opening nights, and social events.

2 Read the situation in the box below and talk together until you all agree on what to do.

3 Each student comes up with ideas for how to proceed. Keep discussing each idea and scenario until you have mapped out a detailed plan *or* until you have decided that your plan to hit the big time can't (or won't) work.

It is time to start your journey on the road to fame and fortune. You want to make it to the big time as quickly as possible. You have identified two routes that could help you to join the rich and famous.

Invent an interesting new past for yourself – become a new person! –one that would make you newsworthy. Will you lie, or just stretch the truth? Will you treat people with respect, or will you stop at nothing to get to the top? What are your limits?

Work your way into the elite group of famous people by hanging out in the right places. Basically, you will party your way to the top! Where will you go? How will you dress? Who will you try to get to know? Will your efforts be enough to make you famous?

What do you think?

When you have finished, discuss these questions.

- In retrospect, did you make any bad decisions? What should you have done?

- How did you make your decisions? Was everybody involved? Did one person dominate? Were your decisions democratic?

- Games such as these are used in management training to practice qualities of good leadership. What are the qualities of a good leader?

LISTENING
An interview with a Hollywood star

1 Drew Barrymore was born into an American acting dynasty. Her grandfather was the famous theater and film actor John Barrymore. Oscar-winning actors Lionel Barrymore and Ethel Barrymore were her great uncle and great aunt. Work with a partner. What do you know about Drew Barrymore? How do you think her famous family influenced her?

2 **CD1 29** Listen to part one of the interview. Are these statements true or false? Correct the false ones.
  1. Drew became famous when she was 6 years old.
  2. Her famous family members forced her into an acting career.
  3. She has close relationships with her family.
  4. She acts because she loves to act.
  5. Her first important acting job was in the movie "E.T."
  6. Steven Spielberg is her father.

3 **CD1 30** Listen to part two. Answer the questions.
  1. What does the interviewer say is the "inherent contradiction" of Drew's life?
  2. Why would Drew feel sorry for herself? Does she?
  3. Why is "A Bill of Divorcement" an emotional movie for her?
  4. Why does Drew say that watching her family's old movies is like a "warm fireplace"?

4 **CD1 31** Listen to part three. How does Drew explain . . .
  1. her desire to have a family?
  2. how damage and pain can teach you?
  3. how her mother's "unorthodox" behavior helped her career?
  4. why people should forgive her mother?
  5. her reaction to being exposed to adult experiences as a child?

Language work

5 Listen again to part one of the interview. Complete Drew's answer.

1. One is I cosmically and _____ , with all of the _____ running through my _____ , felt this connection to this family that I was born into, the Barrymores.

2. I felt a real _____ desire to act.

3. I felt it because they instilled it in my _____ and I never wanted to _____ myself of that.

4. In fact, I was very _____ and _____ of the fact that at such a young age that I was _____ and _____ with that connection with them and wanted to _____ them and _____ and _____ and _____ . I _____ them.

What do you think?

• Drew says she belongs to "another kind of tribe." Who are the people she refers to? Why does she feel connected to them?

• Was her family the only reason she became an actor?

• Does Drew make excuses for her family? Why or why not?

• Why is it so important to her to keep her family tradition alive?

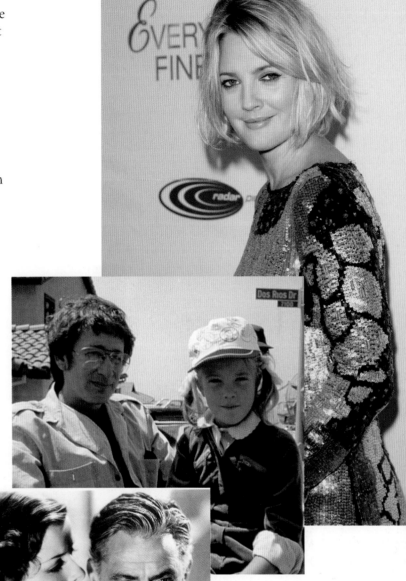

EVERYDAY ENGLISH
You did, did you?

1 Read the exchange below.

A I love your movies.
B Oh, you do, do you?

What kind of question tag is this? What is the second speaker expressing?

2 **CD1 32** Listen and underline the tags and replies in the conversation on the right. Do they rise or fall?

▶▶ **Grammar Reference p. 147**

A Cesária Evora is just fantastic! Her concert was amazing.
B It was, wasn't it? And she puts so much energy into her songs, doesn't she?
A Yes, she does. I love that song about missing home. It's so beautiful, isn't it?
B It is. It was her first big hit. She wrote it about Cape Verde, her home country, I think.
A So she can write as well as sing, can she? What a talent!
B Yeah. She writes most of her songs.
A She's playing again tomorrow, isn't she?
B Yes, I think so. Let's go again, shall we?
A Sure, why not?

3 Work with a partner. Decide where tags and replies can naturally go in these conversations. Do they rise or fall?

1. **A** You haven't seen my car keys.
   B No. You had them this morning.
   A Yes. If I can't find them, I'll be late for work.
   B Panic over. Here they are!
   A Great. You're the best!

2. **A** You didn't like that meal. You were pushing it around the plate.
   B No. Well, it hadn't been cooked properly. Your steak was OK?
   A Yes. It was fine. Let's get the check and go home.
   B OK. We won't be coming back here anytime soon.

3. **A** You forgot the map?
   B Uh-oh. Yes.
   A But I put it next to the car keys.
   B Well, I didn't see it.
   A You're blind.
   B Oh, and you're perfect?

CD1 33 Listen and compare. Practice the conversations with your partner.

4 Respond to these statements in different ways.

1. Jeremy makes an absolute fortune!

   He does, doesn't he?
   Does he? I had no idea. How much?
   So, he's rich, is he? Wow. I didn't know.

2. Peter's new Brazilian girlfriend, Ana, is very beautiful.

CD1 34 Listen and compare.

3. Lisa and Kevin are going to Florida on vacation. They're so lucky.
4. Zidane played really well in the game on Sunday, didn't he?
5. Target is a great store. You can buy everything there.
6. I think our teacher is the best.
7. Carlos is a very experienced traveler. He's been everywhere.

▶▶ **Writing** Expressing a personal opinion **p. 118**

5 Love is ...?

Grammar: Ways of adding emphasis
Vocabulary: Proverbs and poetry
Everyday English: Getting emotional

STARTER

1 Work with a partner. Look at the pictures. How would you describe the types of love portrayed? Which do you think are the deepest forms of love?

2 Which have you experienced in your life? Share some experiences with the class.

3 What is a *soulmate*? Have you found yours? Do you know any couples who you would describe as *soulmates*?

READING AND SPEAKING
Fateful attraction

1 Do you know how your parents met? Tell the class.

2 Read about two couples who met in very unexpected circumstances. Work in two groups.

    Group A   Read about Tina and Andrew on this page.
    Group B   Read about Emma and Ross on page 46.

    In your groups, answer the questions.

    1. How did their relationship start?
    2. What were the stages of its development?
    3. Did physical attraction play any part in their romance?
    4. Do they believe in fate? Why/Why not?

3 Work with a partner from the other group. Compare the two stories using your answers from Exercise 2. Which meeting do you think was most dependent on fate?

Vocabulary work

4 Find these phrases in your article and try to figure out their meaning from the context. Use a dictionary if necessary.

Group A	Group B
8 spur-of-the-moment	2 burst out laughing
13 texting back and forth	20 scrambled to my feet
23 not overly impressed	22 tore off along the path
39 in person	43 blown away
71 make a serious commitment	59 mane of red hair
71 nip it in the bud	67 catapulted into a garden

5 All the words in **A** and some in **B** appear in the texts. Match the synonyms.

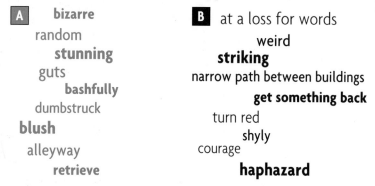

  A   **bizarre**
  random
    stunning
  guts
     bashfully
  dumbstruck
  blush
  alleyway
    retrieve

  B   at a loss for words
     weird
    striking
  narrow path between buildings
     get something back
  turn red
     shyly
  courage
    haphazard

6 **CD2 2** Listen to another couple, Joseph and Mariela, who met in Patagonia in the south of Chile. Tell their story in your own words.

What do you think?

- Which of the three couples had the most romantic meeting? Whose was most dependent on fate? Why?

- Do you believe in fate? Looking back on your life, are there any events where you believe fate played a part?

- Do you believe fate is the best way to meet the love of your life? What alternatives can you think of?

FATEF

"I SENT A RANDOM TEXT MESSAGE AND HE REPLIED!"

Tina Baldwin, 28, sent a random text message. Andrew, 21, instantly sent one back. A year later they were married.

TINA It was like any other day. I was chatting with my best friend in the kitchen. We were bored so I decided
05 to send a text message to a random number and see what happened. Don't ask me why – it was a real spur-of-the-moment thing. I texted, "Feel like talking?" and waited to see
10 if anyone would reply.

To my amazement, someone did – a guy. He just typed "Yes." That day, we had a great hour or two, texting back and forth. When he asked me to
15 call him, I didn't hesitate. We both had the same sense of humor and, although it was strange at first, we talked just as easily as when we'd been texting.

I'd just gotten out of a relationship,
20 so I wasn't looking for a boyfriend. But over the next few months Andrew and I kept in touch every day.

Although I wasn't overly impressed with the photo he sent of himself,
25 when we talked on the phone I found myself becoming more and more attracted to him. It seems bizarre but I'm sure I fell in love with him before I ever saw him. We had so much in
30 common: we loved the same music, the same movies, we laughed at the same jokes.

We met for the first time in a cafe in my neighborhood in Washington,
35 D.C.; he came down from Baltimore. I was very nervous, and met my best friend for a pep talk before I went to meet him. He was much better looking in person and we smiled at
40 each other for ages. Seeing him smile for the first time is something I'll

UL ATTRACTION

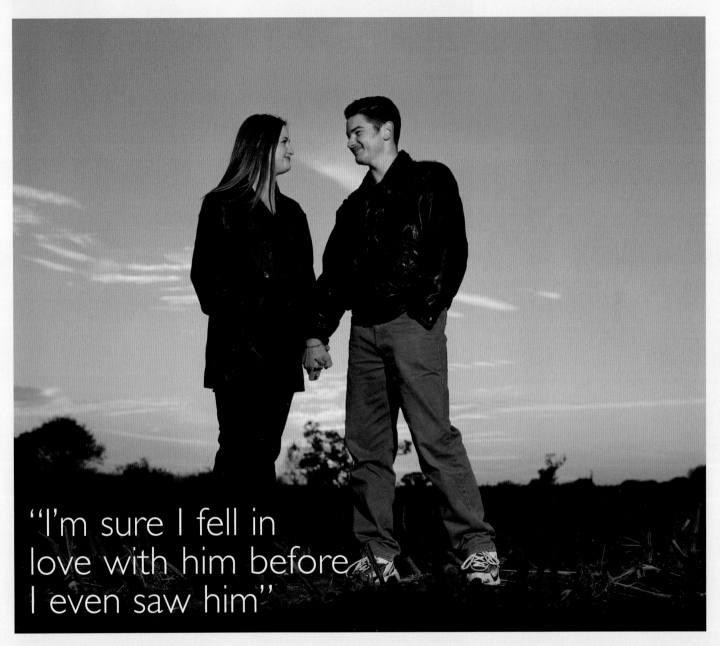

"I'm sure I fell in love with him before I even saw him"

never forget. From then on we saw each other constantly, meeting up at cafes and clubs and getting together on 45 weekends.

Ten months later, we were married. It was a great day – a big white wedding. Now I can't imagine life without Andrew and can't quite 50 believe how we met. I guess he was just out there waiting for me.

ANDREW I've never believed in fate, but when something like this happens, you realize that the odds are billions to one. At first, Tina and I were just 55 having fun but, as time passed, I saw that we had so much in common – we'd say the same thing at the same time, or I'd call her and it would be busy because she was trying to get 60 through to me.

The thing I loved about Tina was her personality, and when, finally, I met her I thought she was stunning. That evening I drove back to Baltimore 65 on my motorcycle, knowing the relationship wasn't going to end there.

During the following months, I'd make the hour long trip to Washington every weekend. It got to a point where it just wasn't practical any more and 70 I said to Tina, "What we do is either make a serious commitment or nip it in the bud."

I left my family and friends in Baltimore, but I've never regretted the 75 move for a second. On our wedding day I was ecstatic. There was nothing I wanted more.

ARTICLE B

"HE KNOCKED ME OFF MY BIKE!"

Emma Allen, 31, ran into Ross, 39, on her bike during a ride in London. Two years later they were married.

EMMA Whenever anyone asks us how we met, we burst out laughing – it's such a ridiculous story. I had gone out on my bike to meet a friend. I always ride too fast, and what happened this
05 time was, as I rounded a corner, an arm appeared out of nowhere. The next minute, I was flying through the air into someone's garden.

Not only was I confused – I didn't
10 know where I was for a moment, and I could hear people saying, "What have you done, Ross? Do you think she's all right?" I was incredibly embarrassed. After all, I was lying in a flowerbed
15 with a bicycle on top of me.

I just wanted to crawl away and, being a redhead with fair skin who blushes really easily, I could feel this heat rising up over my face. So I
20 scrambled to my feet, saying crossly, "I'm fine, I'm fine," got on my bike and tore off along the path, hoping never, ever to see the guy I'd hit and his pals again.

25 I did, though. In a weird stroke of double fate, on my way back, I passed them again. And, hideously, my baseball cap flew off my head right in front of them. It took all my courage
30 to go back, bashfully, and retrieve it.

I'd seen Ross around before but I'd never spoken to him. So when, the next day, a bunch of flowers arrived on my doorstep with a note
35 saying, "Have a happening day," I knew who they were from. The florist confirmed it: Yes, he was tall and blonde, and he worked as a landscape gardener.

40 It took a lot of guts, but I knew I had to go and thank him in person. And I was glad I did – although my knees turned to jelly. I was blown away. We chatted for ages and a few weeks later
45 he invited me out for dinner. That was it. We've now been married 11 years.

"Giving flowers was easy, but when she came to thank me, I was dumbstruck"

I'm a total believer in fate, but what I think is that you have to build your own destiny. If Ross hadn't sent
50 me flowers and if I hadn't gone to thank him, none of this would have happened.

ROSS I had just come back from traveling, surfing, and hitchhiking
55 around South America when I met Emma. I was feeling quite low, having been mugged at gunpoint in Panama.

What I remember is seeing this very striking girl with a wonderful mane of
60 red hair. I'd seen her around before, but we'd never spoken. One day I was with two friends, walking down this little alleyway and recalling some traveling tale. I must have gesticulated
65 too wildly because, the next thing I knew, this girl was coming toward me on a bike and was suddenly catapulted into a garden. On the one hand I felt terrible, but on the other I couldn't
70 believe how gorgeous she was – this gorgeous red hair lying underneath a bicycle. I couldn't take my eyes off her.

For me the meeting was pure romance. What I did was go straight to
75 the local florist and, because she was so identifiable, they knew who she was and delivered flowers to her the next day.

Giving flowers was easy, but when she came to thank me, I was dumbstruck.
80 I had never felt like this before – I knew she was the one.

Finally, I did find the courage to ask her out – and the rest, as they say, is history.

LANGUAGE FOCUS
Ways of adding emphasis

1 Find similar sentences to these in your article. How exactly do they differ? What is the effect of the differences? Compare answers with a partner from the other group.

> **ARTICLE A**
>
> I'll never forget seeing him smile for the first time. L40
> _____
>
> I loved Tina's personality. L61
> _____
>
> We either make a serious commitment or nip it in the bud. L70
> _____
>
> I wanted nothing more. L76
> _____

> **ARTICLE B**
>
> I think you have to build your own destiny. L47
> _____
>
> I remember seeing this very striking girl. L58
> _____
>
> I went straight to the local florist. L74
> _____
>
> Finally I found the courage to ask her out. L82
> _____

There are many ways of emphasizing part of a sentence.

1 Structures that add emphasis

  a I love Tina's personality. (base sentence)

What	
The thing	*I love about Tina is her personality.*
Something	

    It's Tina's personality that I love.
    It's Tina who I love.

  b He criticizes/criticized me constantly. (base sentence)

What	*he does is*	
The thing	*he did was*	*criticize me constantly.*
Something		

2 Negative inversion

  Certain negative expressions can be put at the beginning of a sentence for emphasis.

    I'll never forget seeing him smile for the first time.
    Never will I forget *seeing him smile for the first time.*
    People rarely fall in love at first sight.
    Rarely do people fall in love *at first sight.*

3 Emphatic *do / does / did*

    *Finally, I **did** find the courage to ask her out.*

4 Emphatic structures must sound emphatic!

  Practice saying the sentences from Exercises 1, 2, and 3 above.

▶▶ **Grammar Reference p. 148**

---

2 **CD2 3** Listen and identify the ways in which the speakers add emphasis to these base sentences.

1. I do my homework immediately after class.
2. It was love at first sight.
3. Most couples don't realize how difficult married life can be.
4. I blame the parents for badly behaved kids.
5. The values of society are at risk and the very survival of our nation is threatened.
6. I understood what she meant then.
7. Sam broke the blue vase.
8. I won't marry anybody.

3 Make this sentence more emphatic using these expressions.

We like hiking in the Andes.

1. What we …
2. One thing …
3. The Andes is where …
4. It's …
5. … is something …
6. There's nothing … more than …

CD2 4 Listen and check.
What are the lines that stimulate the different responses? Practice the conversations with your partner, paying particular attention to the stress and intonation.

4 Rephrase these sentences to make them more emphatic.

1. Love changes the course of your life.
2. She repeatedly contradicts me.
3. First you have to decide your priorities.
4. I admire Bill's courage.
5. You should go to the mountains on your vacation.
6. **A** Why didn't you tell Peter the news?
   B I told him – honestly!
7. I've never been so humiliated in my life.
8. We eat out only occasionally.

5 Complete these sentences with your own ideas, using an emphatic structure. Compare answers with the class.

1. What I can't *stand* about …
2. What surprises me *every* time …
3. The thing that annoys me *most* …
4. What we did after class yesterday …
5. It's our *teacher* who …
6. Something I've *never* told you …
7. What the *government* should …
8. *Never* in my *life* have I …

CD2 5 Listen and compare your ideas.

VOCABULARY AND SPEAKING
Proverbs and poetry

1 Match a line in **A** with a line in **B** to make proverbs. Do you have similar ones in your language?

A	B
1. Love is	through his stomach.
2. The course of true love	repent at leisure.
3. All the world loves	the heart grow fonder.
4. Cold hands,	never to have loved at all.
5. All's fair in love	contempt.
6. The way to a man's heart is	and war.
7. Marry in haste,	blind.
8. Better to have loved and lost than	never did run smooth.
9. A little of what you fancy does	you good.
10. Absence makes	warm heart.
11. Familiarity breeds	a lover.

2 Complete the replies with a suitable proverb from Exercise 1.

1. They're back together again, but their relationship's had a bumpy ride.
   You know what they say – the course of true love never did run smoothly.
2. OK, I'll have one more. But that's the last one.
3. You? Going to cooking classes? You *must* be in love!
4. But I don't want you to go off to Mexico for six months. How will I survive?
5. He's always out with his friends, never with her. Can't she see that he's a jerk?

CD2 6 Listen and check.
Write more conversation openers for the remaining proverbs. Ask another pair of students to respond with the correct proverb.

3 Shakespeare added more proverbs to the English language than anyone else. Which one do you think *sounds* like his from the list above?

4 **CD2 7** Close your books and listen to one of Shakespeare's most famous love sonnets. Which season is he comparing his loved one to? Can you remember any words or phrases?

5 **CD2 7** Work with a partner. Choose the correct word to complete the lines of the poem. Listen again and check. Then read the poem aloud.

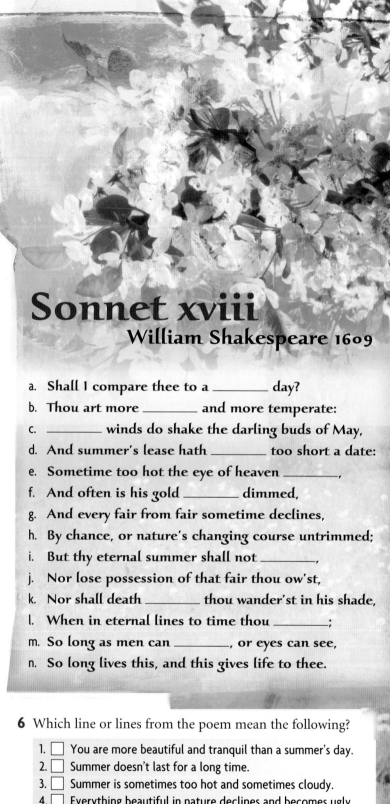

Sonnet xviii
William Shakespeare 1609

a. Shall I compare thee to a _____ day?
b. Thou art more _____ and more temperate:
c. _____ winds do shake the darling buds of May,
d. And summer's lease hath _____ too short a date:
e. Sometime too hot the eye of heaven _____,
f. And often is his gold _____ dimmed,
g. And every fair from fair sometime declines,
h. By chance, or nature's changing course untrimmed;
i. But thy eternal summer shall not _____,
j. Nor lose possession of that fair thou ow'st,
k. Nor shall death _____ thou wander'st in his shade,
l. When in eternal lines to time thou _____;
m. So long as men can _____, or eyes can see,
n. So long lives this, and this gives life to thee.

6 Which line or lines from the poem mean the following?

1. ☐ You are more beautiful and tranquil than a summer's day.
2. ☐ Summer doesn't last for a long time.
3. ☐ Summer is sometimes too hot and sometimes cloudy.
4. ☐ Everything beautiful in nature declines and becomes ugly with time.
5. ☐ You possess such beauty that it will last forever.
6. ☐ You will never die because you are immortalized in poetry.
7. ☐ As long as people exist who read this poem you will have eternal life.

7 What other things could you compare a loved one to? Discuss with the class.

sunny/summer's/perfect
lovely/attractive/stunning
heavy/rough/soft
all/far/way
scalds/shines/burns
complexion/hair/chariot

fade/ebb/wither

boast/brag/proclaim
shrink'st/grow'st/wrinkl'st
write/breathe/think

Glossary
thee/thou = you
art = are
summer's lease = summer season
hath = has
fair = beauty
untrimmed = made ugly
thy = your
fair thou ow'st = beauty you own
eternal lines = immortal verse
this = this sonnet
life = immortality

LISTENING AND SPEAKING
When love lasts forever

1 What and when is Valentine's Day? Is it celebrated in your country?

2 **CD2 8** Olive Hodges is 102-years-old. She is being interviewed on Valentine's Day. The lines below are taken from the interview. Listen and answer the questions.

1. *"She had been looking forward to her 77th wedding anniversary this year."* Why is she not looking forward to it now?
2. *"He came through without a scratch."* Who came through what?
3. *"… he did this about six times."* What did he do?
4. *"I'll put him out of his misery."* What did Olive mean by this?
5. *"I didn't see any need for a hurry."* Any hurry for what?
6. *"I think it was stronger."* What was stronger? When?
7. *"It was quite a job to reassure him."* What did Fred need reassurance about?

3 Answer the questions.
1. How did Olive and Fred's relationship start?
2. What course did their courtship take?
3. What is Olive's recipe for a long marriage?
4. How do we know that they never took their love for granted?
5. How does the presenter show he is moved by the story?

What do you think?

- What's your reaction to Olive's story? How common is her experience?
- Do you know any other couples who have enjoyed such a long marriage?

EVERYDAY ENGLISH
Getting emotional

1 **CD2 9** Read and listen to the lines of conversation. Then discuss with a partner. Who could be speaking? What might the situation be? Discuss with the class.

1. Get this heap of old metal out of my driveway! Now!
2. You mean more to me than words could ever say.
3. I could be wrong, but I think someone in this room is to blame for this.
4. Wow! I could never do anything like that. Stick figures are my limit.
5. I'll have to look at my calendar. Life's just so hectic at the moment. You know me, I'm so much in demand.
6. Come on, you can tell me. I won't breathe a word to anyone. I promise.
7. Could you *not* keep picking on me in front of our friends? It looks so awful.
8. Thank goodness you're here. When I couldn't get you on your cell phone, I thought you'd had an accident.
9. He ranked in the top 2 percent in the country. So his father and I are thrilled.
10. Well, I think you did very well to come in third. Keep up the good work and you'll win next time.
11. Oh, come on now, don't cry. You'll be fine. It's only a scratch. Hardly bleeding at all.
12. It was nothing. Anybody would have done the same.
13. I can't tell you how much I appreciate everything you've done for me. I would've been so lost here on my own.
14. I'm out of here! I don't like the looks of those people.
15. You're kidding me. Nobody gets hitched wearing green rain boots!
16. What do you mean I'm a couch potato?! I go to the gym twice a week.

2 Which of these emotions are expressed by the lines in Exercise 1? Sometimes more than one is appropriate.

admiration	boastfulness	gratitude	reassurance
adoration	curiosity	indignation	relief
amusement	encouragement	irritation	sarcasm
anxiety	fear	modesty	suspicion
astonishment	fury	pride	

3 **CD2 9** Say the lines to your partner according to the emotion. Listen again and compare the stress and intonation.

4 **CD2 10** Listen to someone saying the same name in several different ways. Try and identify the emotions.

▶▶ **Writing** Discussing pros and cons **p. 119**

6 Newspeak

- **Grammar:** Distancing the facts
- **Vocabulary:** Nouns formed from phrasal verbs
- **Everyday English:** Responding to news

STARTER

1 The words in the box are commonly used in newspaper headlines. Why do you think these words are often short and dramatic?

Complete the headlines with the words.

busted	blows up	blow	havoc	cops	slay	raid	slash
freak	snatch	dumps	bid	thug	row	probe	

1 GRANNY-BEATING [ ] CAUGHT

2 J&J to [ ] 5,000 jobs in [ ] to break even

3 Teen confesses in newsman [ ]

4 SENATOR [ ] [ ] OVER POL CARTOON

5 ATTACK DOG SHOT BY [ ]

6 NEW [ ] INTO MURDERS REVEALS FRESH CLUES

7 [ ] summer storm [ ] snow, sleet

8 53 gang members [ ] in Bronx [ ]

9 Minogue in club [ ] with beau

10 New inflation figures deal [ ] to recovery hopes

11 Hi-tech thieves [ ] data from ATMs

12 TAXI DRIVER STRIKE THREAT SPELLS [ ] FOR CITY

2 In the U.S., the main newspapers are regional, not national. Is it the same in your country? Do your newspapers have a political bias?

How do you get your news? Do you read a newspaper, website, or blog regularly? Which one? Why do you choose that one?

READING AND SPEAKING
Tabloid and serious newspapers

1 Look at the front pages of two different newspapers, the *New York Times* and the *New York Post*. Which is the tabloid newspaper, and which is the serious newspaper? What are your immediate impressions of the different presentations?

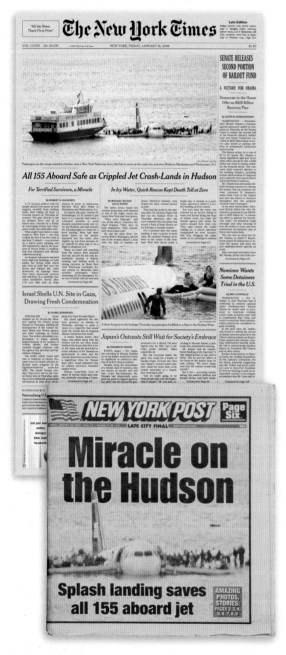

Think about:
- the size of the headline
- the content of the headline
- the photographs
- the layout of the front page
- the length of the text on the front page

2 Read the two articles on pages 53–54. Summarize each story in three or four sentences. Which newspaper:
1. is more factual and objective?
2. is more sensational?
3. relies more on short, dramatic quotations?
4. has longer, more complex sentences?
5. uses more informal, idiomatic, and conversational language?
6. uses more formal, controlled, and concise language?

3 This is the sequence of reporting the events in the *Post*.
1. the crash landing and survival of everyone on board
2. the conditions under which a person could die of hypothermia
3. the reason for the crash
4. eyewitnesses' accounts of the plane crash
5. details about the rescue
6. details about the plane after the rescue

What is the sequence of reporting the events in the *Times*? What is the same? What is different?

4 What are the different ways in which the pilot is referred to in each paper? Which paper prints his nickname? Why?

5 Who or what are these? Why do you think they appear in both articles?
1. Hudson
2. Chesley Sullenberger
3. La Guardia
4. Jeff Kolodjay
5. Michael Bloomberg
6. Charlotte, N.C.
7. New York Waterway

Vocabulary work

6 Find these words in the articles. What do they mean in context?
1. plucked
2. ditch(ed)
3. dumped
4. evoked
5. banked
6. plumes
7. armada
8. charmed

7 Find informal words or idioms in the *Post* and formal words in the *Times* that have similar meanings to the words below.

The *Post* – informal words for . . .	The *Times* – formal words for . . .
big success	praised publicly
act of preventing something undesireable	event causing sudden damage or suffering
someone who excels at something	prevented
damaging something so it stops working	skillful
police officers	carried out
arrived	causing physical or psychological pain
	related to airplanes and flying

CRASH RESCUE A REAL SLAM DUNK

By LARRY CELONA, MURRAY WEISS and DAN MANGAN

What A Save!

An ace US Airways pilot made an astonishing controlled crash landing into the frigid Hudson River after his jet hit geese and lost power minutes after takeoff from La Guardia - and all 155 people aboard were rescued.

One person suffered two broken legs, a paramedic said, but there were no other serious injuries.

Investigators brought in a giant crane and a barge today to help pull the plane from the river.

"We've had a miracle on 34th Street – I believe now we've had a miracle on the Hudson," Gov. Paterson declared.

Cool-headed hero Capt. Chesley B. "Sully" Sullenberger III - a former Air Force fighter pilot and trained glider flier - "masterfully" steered the Airbus A320, originally bound for Charlotte, NC, safely down to the river, Mayor Bloomberg said.

"Both engines cut out, and he actually floated it into the river," passenger Joe Hart marveled.

Bloomberg said Sullenberger, 57, "walked the plane twice after everybody else was off to verify that there was nobody else on board, and assures us there were not."

The crash took place on a 20-degree day, one of the coldest of the season - with the water temperature 36 degrees, a Coast Guard official said.

Hypothermia, at that temperature, can hit within five to eight minutes, experts said.

It would take just a half-hour to lose consciousness - and no more than 90 minutes to die.

Of the 150 passengers and five crew members - including a 9-month-old and a 4-year-old - 35 were rescued from the water. The rest were plucked from the wings of the plane or a life raft, sources said.

US Airways Flight 1549 took off at 3:26 p.m. and was just five miles from La Guardia when the plane hit a flock of birds, knocking out power to one engine, a source said.

As the pilot turned toward Teterboro Airport, where he hoped to make an emergency landing, the plane experienced a second "bird strike" – losing power in its remaining engine.

Sullenberger then radioed the control tower that he was going to ditch the plane - and the Air Force vet's certification as a glider pilot came in more than handy, the source said.

The plane flew over Washington Heights, then cut to the river at 1,400 feet. It went over the 604-foot east tower of the George Washington Bridge, clearing it by about 800 feet.

Patrick Wilder, a 35-year-old social worker, said, "I was riding my bike near 125th Street, and I saw [the plane] coming low.

"I was watching it, and I lost it in the sun. Thirty seconds later, some cops in a car showed up and asked me if I saw a plane come down. It looked like it was landing. It was level. It was very low. It was no higher than the bluff" in New Jersey.

Another witness, Associated Press researcher Barbara Sambriski, was looking toward the river, saw the plane, and thought, "Why is it so low?"

"And - splash! - it hit the water," Sambriski said.

The plane went into the river at about 3:30 p.m., just a few minutes after takeoff.

"The captain said, 'Brace for impact because we're going down,'" Jeff Kolodjay said, noting that his fellow passengers put their heads in their laps and started praying.

"You've got to give it to the pilot. He made a hell of a landing," Kolodjay said.

Almost immediately, ferryboats raced to the aircraft as it bobbed in the Hudson, near the West Side Highway between West 48th and 50th streets.

Passengers sought refuge on the wings of the aircraft - which weighs 169,000 pounds when fully loaded - and shivered in the bone-chilling cold.

A fleet of NY Waterway boats began plucking passengers clad in yellow life vests from the plane and its wings as city firefighters and federal transportation officials sped to the site.

"We came onto the scene, we saw many boats, we saw the plane halfway submerged," said Detective Michael Delaney of the NYPD scuba team.

"One woman was just holding onto the side of the ferryboat, trying to get up onto the ferry and was unable to make it."

The seven-year scuba unit vet dumped his equipment, jumped in with just a mask and snorkel, and held on to the woman until another

ferryboat came over, and its captain and crew lifted her onto the boat.

"She was very frantic at the time," Delaney said of the 35- to 40-year-old woman, who was wearing a life vest. "I just told her to relax. I asked her what her name was. She said, 'Please don't let me go.' She thought that the boat was going to run over us."

It was a massive rescue effort, with the NYPD, FDNY, Office of Emergency Management, NY Waterway, Circle Line and Coast Guard taking part.

NYPD Capt. Richard Johnson, of the Marine Unit, said police boats rescued more than a dozen people.

"We basically came up right alongside of them," he said. "[The passengers] kind of jumped toward the boat and we pulled them over. Their legs were sort of dangling off the boat and we had to heave them over three or four feet of water."

NY Waterway deckhand Wilfredo Rivera, 26, said his craft pulled 56 people to safety.

"People were screaming," he said. "They thought they were going to die. They were saying, 'It's cold! The water's cold!' People were just yelling and nervous."

He said that even when they were safely on the boat, "they were nervous. They were shocked."

NY Waterway spokesman Pat Smith said that within 15 minutes, 14 ferries were put into service in the rescue, and in all, 142 people were finally rescued by its fleet.

"Many passengers never even got wet," said NY Waterway director of operations Alan Warren.

Paterson was effusive in his praise for the rescue effort.

"I think for all the times that we've had to appear at these press conferences in rather dismal circumstances, this is a day to realize how blessed this city is, and how all of us are, as New Yorkers, and . . . the families and those who survived," he said.

He noted another passenger told him he had a brother on 9/11, "so he is no stranger to tragedy, but he said he is a very blessed person today."

Speaking from her Danville, Calif., home, the pilot's wife told The Post she was "shaking" when she heard about the crash and miraculous save.

Authorities said Sullenberger had the plane descend toward the Hudson just as he would if he were landing on a runway.

Once it was on the water, it was only minutes before the doors were opened.

Women and children were let off the plane first as the plane bobbed south in the strong current.

"It would appear that the pilot did a masterful job of landing the plane in the river and then making sure that everyone got out," Bloomberg said.

January 16, 2009 NY Times

Pilot Is Hailed After Jetliner's Icy Plunge

By ROBERT D. MCFADDEN

A US Airways jetliner with 155 people aboard lost power in both engines, possibly from striking birds, after taking off from La Guardia Airport on Thursday afternoon. The pilot ditched in the icy Hudson River and all on board were rescued by a flotilla of converging ferries and emergency boats, the authorities said.

What might have been a catastrophe in New York — one that evoked the feel if not the scale of the Sept. 11 attack — was averted by a pilot's quick thinking and deft maneuvers, and by the nearness of rescue boats, a combination that witnesses and officials called miraculous.

As stunned witnesses watched from high-rise buildings on both banks, the Airbus A320, which had risen to 3,200 feet over the Bronx and banked left, came downriver, its fuselage lower than many apartment terraces and windows, in a carefully executed touchdown shortly after 3:30 p.m. that sent up huge plumes of water at midstream, between West 48th Street in Manhattan and Weehawken, N.J.

On board, the pilot, Chesley B. Sullenberger III, 57, unable to get back to La Guardia, had made a command decision to avoid densely populated areas and try for the Hudson, and had warned the 150 passengers to brace for a hard landing. Most had their heads down as the jetliner slammed into the water, nose slightly up, just three minutes after takeoff on what was to be a flight to Charlotte, N.C.

Many on board and watching from the shores were shocked that the aircraft did not sink immediately. Instead, it floated, twisting and drifting south in strong currents, as three New York Waterway commuter ferries moved in. Moments later, terrified passengers began swarming out the emergency exits into brutally cold air and onto the submerged wings of the bobbing jetliner, which began taking in water.

As the first ferry nudged up alongside, witnesses said, some passengers were able to leap onto the decks. Others were helped aboard by ferry crews. Soon, a small armada of police boats, fireboats, tugboats and Coast Guard craft converged on the scene, and some of them snubbed up to keep the jetliner afloat. Helicopters brought wet-suited police divers, who dropped into the water to help with the rescues.

Brought ashore on both sides of the river, the survivors were taken to hospitals in Manhattan and New Jersey, mostly for treatment of exposure to the brutal cold: 18 degrees in the air, about 35 degrees in the water that many had stood in on the wings up to their waists.

Still, most of them walked ashore, some grim with fright and shivering with cold, wrapped in borrowed coats. But others were smiling, and a few were ready to give interviews to mobs of reporters and television cameras. Some described their survival as a miracle, a sentiment repeated later by city and state officials; others gave harrowing accounts of an ordeal whose outcome few might have imagined in such a crisis.

Mayor Michael R. Bloomberg said that there had been few injuries and that the pilot had done "a masterful job."

W. Douglas Parker, chairman and chief executive of US Airways, and officials of the Federal Aviation Administration said that Flight 1549 had taken off from La Guardia at 3:26 p.m., bound for Charlotte. It headed north, across the East River and over the Bronx on a route that would involve a sweeping left turn to head south. But both engines lost power about a minute into the flight.

The National Transportation Safety Board and state and local agencies are to investigate the cause of the crash, which could take months, but early indications were that the plane's engines had shut down after having ingested a flock of birds — variously described as geese or gulls. It was not clear where the birds were encountered.

The pilot radioed air traffic controllers on Long Island that his plane had sustained a "double bird strike." Without power, returning to the airport was out of the question, aviation experts said. He saw a small airport in the distance, apparently at Teterboro, N.J., but decided to head down the Hudson and make a water landing, a rare event that is mentioned in the safety instructions given by flight crews to all passengers on every flight.

Neil Lasher, 62, a consultant for Sony Music Publishing who lives in a 27th-floor apartment near the shore in Guttenberg, N.J., watched the plane go down. "As soon as the plane hit the water," he said, "I could see the New York Waterway ferries from New York and the Jersey side, within a minute, heading toward the airplane."

One of the passengers who scrambled out onto the wing was Jeff Kolodjay, 31, who had been in Seat 22A in the rear. He said that after the emergency doors were opened, the plane began to take on water. In what he described as "organized chaos," the passengers, all wearing life vests, "just walked through the water" toward the exits.

Tom Fox, president of New York Water Taxi, which sent boats to the scene in the Hudson but did not participate in the rescues, said the setting was, in a sense, ideal for a crash landing on water. "It couldn't have gone down in a better location because there are so many water-borne assets there," he said. "The pilot must have been both talented and charmed."

LANGUAGE FOCUS
Distancing the facts

> Look at these sentences from newspaper articles.
>
> **It would appear** that the pilot did a masterful job.
> These incidents **are reported to have happened** last June . . .
> **It is believed** that the governor was alerted to the problem . . .
> **It is expected** there will be widespread praise . . .
>
> These are all ways of giving information without stating categorically that you know it to be true. The writer is putting distance between himself and the facts.
>
> **1 Passive constructions**
> Look at these sentences.
>
> They say he works on Wall Street.
> People assume he's earning a lot of money.
> Everyone thought he had made his fortune in oil.
>
> These sentences can be expressed in the passive in two ways, beginning with *It* or *He*:
>
> 1 **It is said that** he works on Wall Street.
> **It is assumed that** he's earning a lot of money.
> **It was thought that** he had made his fortune in oil.
>
> 2 He **is said to** work on Wall Street.
> He **is assumed to be** earning a lot of money.
> He **was thought to have** made his fortune in oil.
>
> What differences in form do you notice?
>
> **2 seem and appear**
> He **appears to have** learned his lesson.
> The Post **seems to have** found its information from a
> variety of sources.
> The Times **seems to be** more factual.
> **It appears that** the governor took the incident seriously.
>
> ▶▶ Grammar Reference p. 148

Passive constructions

1 Rewrite these sentences. Use the words in *italics* to start your new sentence.

1. It is reported that *the international criminal Jimmy Rosendale* is living in Canada.
2. People believe that *he* is the head of a gang of bank robbers.
3. Everyone knows that *the gang* has carried out a series of robberies.
4. It is supposed that *they* have escaped with over $10 million.
5. It is thought that *they* are targeting banks in small provincial towns.
6. They say *Jimmy Rosendale* is wanted for questioning by police in three countries.
7. We understand *he* escaped from police custody by bribing a guard.
8. It is assumed that *he* has been involved in criminal activities all his life.
9. People presume that *he* learned his trade from his father.
10. It is alleged that *his father* was the mastermind behind the 2005 gold bullion robbery.

seem and *appear*

2 Change these sentences. Use the words in *italics* to start your new sentence.

1. It seems *the weather* is changing.
2. It appears that *we* have missed the train.
3. Peter appeared to have been attacked by a bull. (*It*)
4. He seemed to have survived the ordeal. (*It*)
5. It would seem that *the government* has changed its policy.
6. It appears that *they* are worried about losing the next election.

Reporting the news

3 In groups, write a short newspaper article for one of these headlines. Include some of the constructions you have practiced.

Athlete loses medal

Governor lied about donations from businessman

PRICELESS PAINTING LOST IN FIRE TRAGEDY

DAYTIME TV STAR RICKY JAILED IN STREET FIGHT

ACTRESS CARRIE MOORE TO WED FOR NINTH TIME

WALL STREET TRADER EMBEZZLES $250 MILLION

DANGEROUS PRISONER ESCAPES BY HELICOPTER

12-year-old math genius admitted to Harvard

4 **CD2** **11** Listen to the news broadcast and use it as a dictation.
Choose one student to write on the board while the rest of the class helps.

I think you spelled that word wrong.
I don't think it was "would." I think it was "had."

VOCABULARY
Nouns formed from phrasal verbs

> **1** There are many compound nouns formed with a verb + preposition, or preposition + verb combination.
>
> *Here is an **update** on the news.*
> *At the **outbreak** of war, I was just three years old.*
> *The arts are suffering from budget **cutbacks**.*
> *The town has a **bypass**, which keeps traffic out of the center.*
>
> Where is the stress on these words?
>
> **2** Some of these nouns operate as phrasal verbs, and some don't.
>
> *Rioting **broke out** in the middle of the night.*
> *Funds allocated to research have been severely **cut back**.*
>
> There is no verb *to date up*. **To pass by** is used literally.
>
> *We **passed by** the park on the way to the station.*

"He says his name is Billy and he's here to update our software."

1 Complete the sentences with a compound noun starting with the word given. Use the definitions to help you.

`out`

1. *the final result of an election, or negotiations, when no one knows what to expect*
   We are all waiting for the __outcome__ of the meeting.

2. *a set of clothes worn together*
   She bought a new _____ for the wedding.

3. *what is expected to happen in the future*
   The _____ for tomorrow's weather is bleak, I'm afraid.

4. *a store or company through which products are sold*
   The Body Shop has retail _____ in major cities throughout the world.

`take`

5. *a meal you buy in a restaurant to eat at home*
   Should we eat out or get _____?

6. *getting control of a company by buying most of its shares*
   Business sections of newspapers are full of company mergers and _____.

`down`

7. *failure or ruin following success*
   She had a great career, but her struggle with weight was her _____.

8. *a lot of rain that falls fast and heavily*
   I got soaked in yesterday's _____.

9. *information obtained from the Internet*
   For free _____, click here.

`break`

10. *new and successful development*
    There have been important _____ in organ transplants in the last 20 years.

11. *a serious mental illness*
    After his wife died, Paul suffered a nervous _____.

Use `up` at the end of these four words.

`shake` `back` `set` `break`

12. *ending a marriage*
    Sarah was very depressed after the _____ of her marriage to Tony.

13. *something used for support if the main one fails*
    At the end of a day's writing, I _____ my work to a separate hard drive.

14. *a situation in which a lot of changes are made*
    There's been a big _____ at work. They fired six managers and introduced new procedures.

15. *a way of organizing or arranging something*
    I don't understand the political _____ of the States. Their political parties seem the same.

2 Work with a partner. Choose some of the words from the box. Write a definition and a sample sentence with a blank. Use a dictionary if necessary. Test the other students.

lookout	setback	outbreak	backlash	upkeep
slip-up	offshoot	comeback	showdown	upturn
write-off	drawback	holdup	outburst	knockout

LISTENING AND SPEAKING
A foreign correspondent

1 Look at the photos. Who are the different people? Where are they? What's happening?

2 *"News is always bad news. We listen for a couple of days, then we lose interest."*

What recent news stories illustrate or contradict this?

3 Check that you know these words.

- do somebody justice
- a pack (of wild animals)
- inconspicuous
- offbeat places
- a patch (of land)
- a skirmish
- to shrink (*pp* shrunk)
- subtlety
- focused

4 **CD2 12** Listen to an interview with Simon Winchester, a foreign correspondent who lives in the U.S., and answer the questions.

Part one
1. What is the interviewer's first question? How does Simon Winchester answer it?
2. What kind of journalist is he? What kind of journalist *isn't* he?
3. What big news story of the 1970s does he mention?
4. What kind of place does he like?

Part two
5. What is the first reason he gives for the change in the foreign correspondent's role?
6. Why did the British press use to have much better coverage of foreign affairs?
7. What does he say about the *New York Times*?
8. What is his attitude toward television news reporting?
9. What sort of news reporting does he like?
10. How have budgets affected foreign news coverage?

Language work

5 What do you think these lines from the interview mean?
- I was very much in the thick of things.
- a more fulfilling time personally
- I've never made a virtue out of danger.
- the echoes of empire
- the little essay that illuminates brilliantly the inner workings of some distant place
- newspapers have become more market driven, and less of a public service
- their hands are tied

6 Simon Winchester often understates his points. For example, he refers to some dangerous situations as *skirmishes*. Find other examples of understatement in the audio script on page 134.

What do you think?

- Do you agree that people aren't so interested in what is happening outside their own country anymore? Has the media numbed our curiosity? How much foreign news coverage is there in your news media?

- How much does the news media report the news and how much does it create it? Think of recent big world stories that exemplify this.

- Do you feel bombarded, or do you appreciate having a wide range of choices provided by newspapers, TV, and the Internet?

EVERYDAY ENGLISH
Responding to news

1 Match the statements and responses. Sometimes there is more than one possible answer.

A	B
1. Guess what! I won $5 million in the lottery!	a. So what? I don't care.
2. My grandfather died last week.	b. In your dreams.
3. One of my students told me I was a bad teacher.	c. Over my dead body.
4. Here we are! Home at last.	d. Now you're talking!
5. I'm broke since I bought all those designer clothes.	e. Nice!
6. Did you hear that Jim's leaving to go to another job?	f. And that surprises you?
7. I missed the last bus and had to walk home.	g. Thank goodness for that!
8. When I get a job, I'm going to be a millionaire.	h. Serves you right.
9. I'm going on vacation to Bali for two weeks.	i. You're kidding!
10. My six-year-old daughter painted me a picture for Father's Day.	j. What a drag!
11. I'm tired of studying. Let's go dancing.	k. What a brat!
12. Susan says she never wants to see you again.	l. Oh no! I'm so sorry to hear that.
13. My team lost again last weekend.	m. Good riddance.
14. *(12-year-old child)* Dad, I'm going to an all-night party. Is that OK?	n. What a sweetheart!

CD2 13 Listen and check. What additional comments do you hear?

2 What ideas do the responses in column B express?

- ☐ surprise at someone's lack of respect
- ☐ sympathy
- ☐ no sympathy
- ☐ pleasure that someone is leaving
- ☐ no surprise
- ☐ no concern
- ☐ relief
- ☐ I like what you're saying.
- ☐ Isn't she cute?
- ☐ How boring!
- ☐ I'm impressed!
- ☐ I don't believe you.
- ☐ What you're saying won't happen.
- ☐ I won't allow this to happen.

3 Work with a partner. Cover the responses and try to remember the complete conversations.

4 **CD2 14** Listen to these lines of conversation. Reply using a response from column B in Exercise 1, then continue the conversations.

5 **CD2 15** Listen to the conversations. What is the second speaker's attitude?

Look at the audio script on pages 134–135 and practice the conversations with a partner. **B** should try to sound sarcastic.

6 In pairs, make conversations from the chart. **B** needs to decide how to sound – sincere or sarcastic.

A	B
I've done all the dishes.	You've been a great help.
I've spilled paint all over your carpet.	Thank you so much.
I've burned the meal.	That's just fantastic.
I've vacuumed everywhere.	I don't know what I'd have done without you.

"That's just fantastic!!"

▶▶ **Writing** A letter to a newspaper **p. 120**

7 Words of wisdom

Grammar: Modal auxiliary verbs
Vocabulary: Rhyme and reason
Everyday English: Breaking the rules of English

STARTER

1 Work with a partner. Which of these people have you heard of? Why are they famous?

2 What do their quotations mean? Which do you agree with? Do you have any favorites?

1 **"**A journey of one thousand miles begins with a single step.**"**
Confucius 551–479 BC

2 **"**Health is the greatest gift, contentment the greatest wealth, faithfulness the best relationship.**"**
Buddha 563–483 BC

3 **"**Our youth now love luxury. They have bad manners, contempt for authority; they show disrespect for their elders; they contradict their parents and tyrannize their teachers.**"**
Socrates 469–399 BC

4 **"**The very atmosphere of firearms anywhere and everywhere restrains evil interference – they deserve a place of honor with all that is good.**"**
George Washington 1732–1799

5 **"**One half of the world cannot understand the pleasures of the other.**"**
Jane Austen 1775–1817

6 **"**When I was fourteen years old, I was amazed at how unintelligent my father was. By the time I turned twenty-one, I was astounded by how much he had learned in the last seven years.**"**
Mark Twain 1835–1910

7 **"**I do not know with what weapons World War 3 will be fought, but World War 4 will be fought with sticks and stones.**"**
Albert Einstein 1879–1955

8 **"**Love is like quicksilver in the hand. Leave the fingers open and it stays. Clutch and it darts away.**"**
Dorothy Parker 1893–1967

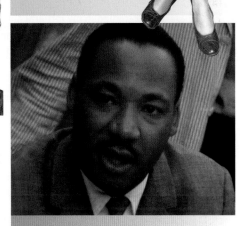

9 **"**The old law about 'an eye for an eye' leaves everybody blind.**"**
Martin Luther King 1929–1968

10 **"**Life is full of misery, loneliness, and suffering – and it's over much too soon.**"**
Woody Allen b. 1935

3 Which quotations do you find relevant to today's world or your own life? In what ways? Discuss with your partner, then the class.

READING AND LISTENING
Letter to a newborn son

Fergal Keane is a BBC foreign correspondent. He recorded this letter to his newborn son for a program called *From Our Own Correspondent* while he was working in Hong Kong. Following the broadcast, hundreds of people jammed the BBC telephone lines in tears because they were so moved by his words.

1 Read these lines from the letter and answer the questions below.

- You are asleep cradled in my left arm and I am learning the art of one-handed typing.
- One man said you were the first baby to be born in our building in the year of the Pig.
- Your coming has turned me upside down and inside out.
- Like many foreign correspondents I know, I have lived a life that, on occasion, has veered close to the edge: war zones, natural disasters, darkness in all its shapes and forms.
- And it's also true that I am pained, perhaps haunted is a better word, by the memory, suddenly so vivid now, of each suffering child I have come across on my journeys.
- But there is something more, a story from long ago that I will tell you face to face, father and son, when you are older. It's a very personal story . . .

1. What do the lines tell you about Fergal's feelings on the birth of his son?
2. What is *the year of the Pig*?
3. What do you learn of his job as a foreign correspondent?
4. What do you think the *personal story* from long ago might be?

2 [CD2] [16] Read and listen to the first part of the letter. Answer the questions.

1. What has Fergal learned about the practicalities of looking after a newborn baby?
2. What do you think *the new grammar* of their daily lives means?
3. Why are the Chinese people in their apartment building so pleased?
4. Is fatherhood as he expected it would be?

Letter to a newborn son

PART ONE

My dear son,

It is six o'clock in the morning on the island of Hong Kong. You are asleep cradled in my left arm and I am learning the art of one-handed typing. Your mother, more tired yet more happy than I've ever known her, is sound asleep in the room next door and there is a soft quiet in our apartment. Since you've arrived, days have melted into night and back again and we are learning a new grammar, a long sentence whose punctuation marks are feeding and burping and diaper changing and these occasional moments of quiet.

When you're older we'll tell you that you were born into Britain's last Asian colony in the lunar year of the Pig and that when we brought you home, the staff of our apartment building gathered to wish you well. "It's a boy, so lucky, so lucky. We Chinese love boys," they told us. One man said you were the first baby to be born in the building in the year of the Pig. This, he told us, was good Feng Shui, in other words a positive sign for the building and everyone who lived there. Naturally your mother and I were only too happy to believe that. We had wanted you and waited for you, imagined you and dreamed about you, and now that you are here, no dream can do justice to you.

3 [CD2] [17] Listen only to part two. Are these statements true or false? Correct the false ones.

1. His Chinese friends say that his son has to be given a Chinese name.
2. He might name him *Son of the Eastern Star* after the beautiful sunrise.
3. He used to be very ambitious in his work.
4. These children he mentions were all hurt in floods.

- Andi Mikail from Eritrea
- Sharja from Afghanistan
- Domingo and Juste from southern Angola
- Three young children from Rwanda

4 **CD2 18** Read and listen to part three. Answer the questions.

1. Who are these people? How are they connected to the places?

a young woman	–	a snowbound big city
a taxi driver	–	a shop doorway
an alcoholic man	–	a one-room apartment
a baby boy	–	the Adventist Hospital

2. What indications are there that Fergal's parents loved him and each other?
3. Describe his father. What is Fergal's attitude to him and his problems?
4. What regrets does he have about his father?

PART THREE

Daniel, these memories explain some of the fierce protectiveness I feel for you, the tenderness and the occasional moments of blind terror when I imagine anything happening to you. But there is something more, a story from long ago that I will tell you face to face, father and son, when you are older. It's a very personal story but it's part of the picture. It has to do with the long lines of blood and family, about our lives and how we can get lost in them and, if we're lucky, find our way out again into the sunlight.

It begins thirty-five years ago in a big city on a January morning with snow on the ground and a woman walking to the hospital to have her first baby. She is in her early twenties and the city is still strange to her, bigger and noisier than the easy streets and gentle hills of her distant home. She's walking because there is no money and everything of value has been pawned to pay for the alcohol to which her husband has become addicted. On the way, a taxi driver notices her sitting, exhausted and cold, in the doorway of a shop and he takes her to the hospital for free. Later that day, she gives birth to a baby boy and, just as you are to me, he is the best thing she has ever seen. Her husband comes that night and weeps with joy when he sees his son. He is truly happy. Hung over, broke, but in his own way happy, for they were both young and in love with each other and their son.

But, Daniel, time had some bad surprises in store for them. The cancer of alcoholism ate away at the man and he lost his family. This was not something he meant to do or wanted to do, it just was. When you are older, my son, you will learn about how complicated life becomes, how we can lose our way and how people get hurt inside and out. By the time his son had grown up, the man lived away from his family, on his own in a one-room apartment, living and dying for the bottle. He died on the fifth of January, one day before the anniversary of his son's birth, all those years before in that snowbound city. But his son was too far away to hear his last words, his final breath, and all the things they might have wished to say to one another were left unspoken.

Yet now, Daniel, I must tell you that when you let out your first powerful cry in the delivery room of the Adventist Hospital and I became a father, I thought of your grandfather and, foolish though it may seem, hoped that in some way he could hear, across the infinity between the living and the dead, your proud statement of arrival. For if he could hear, he would recognize the distinct voice of family, the sound of hope and new beginnings that you and all your innocence and freshness have brought to the world.

---

5 **CD2 16–18** Listen again to the whole letter. Summarize each part in one or two sentences.

Vocabulary work

6 Work with a partner. Who or what do the pronouns in *italics* refer to? What is the meaning of the underlined words? Use a dictionary if necessary.

1. *He* was fed, <u>burped</u>, and <u>put down</u>.
2. *He* <u>gambled</u> with death, <u>veering</u> close to the edge of danger.
3. *He* cried out when the wind blew <u>dust</u> onto *his* <u>wounds</u>.
4. *He* was dying from <u>malnutrition</u>.
5. *It* was <u>ransacked</u> and in ruins.
6. *They* <u>huddled</u> and <u>clung</u> together.
7. *She* <u>pawned</u> her possessions to pay for *his* addiction.
8. *He* was <u>hung over</u> and <u>broke</u>.
9. The <u>cancer of alcoholism</u> ate away at *their* lives.

What do you think?

- What does Fergal Keane mean when he says:
  "So much that seemed essential to me has, in the past few days, taken on a different color."
- How will his relationship with his son differ from the one with his own father?
- What lessons about life does Fergal Keane want his son to learn from this letter?
- Which parts of the letter do you think particularly moved the listeners of the BBC?
- What lessons have you learned from your upbringing that you would like to pass on to your children?

Daniel Patrick Keane
was born on
Thursday, February 4th
in Hong Kong

LANGUAGE FOCUS
Modal auxiliary verbs

Modal verbs in the present and future

> **1** All modal verbs can be used to express varying degrees of likelihood or probability. Match a sentence on the left with an explanation on the right.
>
> | | | | |
> |---|---|---|---|
> | It | will
must
could
may
might
can
can't
shouldn't | be difficult. | I'm not sure, but it's possible. (x3)
All evidence points to this. I predict this strongly.
I have a lot of evidence that it is.
I have a lot of evidence that it isn't.
There are times when it is difficult.
If everything goes according to plan. |
>
> **2** Certain modals can also be used to express *obligation* (mild and strong), *permission, ability, willingness,* and *habit.*
>
> > You **should see** a doctor. (mild obligation/advice)
> > You **may go** in now. (permission)
> > She **will drive** like a maniac. (habit)
>
> Give some more examples.
>
> ▶▶ **Grammar Reference p. 149**

1 Which sentences express a degree of probability?

1. He always looks so stressed. He *must* have a very demanding job.
2. You *must* come with us next time. You'd love it.
3. I *can't* hear you – we have a bad connection.
4. They *can't* be coming. They'd have been here by now.
5. She *might* change her mind if we keep bugging her.
6. You *could* be right.
7. You *can* borrow the car. I don't need it.
8. We *may* stay over at Claire's if dinner runs late.
9. No, you *may* not go out on a school night just before your exams.
10. You *should* have no trouble passing. You're good at exams.
11. You *should* be studying three hours a night.
12. *Will* you give me a hand with this?
13. It's a quarter after ten. She*'ll* be at the airport by now.
14. It's so annoying. He *won't* admit when he's wrong.
15. He *can* read and he's only three.
16. Learning English *can* be difficult.

What are the uses in the other sentences?

Modal verbs in the past

> **1** Modals expressing probability all form their past in the same way.
>
> | Verb + Perfect Infinitive | | |
> |---|---|---|
> | She
It
They | will
must
may | have arrived. |
>
> Give some more examples.
>
> **2** Modals expressing other meanings can have different forms in the past.
>
> > We **must stop** to get gas.
> > (present obligation)
> >
> > We **had to stop** to get gas.
> > (past obligation)
>
> **3** What are the meanings of the modals in these sentences?
>
> > She **could/was able to** read at three.
> > He **wouldn't** admit that he was wrong.
> > You **should have** seen the doctor.
> > He **would** always argue the point.
> > I **needn't have** brought my umbrella.
>
> ▶▶ **Grammar Reference p. 149**

"I've got the bowl, the bone, the big yard,
I know I should be happy."

2 Put the modal in the first sentence into the past to complete the second sentence.

1. It must be raining. Everyone's opening their umbrellas.

    It **must have been raining** . The ground is still wet.

2. I must stop eating so much junk food.

    I _____ eating so much junk food because I was gaining a lot of weight.

3. He should stop gaining weight before it's too late.

    He _____ before it was too late.

4. We can go to Bob's party on Saturday.

    We _____ to Bob's party last Saturday.

5. There's the phone. It'll be Paul.

    Did he have a deep voice? It _____ Paul.

6. My niece can't read very well because she's dyslexic.

    My niece _____ until she was twelve.

7. Let's take a map. We'll get lost if we don't.

    I'm glad we took the map. We _____ if we hadn't.

8. What's wrong with him? He'll just sit for hours staring into space.

    Something was wrong. He _____ staring into space.

3 Look at these pairs of sentences and discuss possible differences in meaning with a partner.

1. He must be on his way.
    I must be on my way.

2. I must stop eating junk food.
    I have to stop eating junk food.

3. They must share an apartment together.
    We must share an apartment together.

4. You don't have to buy her chocolates.
    You mustn't buy her chocolates.

5. The exam will have started.
    The exam will be starting.

6. He can't be married.
    We can't be married.

4 Extend each sentence in Exercise 3 to illustrate its meaning.

He must be on his way **because he said he was leaving at ten o'clock.**

I must be on my way. **I'm meeting John in half an hour.**

SPEAKING
Dilemma!

1 Work in groups. In this game you will predict how one of your classmates would handle a certain situation.

You are a taxi driver. You find a bag in your cab with $20,000 in it. The name of the owner is on the bag, but not the address.	You are offered a prestigious new job with an excellent salary. However, it entails spending six months a year out of the country, away from your family.
You have arranged to meet a friend for dinner. You wait at the restaurant. He/she finally shows up 45 minutes late.	You are at the supermarket when you see an old man, who is obviously not well off, stealing a can of soup.
You are in a restaurant. You have been waiting for a while when the waiter appears and goes to the table of someone who arrived before you.	You open the morning mail. The first letter contains an unexpected check for $500. The second letter is a charity appeal for a famine that is killing hundreds of people every day.
Someone begins telling you a joke that you've heard before.	
You have enrolled at a new language school. At the very beginning of the first class, your teacher comes in and says, "I want you all to take off your shoes, lie on the floor, close your eyes, and relax."	You are on a bus. Someone is listening to music on an MP3 player, and without knowing it, singing very loudly.
	Your ten-year-old child is being bullied.

2 Choose a situation. Then choose someone in the room and discuss with your group how you think he or she would react in that situation. Write down your prediction.

3 When it is your turn, read the situation to the person you chose. Ask for his or her reaction. If your prediction is right, your group scores a point. If it is wrong, challenge the person and explain why you are right. The whole class votes to make a final decision.

LISTENING AND SPEAKING
Words of wisdom

1 **CD2 19** Listen to some people talking about advice they have been given in their lives. Take notes after each person to complete the chart.

Name	Words of wisdom	Given by whom?
1. Emily		
2. Akemi		
3. Justin		
4. Juliana		
5. Young-Il		
6. Victor		
7. Sunny		
8. Chris		
9. Susana		
10. Rob		

2 Work with a partner and use your notes to talk to each other about the people in the chart.

Which pieces of advice are most interesting or relevant to you?

3 Have you ever been given any particularly memorable words of wisdom that have helped you in your life? Tell the class.

VOCABULARY AND PRONUNCIATION
Rhyme and reason

1 Work with a partner. Read the poem on page 65 and discuss which is the best word to complete the lines. Use a dictionary if necessary. Compare your version with others in the class. Justify your choice of words.

2 **CD2 20** Listen and compare with the actual poem. Whose was closest to the original?

3 Listen again and mark the stresses in the first two verses. Read the poem aloud to each other, concentrating on the rhythm.

4 **CD2 21** Read and listen to one of the poems some schoolchildren wrote, modeled on Lewis Carroll's verses.

You are old, Uncle John

"You are old, Uncle John," the young girl did say,

"Yet you spend six hours a day at the gym,

And you jog down the road before break of day

Pray, why keep yourself so very trim?"

"In my youth," Uncle John replied to his niece,

"I was hugely enormously fat,

But now that I've met a young lady from Greece,

Motivation has gotten rid of that!"

---

5 Work with your partner to write some similar verses. Read them to the class.

You are old, Father William

BY LEWIS CARROLL

"You are old, Father William," the young man said,
"And your hair has become very white;
And yet you incessantly stand on your _____.   head/hands/bed
Do you think, at your age, it is _____?"   smart/right/bright

"In my youth," Father William replied to his son,
"I feared it might _____ the brain;   injure/hurt/destroy
But, now that I'm perfectly sure I have _____,   none/one/gone
Why, I do it again and again."

"You are old," said the youth, "as I _____ before,   stated/mentioned/suggested
And have grown most _____ fat,   hugely/uncommonly/unnaturally
Yet you turned a back somersault in at the door,
Pray, what is the reason of that?"

"In my youth," said the sage, as he shook his gray _____,   curls/beard/locks
"I kept all my limbs very _____   supple/fit/nimble
By the use of this ointment – one shilling the box –
Allow me to sell you a couple?"

"You are old," said the youth, "and your jaws are too weak
For anything tougher than _____;   cake/suet/jelly
Yet you finished the goose, with the _____ and the beak   body/feathers/bones
Pray, how did you manage to do it?"

"In my youth," said his father, "I took to the law,
And argued each _____ with my wife;   case/day/night
And the muscular strength which it gave to my _____, tongue/jaw/chin
Has lasted the rest of my life."

"You are old," said the youth, "one would hardly suppose
That your eye was as _____ as ever;   steady/true/focused
Yet you balanced an eel on the end of your nose –
What made you so _____ clever?"   really/awfully/very

"I have answered three questions, and that is enough,"
Said his father. "Don't give yourself _____!   airs/manners/away
Do you think I can listen all day to such _____?   rubbish/stuff/nonsense
Be off, or I'll kick you downstairs!"

EVERYDAY ENGLISH
Breaking the rules of English

1 Look at two quotations on the subject of English grammar rules.
What point is being made by both writers?

> 66 Ending a sentence
> with a preposition is
> something up with
> which I will not put. 99
>
> WINSTON CHURCHILL

> 66 There is a busybody on your staff who devotes a lot of his time
> to chasing split infinitives. Every good literary craftsman splits
> his infinitives when the sense demands it. I call for the immediate
> dismissal of this pedant. It is of no consequence whether he
> decides to go quickly or quickly to go or to quickly go. The
> important thing is that he should go at once. 99
>
> GEORGE BERNARD SHAW in a letter to *The Times* newspaper

2 There are many "rules" in English which linguistic pedants insist should be
taught to children. Work with a partner. Read these tips and say how the "rule"
in each one is broken. Correct them according to the rule where possible.

15 TIPS FOR PROPER ENGLISH

1. A preposition is a terrible word to end a sentence with. Never do it.
2. Remember to never split an infinitive.
3. Don't use no double negatives.
4. And never start a sentence with a conjunction.
5. The passive voice is to be avoided wherever possible.
6. Who needs rhetorical questions?
7. Reserve the apostrophe for it's proper use and omit it when its not necessary.
8. Use fewer with number and less with quantity. Less and less people do.
9. Me and John are careful to use subject pronouns correctly.
10. Verbs has to agree with their subjects.
11. You've done good to use adverbs correctly.
12. Steer clear of incorrect verb forms that have snuck into the language.
13. Take the bull by the hand and avoid mixing your idioms.
14. Tell the rule about "whom" to who you like.
15. At the end of the day avoid clichés like the plague.

3 Which rules above do you think are "good" rules and which are not? Why?

4 Which rules in your language do you think are unnecessary or silly?

▶▶ **Writing** Describing a personal experience **p. 122**

Altered images

🔊 **Grammar:** Metaphors and idioms
🔊 **Vocabulary:** Real and unreal tense usage
Everyday English: Softening the message

STARTER

1 Are these all examples of art? Are some more "arty" than others?
What is the purpose of art? Or does it, by definition, have no point?

2 Work with a partner and try to describe each one. Discuss your reactions to them.

For artwork references see credits

3 **CD2 22** Listen to different people describing these works of art.
Which picture are they talking about? Make notes about what they say and discuss these with your partner.
Which two pictures are not described?

4 Compare the reactions of you and your partner with those of the people you listened to.
Discuss them with the class.

LISTENING AND SPEAKING

At home with an artist

1 Look at the photos. How would you describe Joe Downing's style of painting and sculpting? What's your opinion of it?

2 Read the biographical information. Work with a partner and write some questions you would like to ask Joe Downing if you met him.

3 **CD2 23** These statements about Joe are *all* false. Listen to the first part of an interview with him and correct them. Check any unknown vocabulary in your dictionary.

Part one   The early years

1. Joe wanted to be an artist from childhood.
2. He grew up surrounded by beautiful paintings.
3. He helped at home with the domestic chores, such as making quilts and shelling beans.
4. His mother showed no appreciation of beautiful things.
5. His childhood was idyllic until he had to go to war when he was 16.
6. He celebrated his nineteenth birthday in Germany.
7. After the war he wanted to study optometry in Chicago.
8. As a country bumpkin he found it very difficult to be plunged into city life.
9. He says he would never have become an artist if he hadn't seen Georges Seurat's painting, *La Grande Jatte*.

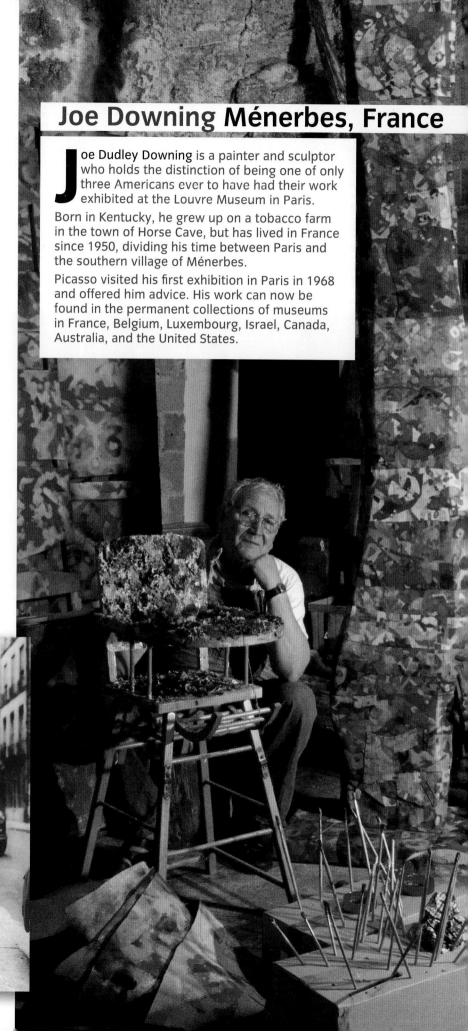

Joe Downing Ménerbes, France

Joe Dudley Downing is a painter and sculptor who holds the distinction of being one of only three Americans ever to have had their work exhibited at the Louvre Museum in Paris.

Born in Kentucky, he grew up on a tobacco farm in the town of Horse Cave, but has lived in France since 1950, dividing his time between Paris and the southern village of Ménerbes.

Picasso visited his first exhibition in Paris in 1968 and offered him advice. His work can now be found in the permanent collections of museums in France, Belgium, Luxembourg, Israel, Canada, Australia, and the United States.

4 **CD2** **24** Before you listen to the second part of the interview, check that you understand the words in *italics*.

Part two On being a painter

1. Has Joe always been an abstract painter? How did he develop as an artist? In what way did he *follow his bent*?
2. How did he *keep the pot boiling* when he moved to Paris?
3. What does he mean when he talks about *a very strong thread, what the French call a "fil conducteur,"* in his work?
4. What does he say is *fragile* for all artists?
5. What is the connection between *velvety-looking lasagna* and *green leather gardening gloves*? Tell Joe's ridiculous story in your own words.

5 **CD2** **25** Listen to the final part of the interview and answer the questions.

Part three On living in the South of France

1. What does Joe believe happens anywhere there's sunshine, olives, and Roman tiles?
2. What do you learn about the village of Ménerbes?
3. Why does Joe feel selfish and mean?
4. Who said: "I'm tired of lugging you two around?" Why?
5. How did he discover his house in Ménerbes?
6. Why was it so inexpensive? What was written on the shoebox?
7. In what way has Joe's life come full circle?
8. Does he have any regrets about his life?

What do you think?

- Which of the questions you wrote with your partner in Exercise 2 were answered?
- In what ways has fate played a part in Joe's life? How might his life have been different?
- What overall impression do you get of Joe as a man? Would his lifestyle appeal to you?

Talking about a work of art

Do you have a favorite work of art? A painting? A sculpture? A piece of music? A building? Where and when did you see/hear it? Make notes describing it and saying why you like it. If you can, bring a picture to show the class.

VOCABULARY AND LISTENING
Metaphors and idioms

1 **CD2 26** Read conversation **A** and listen to conversation **B**. What are the differences?

2 Look at the audio script on page 136 and find the metaphors in conversation **B**. Match the metaphors to their meanings in conversation **A**. What are their literal meanings?

Time flies.
It means to go through the air.
Usually, birds, planes, and insects fly.

3 Work with a partner. Here are some more sentences that contain metaphors. What is the literal meaning? What is the metaphorical meaning?

Conversation A

A Hi, Annie! I haven't seen you in ages.
B I know. Time goes so fast, doesn't it?
A It's true. Work's busy as ever, is it?
B Yes, I'm working very hard as usual, but we have an awful lot of work right now. We're just about coping, but it isn't easy. How about you?
A OK. Business was bad this time last year, and we really had to find ways to save money, but things have improved since then. You've moved, haven't you? Where are you living now?
B We bought an old house in a small town where not much happens. You must come and visit us.
A I'd love to, but we're very busy at the moment. Does it need much work?
B Everything. I hope we haven't given ourselves more work than we can manage.
A You'll be fine. Anyway, I have to go. Great to see you again.
B You, too. Bye!

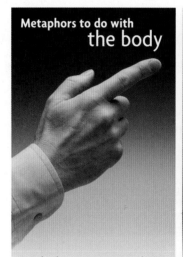

Metaphors to do with the body

1. I don't want to point the finger at anyone for this loss. I think we're all to blame.
2. When we set up the business, we had a few hiccups, but nothing we couldn't get around.
3. It broke his heart when she left him for another man.
4. The view over the snowcapped mountains takes your breath away.
5. Her terrible childhood experiences scarred her for life.

Metaphors to do with light

6. I couldn't solve the problem at all, and then the answer came to me in a flash.
7. When my daughter got her award, she was glowing with pride.
8. It was going to an exhibition that sparked my interest in photography.
9. James has lived his whole life being overshadowed by his famous brother.
10. I didn't know why she was being so nice. Then it suddenly dawned on me. She wanted my money.

Metaphors to do with nature

11. Joe and Helen have a stormy relationship. They have some huge fights.
12. His career blossomed after he was nominated for an Oscar.
13. She cried a river of tears when she was told she was being fired.
14. The root of all my problems is lack of money.
15. Sorry. I don't have the foggiest idea what you're talking about.

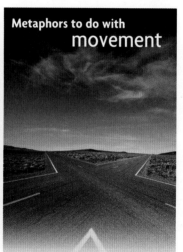

Metaphors to do with movement

16. Help! I've reached a crossroad. What should I do next?
17. He followed in his father's footsteps and became a doctor.
18. The politician gave a long, rambling speech about the budget.
19. We aren't getting any closer to solving our problem. We're going around in circles.
20. There have been great strides in medical technology over the past fifty years.

4 **CD2** **27** Listen to the conversation. Who and what is being talked about? The speakers use a lot of idioms. Which can you remember?

5 **CD2** **27** These sentences are similar to some of those in the conversation. Replace the words in *italics* with the idioms you heard. Listen again and check.

1. *It was a complete surprise when* he inherited a fortune.
2. When he heard about it, he was *thrilled*.
3. He's *in real trouble* because he spent the whole amount in a month.
4. He was going to ask her to marry him, but then he *lost the courage*.
5. He'll have to *change his attitude, try harder* and get a job.
6. Marilyn – no, that's not it. *I can almost remember* her name.
7. She told him he was *useless*.
8. I'm glad you told me, otherwise I might have *said something really insensitive*.

6 Replace the words in *italics* with a metaphor or idiom from Exercises 3–5. Make any necessary changes.

1. I *did what my mother did* and became a teacher.
2. The actors had a few *small problems* at the beginning of the play, but then it went smoothly.
3. My neighbors *fight a lot*.
4. When I heard I'd gotten the job, I was *very, very happy*.
5. When Jane's marriage ended, she knew she *had to make an important decision that would affect the rest of her life*.
6. This argument is stupid. We're *making no progress at all*.
7. When she showed him the finished statue, it *left him stunned and he couldn't speak*.
8. The business *developed successfully* when they won a ruling worth $1 million.
9. I was going to ask the movie star for his autograph, but then I *lost the courage* and couldn't do it.
10. I went to the lecture on nuclear physics, but I didn't have *a clue* what it was about.
11. The book got a *review with a lot of praise*, so I went out and bought it.
12. You're *in real trouble*. I saw you steal that book.

READING AND SPEAKING
The man behind the mouse

1 What Disney movies can you name? Have you ever been to a Disneyland® theme park? What do you know about them?

2 Which of these words or expressions would you relate to the world of Disney?

airbrushed reality	harmonious	romanticized
cruel	harsh	troubled
a dream factory	imaginative	a tormented childhood
fantasy land	idealized	violent
happy endings	magical	

3 Read the opening lines of the article. What first impression do you get of Walt Disney's childhood?

4 Read the rest of the article. Which of the words in Exercise 2 on page 71 relate to the life of the man, Walt Disney?

5 Imagine that Walt Disney lied about his life, and said these things. What in fact was the truth?

1. I had an idyllic childhood with everything I could have wanted.
2. We were a tight family unit, and we all got along.
3. I wasn't particularly close to my brother.
4. I put all of my childhood experiences into my work.
5. Success came to me easily. I didn't have to work hard.
6. I was a self-made man. Nobody helped me.
7. I always put my family before my work, and I was always blessed with good health.
8. The idea for Mickey Mouse was mine. I created every aspect of the character.
9. There were never any hiccups in my career.
10. I wasn't particularly involved in the creation of Disneyland.

Language work

6 Who might have said these things? About what?

1. He'd beat us regularly for no reason.
2. You'd better not do that again or I'll run away.
3. I would've been able to do more drawing if we'd been less poverty-stricken.
4. If he'd asked our permission, we would never have allowed him to go.
5. What if we'd kept the name Mortimer?
6. I know he would rather we'd had a son.
7. I would've have slept at home if she'd been quieter.

7 Work with a partner. Discuss the meaning of the words highlighted in the article.

What do you think?

- In what ways was Walt Disney a workaholic? What drove him?
- Successful people often have unhappy childhoods. Why is this? Do you know any examples?
- Are there features that all creative geniuses have in common?
- Compare the lives of Walt Disney and Joe Downing.

Walt
The man

It was 3:30 in the morning and 8-year-old Walt Disney was doing what he did at that time every morning – rolling hundreds of copies of the Kansas City *Morning Times* that he would soon place behind the screen door of subscribers along his route.

It was hard work for a little kid who also had to go to school, then deliver another round in the evening. Sometimes he had to trudge through three feet of snow. Other times he got so tired he'd sneak into an alley for a catnap. But the paper route beat picking apples for a living. That's what he'd been doing before, on his family's failing farm in Marceline, Missouri. The problem was that his boss – his stern father, Elias – had the nasty habit of delivering daily beatings both to Walt and his brother Roy, eight years Walt's senior. After a disgusted Roy left home, the brunt of the work, and the beatings, fell on Elias' youngest son.

Walt Disney, born on December 5, 1901, never had time for a childhood. As a result, he spent all of his adult life attempting to invent one for himself. In the process – almost by accident – he created wonderful childhood memories for generation after generation of children worldwide.

An airbrushed boyhood

Later, Walt would paint a nostalgic picture of life in Missouri, carefully airbrushing away the difficult times. He'd talk about sketching the farm animals, which he did when he could find pencil and paper – rare commodities in the dirt-poor Disney home. Once he was punished for painting a cartoon on the wall of the house. As always, it was his teenage brother, Roy, who comforted him, rocking him to sleep.

When the Disneys moved to Chicago, Walt signed up for cartooning classes at the Chicago Academy of Fine Arts, working three part-time jobs to pay for them. But all these were abandoned during World War I, when, at the age of 16, he forged his parents' signatures and became an ambulance driver for the Red Cross in France.

Home again, Walt joined Roy in Kansas City and found work as a commercial artist. Here he met another artist, Ub Iwerks, and together they developed a series of short films called *Alice in Cartoonland*. Walt moved to Los Angeles, where Roy was in the hospital with tuberculosis. He searched desperately for a distributor. The night he got a telegram offering him $1,500

Disney
behind the mouse

by MELISSA BURDICK HARMON

apiece for six *Alice* shorts, Walt raced to the hospital where Roy was a patient, and persuaded him to leave the hospital and come to work for him the next day.

Roy Disney would devote the rest of his life to helping his little brother, skillfully handling the business end of the Disney empire. Walt also employed Ub Iwerks as chief animator.

Of mice, marriage, and men

When he was 24, he married one of his employees, Lillian Bounds. It was a union that would last – although not always happily – until his death 41 years later. At 24, Walt was already married to his work. He created a cartoon character called *Oswald the Lucky Rabbit*, who was a great success. He then shifted his attention to mice, or one particular mouse named Mortimer. Lillian dismissed the name Mortimer as "too sissy," so Mortimer became Mickey. Surprisingly, it was Ub Iwerks, not Walt, who first drew him. Walt, however, provided Mickey's voice. They made a talkie, *Steamboat Willie*, which premiered on November 18, 1928, to rave reviews, and Mickey Mouse became an overnight sensation.

Success followed success, but Walt pushed himself ever harder. In 1930 he suffered a nervous breakdown due to overwork, and when Lillian surprised him with the news that she was pregnant, he became severely depressed. How could a man whose whole life was dedicated to giving *himself* a childhood take on the burden of becoming a parent?

He produced his first feature-length cartoon, *Snow White and the Seven Dwarfs*, for which he won a special Oscar. Then came the birth of a second daughter, Sharon, who started crying all night. Walt, who had wanted a son, started sleeping at the studio.

In many ways Walt was a benevolent employer, but like his father, he was subject to terrible fits of rage. Feeling totally betrayed when his animators went on strike because they wanted to join a union, he started working for the "House of Un-American Activities Committee," which investigated "communists" in Hollywood, and informed on the strike leader.

The last, best times

Post-Second World War, Walt continued to work prolifically. In 1950 he produced his first live-action film, *Treasure Island*. Then came Disneyland®. Everyone tried to dissuade him, saying it was too costly a dream, but he wouldn't listen. He oversaw every nut and bolt of its creation. His great world of fantasy opened on July 17, 1955. In the next seven weeks, more than one million people walked down Disneyland®'s Main Street USA, an idealized version of Main Street in Marceline, Missouri, circa 1900. The man who had spent his painful childhood in the real-life version of that town now stood in the window of an apartment decorated exactly like his boyhood home, tears streaming down his face, watching other people enjoy the perfect childhood world that he had created.

In November 1966 he was diagnosed with lung cancer. He was given six months to two years to live, but two weeks later, after spending the evening with Roy working on a new Florida theme park, Walt Disney died. He had just turned 65.

Walt Disney used to say jokingly, "I hope we never lose sight of one thing ... none of this would have happened if it hadn't been for a mouse." But in truth, it was started by a tormented childhood and became reality through Walt's irrepressible drive and imagination and the tireless help of a devoted brother.

LANGUAGE FOCUS
Real and unreal tense usage

would

> **1** *Would* has several different uses. Look at these examples from the text.
>
> a. Roy Disney **would** devote the rest of his life . . .
> It was a union that **would** last . . . until his death . . .
>
> b. . . . he**'d** sneak into an alley for a catnap.
> He**'d** talk about sketching the farm animals . . .
>
> c. . . . but Walt **wouldn't** listen.
>
> **2** Which sentences, a, b, or c, express . . . ?
> - past habits
> - refusal on a past occasion
> - the future in the past
>
> ▶▶ **Grammar Reference p. 150**

1 Which use of *would* is expressed in these sentences?

1. My car wouldn't start this morning. I had to take the bus.
2. When I was a kid, I'd get up at 7:00 and take the dog for a walk.
3. In New York, Kevin met Angela, who he would marry five years later.
4. Whenever we had time, we'd go hiking. Those were the days!
5. When he was first going out with Ana, he'd buy her flowers all the time.
6. So he took the job, did he? I knew he'd change his mind.
7. I asked him why he'd lied, but he wouldn't tell me.
8. Sorry about the noise. I didn't think you'd hear it.

2 Complete these sentences in a suitable way.

1. I could have smashed my computer this morning.
It just wouldn't . . .

2. My grandfather was such a kind man.
He'd . . .

3. I don't know why she got so angry.
I told her a thousand times I'd . . .

4. My mother used to drive me crazy.
She'd always . . .

5. I can't believe they lost 2–0!
I thought they'd . . .

6. Why did you clean the apartment?
I said I'd . . .

Past tenses to express unreality

> **1** The examples of *would* in Exercises 1 and 2 express real time. *Would* is also used in conditional sentences to express a situation that is contrary to reality.
>
> I **would** sleep at home if the baby didn't make so much noise.
> . . . none of this (success) **would** have happened if it hadn't been for a mouse.
>
> Which is a second and which is a third conditional? What are the rules of form and use?
>
> **2** There are other ways of expressing a situation that is contrary to reality. Identify the tenses in the examples below. What is the reality in each one? Complete the sentences.
>
> I wish I didn't eat so much junk food. (But . . .)
> She wished she hadn't opened her big mouth. (But . . .)
> I wish you'd think before you speak. (But . . .)
> I wish I could drive. (But . . .)
> If only we'd left home earlier! (But . . .)
>
> ▶▶ **Grammar Reference p. 150–151**

3 These sentences all have verbs in the Past Simple. Which ones refer to real past time?

1. What if we called him Mickey?
2. He would become nostalgic when he told stories about his upbringing.
3. I couldn't swim until I was fourteen.
4. If I could afford it, I'd buy it.
5. Isn't it time we had a break?
6. My childhood was poor. If we had any money, it went to pay debts.
7. He acts as if he owned the place.
8. I wish you didn't have to go.

4 These sentences all have verbs in the Past Perfect. Which ones refer to real past time?

1. I wish you hadn't said that. It was cruel.
2. I knew I'd seen her before.
3. Had he known the truth, he would have acted more cautiously.
4. She apologized, saying she hadn't had time to call me.
5. I'd rather you'd kept the news to yourself, but it's too late now.
6. They looked as though they'd had a good time.

5 Put the verbs in the correct tense or verb form.
Where there is no verb given, use an auxiliary verb.

Seth and Amy are having an argument in a hotel. They're on their way to New York.

Amy Ugh! This hotel is horrible. I wish we (1)_____
(not come) here. I (2)_____ never
_____ (see) such a dirty hotel in my life!
It (3)_____ (not be) so bad if the bathroom
(4)_____ (be) clean, but it (5)_____
(be) filthy. I (6)_____ even _____
(not wash) my socks in it.

Seth I know, but it (7)_____ (get) late, and we
(8)_____ (drive) all day, and I (9)_____
(want) to stop. If we (10)_____ , we might
not have found a hotel and we (11)_____
still _____ (drive). That (12)_____
(be) awful. This is better than nothing.

Amy Well, I wish we (13)_____ (leave) home
earlier. Then we (14)_____ (can arrive) in
New York today, and we (15)_____ (have)
a whole day to go to galleries and museums.
As it is, we (16)_____ (not get) there till
tomorrow lunchtime, and we (17)_____
only _____ (have) a few hours.

Seth I (18)_____ (like) (19)_____
(spend) more time in New York, too, but I (20)
_____ (have) to go to work this morning. If I
(21)_____ , we (22)_____ (stay) in a
nice hotel in New York now instead of this dump.

Amy I (23)_____ (like) (24)_____ (see) a
show, but we can't, so that's all there is to it. Anyway,
it's time we (25)_____ (think) about getting
something to eat. If it (26)_____ (not be) so
late, I (27)_____ (suggest) going into town,
but if we (28)_____ (do) we might not find
anything. It's pretty late already.

Seth I wish you (29)_____ (not complain)
about everything. I (30)_____ (not mind),
but you're so indecisive. If it (31)_____
(leave) up to you, we (32)_____ never
_____ (do) anything or go anywhere.

Amy OK, OK. I'm sorry. Let's go.

CD2 28 Listen and check. Practice the conversation with a partner.
Pay attention to short forms and contractions.

EVERYDAY ENGLISH
Softening the message

1 Sometimes we want to express ourselves in a tactful, polite way. We don't want to be too direct or confrontational.

Could you possibly lend me some money? is less direct than *Lend me some money.*

Read the lines and number them in order, 1 being most direct. What makes each message less direct?

CD2 29 Listen and repeat. Practice the stress and intonation.

▶▶ **Grammar Reference p. 152**

a. ☐ I wonder if you could help me?
   ☐ Could you help me?
   ☑ Can you help me?
   ☐ I was wondering if you could possibly help me?

b. ☐ Do you mind if I open the window?
   ☐ Would you mind if I opened the window? It's so stuffy in here.

c. ☐ I want to speak to you.
   ☐ I wanted to have a word with you, if that's all right.

d. ☐ If I were you, I'd dye it black.
   ☐ I'd have thought the best idea would have been to dye it black, but it's up to you.
   ☐ You could dye it black.
   ☐ Dye it black.

2 **CD2 30** Listen to some conversations. How is the message softened in each one?

Look at the audio script on page 137 and practice with a partner.

3 Rephrase these sentences so that they sound softer. Use the words in parentheses.

1. I want to use your phone. (*mind*)
2. Don't paint the wall red. (*If I … you*)
3. We should go in my car. (*better*)
4. Call back later. (*possible / possibly*)
5. We should call to say we'll be late. (*Don't … ?*)
6. Give me a ride to the station. (*hoping*)
7. She's French. (*think / thought*)
8. Would you like to come to the movies with me? (*wondering*)
9. Fill out this form, please. (*mind*)
10. It'll rain this afternoon. (*surprised*)
11. I'm going for a walk. Anyone interested? (*thinking*)
12. I've dropped by to see if you need anything. (*thought*)
13. It's a bad idea. (*say / said*)
14. Apologize to her. (*'d have said … best idea*)
15. I gave her a present. She didn't say thank you. (*You'd have thought*)

CD2 31 Listen and check. Practice saying the sentences, paying attention to short forms and rhythm.

4 With a partner, write some conversations for these situations. Use tactful, polite language. Choose one and act it out in front of the class.

- You want to invite someone to go out with you. Meal? Movies? Dance? Picnic?
- You call a hotel. You want to stay three nights, and you'd like a quiet room.
- Your friend has just moved into a new apartment. He/She wants some ideas about how to decorate it.
- Someone calls to speak to your roommate. She's out. What time will she be back? (*I'd have thought …*)

CD2 32 Listen and compare.

▶▶ **Writing** Reviewing a movie or book **p. 123**

History lessons

STARTER

1 Work in groups. Which historical events do the pictures illustrate? Match them to the events.

2 Put the twelve events in chronological order. In which century did they happen?
Give any precise dates that you know.

☐ **First World War begins**

☐ **Great Wall of China built**

☐ **Charles Darwin publishes** *On the Origin of Species*

☐ **Panama Canal built**

☐ **Terrorist attack demolishes World Trade Center in New York**

☐ **Steve Jobs and Steve Wozniak produce the first personal computers**

☐ **Leonardo da Vinci paints the Mona Lisa**

☐ **First Olympic Games held in Greece**

☐ **U.S. drops first atomic bombs on Hiroshima and Nagasaki**

☐ **American War of Independence begins**

☐ **AIDS becomes a major health threat throughout the world**

☐ **Berlin Wall demolished**

3 Write down the three events that you feel are most important. Add any others that you feel have been omitted from the list. Compare and justify your ideas in your groups and then with the whole class.

4 Which recent news events do you feel will go down in history?

READING AND SPEAKING
I was there

1 Where do these historical events fit chronologically with those on page 77?
   - The destruction of Pompeii by Mount Vesuvius
   - The first transatlantic radio message
   - The sinking of the Titanic
   - The first men on the moon

2 Match the events in Exercise 1 with these excerpts from eyewitness accounts.
   1. It stood upright in the water for four full minutes, then it began to slide gently downwards.
   2. It had been awaiting its first visitors for a long time.
   3. We saw the sea sucked away and apparently forced back by the earthquake.
   4. The result meant much more to me than the mere successful realization of an experiment, it was an epoch in history.

   Quickly scan all the texts to check your ideas.

3 Work in pairs. Look at the historical events on pages 78–81. Choose two that interest you and divide them between you. Read them and answer the questions.
   1. What was the exact date of the event?
   2. Who is describing it? Is the person a protagonist or an observer? In what way?
   3. What kind of event is it? Natural or man-made? Good or bad? Describe it.
   4. Who were the people involved? How did they react?
   5. Why was it so important? What repercussions have there been since it took place?

   Compare the answers with your partner and share information about the events with another pair.

Vocabulary work

4 Which of these words are from the texts you chose? Divide them into nouns, verbs, and adjectives. Use a dictionary if necessary.

amplifiers	crude	shriek	toss
ashes	deploy	slant	trunk
blaze	jettison	slide	unimpeded
blot out	lunar	snowdrift	valves
bow	mob	stern	violent
cart	overwhelmed	stranded	wailing
coils	panic-stricken	swarm	
condensers	pungent	sway	

5 Explain the words from your texts to your group.

6 Which words are technical words? Which texts are they from?

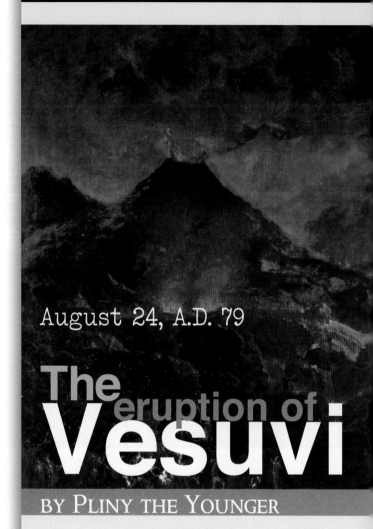

① I was there...

August 24, A.D. 79

The eruption of Vesuvi
BY PLINY THE YOUNGER

This was the eruption that destroyed and buried the towns of Pompeii and Herculaneum.

On August 24, in the early afternoon, my mother drew attention to a cloud of unusual size and appearance. It was not clear at that distance from which mountain the cloud was rising. (It was afterwards known to be Vesuvius.) Its general appearance can best be expressed as being like an umbrella pine, for it rose to a great height on a sort of trunk and then split off into branches. Broad sheets of fire and leaping flames blazed at several points. By this time the courtyard was full of ashes so that its level had risen. The buildings were now shaking with violent shocks and seemed to be swaying back and forth.

My mother and I finally decided to leave the town. We were followed by a panic-stricken mob of people. Once beyond the buildings we stopped, and there we had some extraordinary experiences which thoroughly

December 12, 1901

The first radio signal
across the Atlantic

BY GUGLIELMO MARCONI

The signal was sent from Poldhu in Cornwall to Guglielmo Marconi, waiting on a cliff in Newfoundland.

Shortly before midday I placed the single earphone to my ear and started listening. The receiver on the table before me was very crude – a few coils and condensers – no valves, no amplifiers, not even a crystal. But I was at last on the point of putting the correctness of all my beliefs to the test. The answer came at 12:30 when I heard, faintly but distinctly, pip-pip-pip. I handed the phone to Kemp, "Can you hear anything?" I asked. "Yes," he said, "the letter S" – he could hear it. I knew then that all my anticipations had been justified. The electric waves sent out into space from Poldhu had traversed the Atlantic – the enormous distance of 1,700 miles – unimpeded by the curvature of the earth. The result meant much more to me than the mere successful realization of an experiment, it was an epoch in history. I now felt for the first time absolutely certain that the day would come when mankind would be able to send messages without wires not only across the Atlantic but also between the furthermost ends of the earth.

us

alarmed us. We saw the sea sucked away and apparently forced back by the earthquake: it receded from the shore so that quantities of sea creatures were left stranded on dry sand. On the landward side a fearful black cloud parted to reveal great tongues of fire, like flashes of lightning magnified in size. Soon afterwards the cloud sank down to earth and covered the sea; it had already blotted out Capri. You could hear the shrieks of women, the wailing of infants, the shouts of men. Many besought the aid of gods, but still more imagined there were no gods left, and that the universe was plunged into darkness forevermore.

At last the darkness thinned. Then there was genuine daylight, and the sun actually shone out. We were terrified to see everything changed, buried deep in ashes like snowdrifts.

I was there...

April 15, 1912

The Titanic
from a lifeboat

BY MRS. D.H. BISHOP

The "unsinkable" Titanic had only 1,178 lifeboat spaces for 2,224 people on board. A total of 1,513 lives were lost.

We did not begin to understand the situation till we were perhaps a mile or more away from the Titanic. Then we could see the rows of lights along the decks begin to slant gradually upward from the bow. Very slowly these lines of light began to point downward at a greater and greater angle. The slant seemed to be greater about every quarter of an hour.

In a couple of hours, though, she began to go down more rapidly. Then the fearful sight began. The people in the ship were just beginning to realize how great their danger was. When the forward part of the ship dropped suddenly, there was a sudden rush of passengers on all the decks towards the stern. It was like a wave. We could see the great black mass of people in the steerage sweeping to the rear part of the boat. We could make out the increasing excitement on board as the people, rushing to and fro, caused the deck lights to disappear and reappear as they passed in front of them.

This panic went on for an hour. Then suddenly the ship seemed to shoot up out of the water and stand there perpendicularly. It stood upright in the water for four full minutes, then it began to slide gently downwards. Its speed increased as it went down head first, so that the stern shot down with a rush. The lights continued to burn until it sank. We could see the people packed densely in the stern till it was gone and we could hear their screaming a mile away. Gradually this became fainter and fainter and died away. Some of the lifeboats that had room for more might have gone to their rescue, but it would have meant that those who were in the water would have swarmed aboard and sunk her.

I was there...

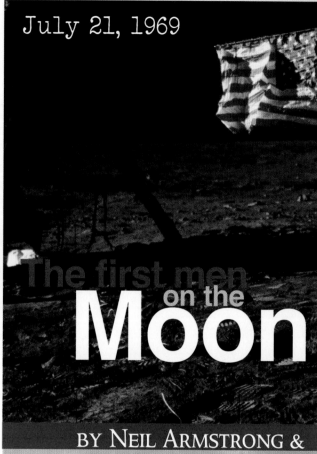

July 21, 1969

The first men
on the
Moon

BY NEIL ARMSTRONG &

Apollo 11, carrying Neil Armstrong, Edwin (Buzz) Aldrin and Michael Collins, was launched on July 16. Five days later they stepped down onto the moon.

NEIL ARMSTRONG

On the way there Of all the spectacular views we had, the most impressive to me was on the way to the Moon when we flew through its shadow. We were still thousands of miles away, but close enough so that the Moon almost filled our circular window. It was illuminated only by earthshine. It made the Moon appear blue-gray, and the entire scene looked decidedly three-dimensional. It seemed almost as if it were showing us its roundness, its similarity in shape to our Earth, in a sort of welcome. I was sure it would be a hospitable host. It had been awaiting its first visitors for a long time.

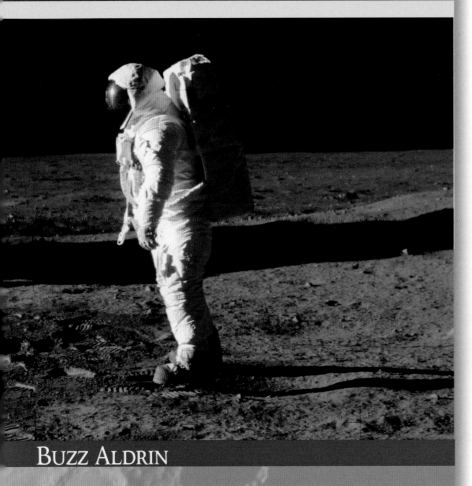

BUZZ ALDRIN

After touchdown The sky is black, you know. It's a very dark sky. But it still seemed more like daylight than darkness as we looked out the window. It's a peculiar thing but the surface looked very warm and inviting. From the cockpit it seemed to be tan. It's hard to account for that, because later when I held the material in my hand, it wasn't tan at all. It was black, gray and so on.

BUZZ ALDRIN

On the Moon The blue color of my boot has completely disappeared now into this — still don't know what color to describe this other than grayish-cocoa.

Back on board The Moon was a very natural and pleasant environment in which to work. On the Moon, in one-sixth gravity, you have a distinct feeling of being somewhere. As we deployed our experiments we had to jettison things, some objects we tossed away and they would go in a slow, lazy motion.

Odor is very subjective, but to me there was a distinct smell to the lunar material — pungent, like gunpowder. We carted a fair amount of lunar dust back inside the vehicle, on our suits and boots, and we did notice the odors right away.

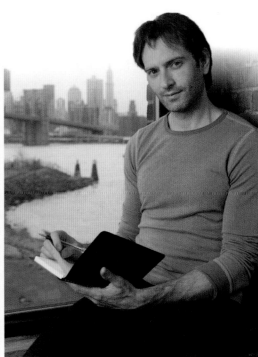

7 **CD3 2** Listen to Justin Baines' eyewitness account. Which historical event did he witness? Where was he at the beginning of the story? From where did he watch events unfold?

Describe what he saw in your own words.

Do you remember where you were on that day? How did you hear about what happened? What were the repercussions of this event?

Personal history

- Close your eyes and select an important event in your own life.
- Write brief notes on what, where, and when.
- Discuss its significance with your group. Ask and answer questions.

VOCABULARY AND PRONUNCIATION
Homonyms, homophones, and homographs

1 The word *bow* is both a homonym (same pronunciation, same spelling, but different meanings) and a homograph (same spelling, but two pronunciations with different meanings).

bow /baʊ/	
noun	1 The front of a ship is called the **bow**.
	2 The cast took their **bows** after the performance.
verb	The Japanese **bow** when they greet each other.

bow /boʊ/	
noun	1 The ribbon made a beautiful **bow** in her hair.
	2 Robin Hood used a **bow** and arrow to fight.
	3 You play the violin with a **bow**.

1. Read aloud all the sentences in the boxes.
2. Which meaning is both a noun and a verb?
3. Choose sentences to illustrate *bow* as a homonym.
4. Choose sentences to illustrate it as a homograph.

2 *bow* /baʊ/ is also a homophone. *bough* /baʊ/ has the same pronunciation, a different spelling, and a different meaning. What is the meaning?

Homonyms

1 These sentences all contain words that have homonyms in the texts on pages 78–81. Use your dictionary to check meanings and find the homonyms in the texts.

1. Our company has branches in New York, Frankfurt, and Singapore. (text 1)
2. It's time I replaced my battered old trunk with a new suitcase. (text 1)
3. Don't pine for him, Kristin. Cheer up! He isn't worth it! (text 1)
4. We were given a stern warning about the dangers of swimming in rough seas. (text 3)
5. Both jokers are missing in this deck of cards. (text 3)

2 Identify the homonyms in these sentences. Make sentences for the other meanings.

1. A swallow made a nest near my house.
2. We spotted a rare bird in the forest.
3. Don't go making any rash promises that you can't keep!
4. Classes were interrupted for a fire drill.
5. I think we should scrap that idea. It won't work.
6. Stop rambling and get to the point!

Homophones

3 Read these words aloud. Think of a homophone for each one.

wail	whirled	heir	site	hire	soar

4 Complete the sentences with the correct homophone.

1. They tied their boat to a small _____ in the harbor.	a. buoy	b. boy
2. His _____ remarks upset everyone.	a. coarse	b. course
3. Public speaking makes my voice go _____.	a. horse	b. hoarse
4. They say it was a _____ gunman who shot the president.	a. loan	b. lone
5. The thieves got away with a large _____ of old bank notes.	a. hall	b. haul
6. Squirrels _____ nuts in woods and gardens.	a. berry	b. bury
7. She lifted her _____ and smiled at her new husband.	a. vale	b. veil

Homographs

5 **CD3 3** Listen and write the homograph you hear in each pair of sentences. What are the different pronunciations?

After the performance she took five bows.
She wore five bows in her hair.

6 Divide into two groups. Use your dictionaries to find the two pronunciations and meanings of the words in your box. Make sentences to illustrate the meanings to the other group.

GROUP A			**GROUP B**		
wind	refuse	defect	wound	minute	object

LISTENING AND SPEAKING
Peace and goodwill

1 Many historical events are concerned with war. Which major wars have there been over the last hundred years? What conflicts are in the news at the moment?

2 **CD3 4** Listen to an excerpt from a musical called *Oh, What a Lovely War!*

1. Which war is it? Who is fighting who?
2. What nicknames do the two sides have for each other?
3. Where are they standing?
4. What is surprising about this enemy interaction?
5. The scene depicts the beginning of the so-called Christmas Truce, which took place on Christmas Eve in the first year of the war. What do you think happened next?

3 **CD3 5** Listen to an interview with Graham Williams and Harold Startin, who were on sentry duty that night. Complete the sentences with the exact words you hear.

1. … lights began to appear all along the _____.
2. They sang this _____ right through.
3. … when I woke up I found everyone was walking out into _____.
4. They were giving us _____ about as big as your arm.
5. … we'd got no _____ against them, they'd got no _____ against us.
6. We were the best of _____, although we were there to kill one other.
7. They helped us _____ our dead, and we _____ our dead with their dead.
8. … they'd come and help you _____ your defenses against them.

4 Answer the questions.

1. How is Graham Williams' account similar to the scene in the play?
2. In what ways did the two sides communicate at first?
3. What is "no-man's land"?
4. In what ways did they show goodwill toward each other?
5. How long did the truce last?
6. Who was Otto?

What do you think?

- Do you find the story depressing or uplifting? Why?
- How is it possible that enemies become friends in the middle of a war?
- Do you think that commanding officers could become friends in the same way?
- Could such an incident happen in modern warfare? If so, under what circumstances? If not, why not?

LANGUAGE FOCUS
Verb patterns

1 Complete these common verb patterns from this unit with a verb on the right.

verb + infinitive	The buildings **seemed** _____ back and forth.	appear
	We finally **decided** _____ the town.	burn
	The lights **continued** _____ until it sank.	bury
	I placed the earphone to my ear and **started** _____ .	hate
verb + object + infinitive	They had **trained us** _____ the Germans.	leave
	They **helped us** _____ our dead.	listen
	It **made the Moon** _____ blue-gray.	make
verb + preposition + -ing	The Germans **joined in** _____ with the British.	see
	Not speaking German **didn't stop him from** _____ friends.	sing
verb + adjective + infinitive	We **were terrified** _____ everything changed.	sway

▶▶ **Grammar Reference p. 152**

2 Read the *Oxford Dictionary of American English* entry on verb patterns with the verb *agree*. Use it to help you decide which of the sentences below are correct. Correct the others.

> **agree** /əˈɡriː/ *verb*
> SHARE OPINION | **1** (I,T) **agree (with sb/sth)**; **agree (that …)** to have the same opinion as sb; *"I think we should talk to the manager about this." "Yes, I agree."◇ I agree with Paul.◇ Do you agree that we should go by train?.◇ No, I don't agree.* OPP **disagree**
> SAY YES | **2** (I) **agree (to sth)** to say yes to sth; *I asked if I could go home early and she agreed. ◇ Andy has agreed to loan me his car for the weekend.* OPP **refuse**[1]
> MAKE AN ARRANGEMENT | **3** (I) **agree (to do sth)**; **agree (on sth)** to make an arrangement or agreement with sb; *They agreed to meet again the following day. ◇ Can we agree on a price? ◇ We agreed that Leah would contact us if she needed help.*
> ACCEPT | **4** (I) **agree with sth** to think that sth is right; *I don't agree with experiments on animals.*
> BE THE SAME | **5** (I) to be the same as sth; *The two accounts of the accident do not agree. ◇ In French the adjective must agree with the noun in number and gender.*
> PHRV **agree with sb** to be pleasant for sb or good for sb's health; *No, thanks. Onions don't agree with me.*

1. She thinks the war ended in 1918 and I am agree.
2. He agreed that they should spend some time apart.
3. They agreed on fighting the proposal was a bad idea.
4. He agreed to give us more time to finish the project.
5. They always agree to each other about the major decisions in life.
6. We agree to differ about politics.
7. They agreed to me about the time we should start the meeting.

3 Do the same with this entry.

> **persuade** /pərˈsweɪd/ *verb* (T) **1 persuade sb (to do sth)** to cause sb to do sth by giving him/her good reasons; *It was difficult to persuade Louise to change her mind.* OPP **dissuade 2 persuade sb (of sth)**; **persuade sb (that …)** to cause sb to believe sth; *The jury was persuaded of her innocence. ◇ The attorney persuaded the jury that she was innocent.* ⊃ Look at **convince.**

1. He persuaded his mother into lend him the money.
2. We were persuaded that it was the best course of action.
3. What do I have to do to persuade you that I love you?
4. You'll never persuade me of taking up mountaineering.
5. Eventually I was persuaded of all their arguments.

"Rugged romantic seeks elegant lady. Must like hunting and gathering."

4 Choose the verb that completes each sentence correctly. Change the verb patterns to make correct sentences with the other verbs.

1. He	enjoys used is used would rather	to be a soldier.
2. We	are trying have decided are thinking of had better	selling our apartment.
3. They	stopped wanted hoped let	us to go.
4. I	am looking forward to happened avoided suggested that he	meet her.
5. Did you	mind see him remind him manage	do it?
6. She	didn't feel like made me couldn't help promised not	to laugh.
7. Why	didn't you dare were you made are you threatening were you forced into	resigning?
8. He	is interested in helped me encouraged me can't stand	learn English.

*"'Society for the preservation of dragons' –
You don't want them to become extinct, do you ?!!"*

5 **CD3** **6** Listen and report the conversations using different verb patterns.

1. She was delighted _____.
   He congratulated _____.

2. She was concerned _____.
   He urged _____.

3. She was annoyed _____.
   They offered _____.

4. She complained _____.
   They denied _____.

5. She promised _____.
   He threatened _____.

6. She accused _____.
   He apologized _____.

7. He's really scared _____.
   She advised _____.

8. He bragged _____.
   He challenged _____.

6 Complete these sentences in your own words, using the correct verb pattern. Compare with a partner.

1. I remember _____ when I was young.
2. I'll never forget _____ for the first time.
3. I like _____ when it's raining.
4. I'm thinking of _____ next year.
5. I find it difficult _____.
6. I can't forget _____.
7. I've always tried _____.
8. I'm looking forward to _____.
9. I try to avoid _____.
10. Our teacher always makes us _____.

EVERYDAY ENGLISH
Telling jokes

1 Work with a partner. Match the questions and answers to make jokes.

HISTORY JOKES

1. ☐ Who invented King Arthur's round table?
2. ☐ Why were the early days of history called the Dark Ages?
3. ☐ Who was the greatest robber in history?
4. ☐ What did Noah do for a job?
5. ☐ What did the Sheriff of Nottingham say when Robin Hood fired at him?
6. ☐ Who was the famous Mongolian who conquered nothing?
7. ☐ Which famous French general stepped on a land mine?
8. ☐ What Native American tribe has the most lawyers?
9. ☐ Which letters of the alphabet are like a Roman Emperor?
10. ☐ Why is an archaeologist never successful?

a. Atlas, he held up the whole world!
b. Because his career lies in ruins.
c. Because there were so many knights!
d. Genghis Khan't.
e. The Cs are.
f. Napoleon Blownapart!
g. The Sioux. /su/
h. Sir Cumference!
i. That was an arrow escape!
j. He was an *ark*itect!

2 [CD3] [7] Listen and check.
Each joke depends on a play on words. Explain how. Which jokes rely on homophones and homonyms for their humor?

3 [CD3] [8] Notice which words are stressed in the way jokes are told.

> Who invented King Arthur's round table?

> I don't know. Who did invent King Arthur's round table?

> Sir Cumference! Do you get it?

> Aaah! Of course I get it! How corny is that!

Practice telling the jokes and responding with your partner.

4 [CD3] [9] Mark the main stresses in **B**'s replies in these conversations. Listen and check.

1. **A** Have you heard the one about the old man and his dog?
   B I told it to you!
2. **A** I invited Lara, but she isn't coming.
   B I told you she wouldn't.
3. **A** Paolo hasn't told anybody.
   B He told me.
4. **A** I hope you didn't tell Sunny.
   B I didn't tell anyone.
5. **A** Who told Sunny?
   B I didn't tell her.
6. **A** John won't like it when you tell him.
   B If I tell him.
7. **A** It's the worst movie I've ever seen.
   B Tell me about it!
8. **A** He dumped me.
   B I don't want to say, "I told you so!"

Practice them with your partner.

5 Do you know any jokes in English? Tell the class.

10 The body beautiful

STARTER

1 Think of ten sports in which you have to compete against an opponent, and ten physical activities that you can do as an individual.

Competitive
squash
wrestling
football

Individual
yoga
aerobics
skateboarding

Compare your ideas with the class.

2 **CD3 10** Listen to radio commentaries of six different sports. Can you identify each one? What were the clues that helped you?

3 Which sports do you like to take part in? Which sports do you like to watch? What do you do to keep fit?

READING AND SPEAKING
The age of sports

1 What sports are these people renowned for?
Why, do you think?
- Australians
- African Americans
- Kenyans
- Brazilians
- Chinese
- Russians

2 Who is the most highly paid sportsperson in your country?
In the world?

Is he/she in … ?
- auto racing
- golf
- boxing
- soccer
- athletics
- baseball

3 What are the biggest sporting events in your country?
In the world?

4 Look at the paragraph headings in the article and make
some notes on what the text might be about. Compare your
ideas with the class before reading the article.

5 Read the article and answer the questions.
1. What is the correlation between sports and strawberries?
2. The first paragraph describes various aspects of the
current "Age of Sports". What, by implication, were
these aspects like before this era?
3. "Sports knew their place." What does this mean? Why
don't they know their place any more?
4. How has TV changed sports? Has this change been
beneficial or not?
5. Why is the New York Marathon mentioned?
6. In what ways are most sports stars like everyone else?
7. What is the correlation between modern sports stars and
ancient gladiators?
8. What can sports offer that a rock concert can't?
9. What is special about the Olympics and the World Cup?
10. Why is the besotted fan in a minority?

Vocabulary work

6 Figure out the meanings of the highlighted words in
the article.

What do you think?

- Do you agree that our culture is obsessed by sports?
- Which sporting events are taking place now? Do you think
there is too much sports in the world? Too much sports
on television?
- *"As individuals become rich, sports become impoverished."*
Can you think of any examples that support this opinion?
- Who are the sports icons of the moment? Why are
they famous?
- Who do you think is more interested in sports, men or
women? Why?

the
"It's not just a pastime

Sports used to be like fresh fruit and
vegetables. Football had its season,
then it ended, and you had to wait a
while to get some more. Tennis was
an explosion of Wimbledon at the
end of June, Flushing Meadow in September,
and the Australian Open in January, and that
was that. Now, just as you can get fresh
strawberries all year round, there are major
championships for every sport taking place
somewhere in the world all of the time.

Sports are everywhere

Sports are ubiquitous. Sky TV has at least thirteen
sports channels. Throughout the world there is a
proliferation of newspapers and magazines totally
dedicated to sports. Sports personalities have become
cultural icons, worshiped like movie stars and sought
after by sponsors and advertisers alike. Where sports
were once for fun and amateurs, they are now the
stuff of serious investment.

Of course, sports have always mattered. But the
point is that in the past sports knew their place. Now
they invade areas of life where previously they had
no presence: fashion, showbiz, business. They are a
worldwide obsession.

Why this obsession with sports?

What is it that makes sports so enjoyable for so many?

First, we seriously believe that sports are something
we can all do, however badly or however well. Tens
of thousands set off on the London and New York
Marathons. Amateur soccer matches take place all
over the world every weekend. Playing a sport is a
democratic activity.

Second, sports stars are self-made people. Sports are
dominated by athletes from ordinary backgrounds.
This is why it is a classic means by which those from
the poorest backgrounds can seek fame and fortune.

Third, we enjoy watching sports because we like to see
the supreme skill of those who act like gladiators in the

age of sports

or a hobby. Sports have become a world-wide obsession," writes Simon Carter

modern arena. There is the excitement of not knowing who is going to win. No rock concert, no movie, no play can offer that kind of spontaneous uncertainty. This gut-wrenching experience can be shared with a crowd of fifty around a widescreen TV, or a thronging mass of 100,000 live in a stadium.

The role of television

Television has been absolutely crucial to the growing obsession with sports. It gives increased numbers of people access to sporting events around the globe. With this, certain sports have accumulated untold riches via advertising, sponsorship, and fees. Television changes sports completely, nearly always for the worse. We are saturated with soccer nearly every night of the week with the same top clubs playing each other again and again. TV companies dictate tennis players' schedules. The most important matches must take place at a time when most people are at home, even if this is late at night. Only in this way are the highest advertising fees commanded.

Sports as big business

The growing importance of sports is reflected in the money that surrounds them. Sky TV's sports channels are worth more than $8 billion. Manchester United football club is a public limited company worth more than $1 billion. It has even formed a superclub with baseball's New York Yankees, so that they can package themselves collectively.

The rise of sports has been accompanied by the growing prominence of sports stars. They have become public figures, hence in great demand for TV commercials. For advertisers, they convey glamour, success, credibility, and authenticity. The rise of the sports star is mirrored by the rise of sports companies such as Nike and Adidas. Along with pop music, the Internet, and multinational companies, sports are one of the key agents of globalization.

The global unifier

"Sport probably does more to unify nations than any politician has ever been capable of." So said Nelson Mandela. The only truly global occasions are the Olympics and the World Cup, watched by thousands of millions across the world. These great sporting events bring together players and athletes from different races like no other. Not only that, but sports provide just about the only example of global democracy where the rich do not dominate: On the contrary, Brazilians have long been supreme at soccer, the Kenyans at middle-distance running, and Americans at boxing.

The ultimate risk

However, there are signs of disquiet in this vast, global industry. The sheer volume of sports is reaching the bursting point for all but the most besotted fan. In soccer, the president of FIFA has suggested staging the World Cup every two years instead of four, and overpaid tennis players and golfers fly endlessly in personal jets from one meaningless tournament to the next. Sports are at risk of killing themselves through greed and overexposure. The danger is that we will all become satiated and ultimately disillusioned.

LANGUAGE FOCUS
Intensifying adverbs

> Intensifying adverbs often go together with certain verbs and adjectives. Look at these examples from the article on pages 88–89.
>
> | | |
> |---|---|
> | **totally** dedicated | change **completely** |
> | **seriously** believe | **absolutely** crucial |
>
> ▶▶ **Grammar Reference p. 153**

1 Choose the *two* correct adverbs in these sentences.

1. I *totally / perfectly / quite* agree with you.
2. She *totally / quite / strongly* disagrees with me.
3. Some people *sincerely / seriously / entirely* believe there's life in space.
4. I *perfectly / strongly / completely* understand what you're trying to say.
5. I *totally / really / quite* like spicy food.

2 Choose the *one* correct adverb in these sentences.

1. I *absolutely / completely / sincerely* adore ice cream.
2. I *perfectly / strongly / totally* forgot about her birthday.
3. What you believe depends *entirely / seriously / sincerely* on your point of view.
4. I *really / quite / completely* can't stand getting up in the morning.
5. I have *absolutely / entirely / thoroughly* enjoyed the evening with you.

3 Match a gradable adjective with an extreme adjective.

Gradable adjective	Extreme adjective
stupid	delightful
expensive	brilliant
pleasant	exorbitant
unusual	devastated
upset	extraordinary
smart	ridiculous

With which group or groups of adjectives can we use these intensifying adverbs?

very	absolutely	really	quite

CD3 11 Listen and check. Practice the sentences.

4 Choose the *two* correct adverbs in these sentences.

1. Kate thinks math is hard, and she's *absolutely / very / quite* right.
2. Personally, I find math *extremely / totally / quite* impossible.
3. She's *absolutely / completely / very* terrified of dogs.
4. I was *absolutely / very / really* pleased to hear you're getting married.
5. I'm sure you'll be *totally / extremely / really* happy together.

CD3 12 Listen and check. Practice the sentences, paying attention to stress and intonation.

5 Choose the *one* correct adverb in these sentences.

1. This cheese is *absolutely / totally / really* good. You should try it.
2. I'm *absolutely / terribly / very* determined to lose weight.
3. The restaurant was *pretty / utterly / absolutely* nice, but I wouldn't recommend it.
4. The movie was *totally / utterly / quite* interesting. You should see it.
5. If you ask her, I'm *terribly / pretty / completely* sure she'll say yes.

CD3 13 Listen and check. Practice the sentences, paying attention to stress and intonation.

6 Work with a partner. Write questions to prompt responses that use some of the adverb collocations you have practiced. Ask and answer questions with another partner.

A *Are you going to take the exams?*
B *Yes, I'm absolutely determined to pass.*

"He's not totally lacking in ambition. He dreams of one day owning a bigger TV set."

VOCABULARY AND SPEAKING
Words to do with the body

1 Label the numbered parts of the body, using the words in the box. The numbers in black boxes are inside the body.

ankle	earlobe	jaw	neck	throat
armpit	eyebrow	knee	rib	thumb
bone	forehead	kidney	shin	toe
brain	groin	knuckle	shoulder	vein
calf	heart	lip	spine	waist
cheek	heel	liver	stomach	wrist
chest	hip	lung	temple	
chin	intestines	muscle	thigh	

What other body parts can you name?

2 Complete the sentences with a part of the body used as a verb in the correct form.

1. In the final seconds of the match, Martin _____ the ball into the back of the net.

2. After his father's death, Tom had to _____ the responsibility for the family business.

3. When a couple gets married, it's usually the bride's family who _____ the bill.

4. The boys stood on one side of the room, _____ the girls on the other side.

5. You've got to _____ facts, Jack. You're in debt, and you have no income.

6. Old ladies are the worst people in line. They just _____ everyone else out of the way.

7. I ran out of gas, so I had to _____ a ride to the nearest gas station.

8. Maria, could you help me by _____ out these books to the other students?

9. My friend Pat loves _____ around other people's houses, looking in drawers and reading their letters.

10. When a mugger tried to attack Jane, she _____ him in the groin and left him collapsed on the ground.

3 What part of your body do you use to do these things?

tickle	stroke	nudge	thump	sniff	pat
pinch	squeeze	grin	rub	clap	crunch
shove	spit	wink	scratch	slap	hug

Why might you do these things?

You tickle someone to make them laugh.

4 Close your books and work with a partner. Take turns miming a verb for your partner to guess.

LISTENING AND SPEAKING
Sports heroes and heroines

The cycler and the gymnast

1 Do you have a particular sports figure that you admire? Who? Why? Discuss as a class.

2 What do you think the life of a professional athlete is like? What are the highs and lows?

3 Look at the photos and read the quotations on the right. Who do you think says what?

> " I've done it before. It won't be the last time. You're going to go years where you just don't win. That's OK, as long as you keep trying to improve. "

> " I know if I put my heart and mind to it, nothing is impossible. "

LANCE ARMSTRONG – professional cyclist and the only person to win the famous bike race, Tour de France, a record-breaking seven times in a row, from 1999 to 2005. He has survived cancer, a serious tumor, and cancer treatment and was named ESPN'S Best Male Athlete four times. In 2009 he finished wthird in the Tour de France.

NASTIA LIUKIN – world-class gymnast, has been at the top of her profession since she was 12 years old, winning nine World Championships medals and the hearts of people the world over.

4 Work in two groups.

Group A **CD3 14** Listen to Marco and James talk about Lance Armstrong, the famous cyclist.

Group B **CD3 15** Listen to Alicia and Kate talk about Nastia Liukin, the gymnast.

Answer the questions.

1. Why are the speakers interested in Lance/Nastia?
2. What have been the best moments of Nastia's/Lance's career?
3. What health problems has he/she had?
4. What is her/his training program?
5. What does his/her diet consist of?
6. What sacrifices has he/she had to make?
7. What are his/her ambitions for the future?
8. What kind of a relationship do the two speakers have? What do you learn about them?

5 Work with a partner from the other group. Compare and exchange information.

What do you think?

1. Whose training program is harder, Nastia Liukin's or Lance Armstrong's? Who has suffered more?
2. What sort of person do you have to be to succeed in sports? Why do you think they do it?
3. Do you know any examples of athletes burning out? What were the pressures on them?

SPEAKING

How healthy and fit are you?

1 *"If you're fit, you don't need to exercise. If you aren't fit, exercise is dangerous."* Do you agree with this logic or not? How can you injure yourself exercising?

2 Work with a partner and ask each other the questions in the quiz. Tally and compare your scores, and decide on your priorities for action.

What do you think?

- How effective and useful are these quizzes?
- Will you pay attention to the results and alter your lifestyle?

"My doctor wants me to walk a mile after every meal, but, frankly, ten miles a day is killing me."

HEALTH & FITNESS QUIZ

How healthy & fit are you? How healthy & fit could you be?

How **true** are these statements for you?

| 5 | Always | 4 | Often | 3 | Sometimes | 2 | Rarely | 1 | Never |

1 I start the day with a sensible breakfast. ☐

2 I tend to have 4 or 5 smaller meals a day. ☐

3 On an average day, my diet includes 5 portions of fruit and vegetables. ☐

4 Less than 30 percent of my daily calorie intake is fat. ☐

5 I regularly take food supplements of vitamins and minerals. ☐

6 I don't eat a lot of fried foods. ☐

7 I don't eat red meat. ☐

8 I make sure I drink 6–8 glasses of water a day. ☐

9 My sugar consumption is generally low. ☐

10 I exercise aerobically at least 3 times a week. ☐

11 I work out with weights or exercise machines twice a week. ☐

12 As well as a proper lunch break, I take a couple of breaks during the work day. ☐

13 I get about 7–8 hours of sleep a night. ☐

14 I actively cultivate relationships and interests outside of work. ☐

15 I have several close friendships with people I trust. ☐

16 I probably break into laughter about 20 times a day. ☐

17 I allow myself adequate vacation time. ☐

18 I meditate, pray, or practice some form of relaxation technique daily. ☐

19 I feel in charge of my health and take full responsibility for it. ☐

20 I generally have a positive mental attitude. ☐

Check your answers to each question. To find your score, add up the numbers.

My total score is: ☐

If your total score is:

100–80 you have **excellent** health habits (great job, keep up the good work!)

79–70 you have **good** health habits (good, but let's work on it a little)

69–60 you need **special** attention (let's go to work on it now)

59–0 is a **red alert!** (do something about it now!)

Decide on your top three priorities for action from your lowest scores in the quiz:

1. _____

_____

2. _____

_____

3. _____

_____

EVERYDAY ENGLISH
Clichés

1 **CD3** **16** A cliché is a phrase that has been used so often that it has lost much of its force. Read and listen to the conversations and identify the clichés. What do they mean?

1. A You should get a new job, stop eating so much junk food, and have a healthier lifestyle.
B Easier said than done.

2. A I don't know whether to apply for that job or not. What do you think?
B Well, I'm not sure. At the end of the day, it's your decision.

3. A Jamie and I are going out for the evening.
B Have a great time! Don't do anything I wouldn't do.

2 Match a line in **A** with a line in **B**. Where are the clichés? What do they mean?

1. Mom! Tommy broke the vase!	a. Well, you know what they say. No pain, no gain.
2. I just need to go back in the house and make sure I've turned off the iron.	b. Good idea. Better safe than sorry.
3. It's been raining nonstop for weeks! We need some sunshine!	c. Uh-oh! They say bad luck comes in threes.
4. I got a card from Jeremy a week after my birthday.	d. You can say that again.
5. We're going away for two weeks.	e. It takes all kinds.
6. Took me ten years to build this business. Nearly killed me.	f. It boggles the mind.
7. Tom failed his exams, Amy has chicken pox. What's next?	g. Oh, well. Better late than never.
8. They have ten kids. Goodness knows what their house is like.	h. Sounds like just what the doctor ordered.
9. Bob's a strange guy. Did you hear he's going to walk across Europe?	i. It's OK. Accidents happen.

CD3 **17** Listen and check. Do you have any similar clichés in your language?

3 **CD3** **18** Listen and respond to the statements, using an appropriate cliché.

▶▶ **Writing** Entering a competition **p. 125**

11 The ends of the earth

- **Grammar:** Relatives and participles
- **Vocabulary:** Compound nouns and adjectives
- **Everyday English:** Idiomatic expressions

STARTER   **1** Work in groups and answer the questions.

EARTH QUIZ

1 How old is the earth?
a. 4.6 billion years
b. 6.7 billion years
c. 10.5 billion years

2 The earth is considered to have a maximum of seven continents. What are they?

3 How many countries are there in the world?
a. 123   b. 146   c. 193

4 Which continent has the most countries?

5 What is the population of the world?
a. 4.7 billion people
b. 5.7 billion people
c. 6.7 billion people

6 Which country has the largest population?

7 What proportion of the earth is covered by water?
a. 61%   b. 71%   c. 81%

8 How many oceans are there? What are they?

9 How much of the earth's land surface is used to grow food?
a. 11%   b. 16%   c. 21%

10 Where is the world's largest desert? What is it called?

11 What's the difference between a political and a physical map?

12 What is the world's largest island?
a. Greenland
b. Iceland
c. Madagascar

2 **CD3** **19** Listen and check. What extra information do you learn about each?

3 Read these funny mistakes from some students' geography exams. Explain them.

1 The chief animals of Australia are the kangaroo and the boomerang.	**4** The Mediterranean and the Red Sea are connected by the Sewage Canal.
2 Floods from the Mississippi may be prevented by putting big dames in the river.	**5** The Pyramids are a range of mountains between France and Spain.
3 The inhabitants of Moscow are called Mosquitoes.	**6** In the West, farming is done mostly by irritating the land.

READING AND SPEAKING
Three island stories

1 Did you know that one in ten people in the world live on an island? Which islands have you visited? When? What were they like?

2 Match the photos above to the islands of **Greenland**, **Tristan da Cunha**, and **Zanzibar**. Which island do you know most/least about? Compare ideas with the class.

3 Work in groups of three.

Student A Read about Greenland on page 97.

Student B Read about Tristan da Cunha on page 98.

Student C Read about Zanzibar on page 99.

As you read, underline at least three things that you find interesting or surprising. Tell your group about them.

4 Answer the questions by comparing information about the islands.

1. What do you learn about the islands' names?
2. Which island lies farthest west?
3. Which has the smallest population?
4. Which is the most economically successful?
5. Which has the most varied history in terms of colonization?
6. Do any of the islands share the same native tongue?
7. Which imports the most goods?
8. Which is the most self-sufficient?
9. Which is the most colorful? Which the least? Why?
10. Which do you think attracts the most tourists?

Language work

5 Geographical expressions

Complete the sentences with the correct prepositions. Which island is being referred to in each sentence?

1. It is situated _____ the South Atlantic, 1,740 miles _____ the nearest mainland and south _____ the island of St. Helena.
2. Temperatures range _____ 32°F _____ 59°F in summer.
3. Its landscape is made _____ _____ gray granite rock.
4. It lies just _____ the coast of East Africa.
5. It is equal _____ size _____ half of Western Europe.
6. If all this ice were to melt, the world's oceans might rise _____ six _____ seven meters.
7. He didn't settle _____ the island but, nevertheless, he named it _____ himself.
8. The history of the island is _____ _____ proportion _____ its size.
9. It is divided _____ three areas.
10. It is an island burgeoning _____ spices and subject _____ favorable trade winds.
11. The population now numbers just _____ 300.
12. The population is estimated _____ _____ 800,000.
13. It lacks the abundance _____ wildlife found _____ the mainland.

What do you think?

• In what ways does the location influence life on the islands?

• In what ways has its history influenced present island life?

• Which of these islands would you like to visit? Which not? Why?

GREENLAND

The largest island in the world

Geography

Greenland is the largest island in the world, measuring 1,659 miles from north to south, but with a population of only about 56,000, one-quarter of which lives in the capital, Nuuk. It lies just south of the Arctic Circle, so its summer temperatures range from just 32°F to 59°F. Eighty-five percent of its 840,000 mi^2 area is covered with a massive ice cap, which holds 9 percent of the world's fresh water. If all this ice were to melt, the world's oceans would rise by 19 to 22 feet. Despite its name, Greenland is anything but green. Its bare haunting landscape is made up of gray granite rock and massive icebergs, with only tiny pockets of greenery.

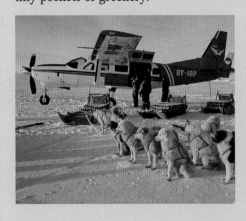

History

The Inuit people (previously known as Eskimos) were the first people of this island. Then, around 980 A.D., Eric the Red, a bloodthirsty Norwegian Viking, fled to the island and founded a colony. Despite the desolate grayness, Eric cunningly named the island "Greenland," so as to attract settlers. His trick worked and the colony grew but then died out suddenly and mysteriously in the 1400s. In 1721, the Danish established a settlement there, and ruled for over 200 years, until 1979, when Greenland was declared an autonomous nation within the Kingdom of Denmark.

Greenland today

Regional boundaries divide the country into three areas: North, East, and West Greenland. East Greenland, known as Tunu, is the most isolated, blocked by ice for 9 months out of 12. Only 4,000 people live here, despite it being equal in size to half of Western Europe. In the harbor there are corpses of hunted seals, sunk in the cold water, which acts as a natural refrigerator. The presence of polar bears is always a possibility. These dangerous, man-eating creatures are feared but also loved as the embodiment of the human spirit in a harsh land.

This is also the region of the semi-permafrost. Tombs are shallow and the dead are often stored for months before being buried in warmer months, when the soil can be dug. There are serious social problems, such as alcoholism and suicides, as a result of unemployment and seasonal depression. The latter is a common syndrome in places where winter lasts more than half the year, where there is no light at all.

These days Greenlandic, or East Inuit language, has become the first language, and Danish the second. The Civil Service is largely Greenlandic as well and there are more Inuit signs than Danish ones. However, like most small remote nations, economic independence is non-existent. Most of the national budget is funded by Denmark. Everything in the supermarket is Danish. Job prospects remain poor and most services, from air transportation to seal hunting, are subsidized by the Danish taxpayer.

TRISTAN DA CUNHA

The most remote island in the world

Geography

Tristan da Cunha is the most remote island in the world. Situated in the South Atlantic, it is 1,740 miles from the nearest mainland, South Africa, and 1,600 miles south of the island of St. Helena. The island is roughly circular with an average diameter of 6 miles. It rises out of the ocean, its volcanic peak crowned with an almost permanent cap of white cloud, and its 24 miles of wild, storm-tossed coastline comprising magnificent, massive basalt cliffs. The surrounding seas are rich in fish, providing Tristan da Cunha with its main export.

History

The island was discovered in 1506 by a Portuguese explorer, Tristao da Cunha, who, despite being unable to land there, named the island after himself. The first actual settler was an American, Captain Jonathan Lambert, in 1811. Unfortunately, he drowned a year later.

In 1816, the British annexed the island as a defense against the French, who, it was thought, were planning to rescue Napoleon from exile on the island of St. Helena.

The British left, leaving the founder of the present community – a Scot, Corporal William Glass, who settled on the island with his family, two companions, and a woman from St. Helena, making a total of six inhabitants. The community comprised still no more than eleven thatched cottages when, in 1867, Alfred, Duke of Edinburgh and second son of Queen Victoria, visited the island and gave his name to the capital, which is called the Edinburgh of the South Seas. Throughout the nineteenth century the population slowly increased but Tristan da Cunha passed into obscurity. Then, in October 1961 a dramatic volcanic eruption forced the evacuation of the entire island. Its people were taken to what was glibly referred to as "civilization" in South Africa and England. By August 1962 the eruptions had died down and in November 1963 the islanders chose to return home.

Tristan today

To visit Tristan da Cunha is to visit another world, another life, another time. The settlement of Edinburgh has a distinct air of yesteryear about it, although it has all modern conveniences. There is a small museum, a large supermarket, a swimming pool, and a radio station, but no television.

The population now numbers just under 300 – a proud and hospitable people with only seven last names among them: Hagan, Rogers, Glass, Lavarello, Swain, Green, and Repetto. Through their veins flows the blood of English sailors from Nelson's fleet, Americans, Italians, two Irish girls, Dutch, and mulattos from St. Helena and South Africa. English is the native tongue, albeit a slightly strange, old-fashioned dialect, laced with a few early Americanisms.

The island is self-supporting with a thriving economy. Income tax is low (although imported goods are very expensive). Serious crime is unknown, and unemployment is virtually nonexistent.

As well as the fishing industry, a main source of income on the island is the sale of postage stamps, which are prized by philatelists worldwide.

3

ZANZIBAR
The most exotic island in the world

Geography

A large proportion of the world's population has heard of Zanzibar. The name conjures up all sorts of exotic images: sultans, slaves, spices, ebony, ivory, gold, and explorers — words that start to tell the story of Zanzibar. However, only a small proportion of the world's population knows exactly where Zanzibar is. It is located in the Indian Ocean, just off the Tanzanian coast of East Africa, immediately south of the equator. Zanzibar Island is 51 miles long and 23 miles wide with magnificent, golden, sandy beaches fringed by coconut palms and coral reefs. Zanzibar lacks the abundance of wildlife that is found on mainland Africa. No giraffes, elephants, or lions here today, just a few monkeys and small antelopes. However, in 1295, when visiting the island, Marco Polo recorded that Zanzibar had "elephants in plenty."

History

The history of Zanzibar is one out of proportion to its size. It was the richest place in Africa for centuries, an island burgeoning with spices and subject to such favorable winds that it has served as the center of trade between Africa, Arabia, and India for over five thousand years. The islands have always been highly prized by empire builders: Egyptians, Arabs, Portuguese, Chinese, Dutch, and British have all taken possession, valuing it not only for its strategic trading position, but also because of its fertile soil and temperate climate. Zanzibar used to be the world's largest producer of cloves, grown on plantations established in the early 1800s by Sultan Said of Oman.

In 1964, the islands joined with the country of Tanganyika on the East African mainland, to become the United Republic of Tanzania. "Zanzibar" forms half the name of "Tanzania."

Zanzibar today

The population is estimated at about 800,000, an incredible mixture of ethnic backgrounds, indicative of the island's colorful history. Zanzibaris speak Swahili, a language that is spoken extensively in East Africa. Many believe that the purest form is spoken in Zanzibar as it is the birthplace of the language. Fishing and agriculture are the main economic activities of the local people. Although cloves are still a major export along with coconut products and spices, tourism has been earmarked as the primary foreign exchange earner, with more visitors coming to Zanzibar each year. Some of these come to visit the birthplace of the late Freddie Mercury, lead singer of the band Queen, who was born Farouk Bulsara in Zanzibar City on September 5, 1946. However, the numbers of tourists are still relatively low (less than 100,000 annually) and the potential for tourism is still largely untapped. The island is trying hard to develop sensitive tourism that benefits both visitors and community, without losing the magic that is Zanzibar.

VOCABULARY AND LISTENING
Compound nouns and adjectives

Weather words

1 How many compound nouns and adjectives can you make using the weather words on the left?

sun
rain
wind
snow
ice
+

Nouns	Adjectives
berg	-blown
cap	burned
drift	-capped
drop	-drenched
fall	-soaked
plow	swept
flake	tanned
roof	
storm	
stroke	

2 Complete these sentences with compounds from Exercise 1.

1. The annual _____ in San Francisco is 20 inches.
2. My sister stayed out in the sun for too long, and she was sick for two days with _____.
3. One winter's night there was a terrible _____. In the morning the _____ were so deep that even the _____ couldn't get through to our town.
4. I'd love a convertible on warm days like these. My car doesn't even have a _____.
5. The *Titanic* sank because it hit a huge _____.
6. Did you know that Kilimanjaro is a _____ mountain even though it's on the equator?
7. After a hot day's sailing my face was _____ and my hair was _____.
8. Did you know that the pattern of every single tiny _____ is different?
9. I love the sight of _____ on rose petals after a shower.
10. I love both the hot _____ beaches of the Caribbean and the wet _____ hills of Scotland for my vacation.

Adjective order

3 Look at these examples of adjectives before nouns. Which adjectives are more factual? Which are more opinion? What is their position? Try to figure out some rules.

1. Beautiful, old, thatched cottages
2. Glorious, golden Mediterranean beaches
3. Amazing, huge, gray, granite rocks
4. Strange, old-fashioned English dialect
5. Wild, storm-tossed Atlantic coast
6. Dangerous, man-eating polar bears

▶▶ **Grammar Reference p. 153**

4 Put the adjectives into a natural-sounding order.

1. He gave us some bread. (whole wheat; delicious; homemade)
2. A lady arrived. (little; funny; old; Irish)
3. I bought a shirt. (silk; red and white; gorgeous; striped)
4. She just had a boy. (baby; beautiful; bouncing; fat)
5. He showed me into a room. (airy; light; high-ceilinged; delightful; living)
6. I met a student. (young; trendy; art; Venezuelan)
7. She's wearing pants. (leather; black; shiny; tight-fitting)
8. It's a rose bush. (sweet-smelling; exquisite; apricot-colored)

5 Add some extra information for each sentence in Exercise 4.

It's a beautiful, old thatched cottage **with a beautiful garden./ hidden from the road.**

CD3 20 Listen and compare your answers.

Far-flung spots

6 **CD3 21** Listen to some people describing the most far-flung place they have visited and write down the adjectives they use.
Then answer these questions about each person, using the adjectives you wrote down to help you.

1. Where did they go?
2. What did they do and see?
3. Why was it unusual and memorable?

7 Which of the places would you like to visit and why? What is the most unusual place you've been to?

8 Write a short description of a place you have visited, using both factual and opinion adjectives.

LISTENING AND SPEAKING
A meeting in the desert

Simon Winchester is a foreign correspondent who travels widely, often to the more remote parts of the world.

1 Look at the illustrations, which tell Simon's unusual story about a train trip in the far west of China. Work with a partner to try to predict what happens.

2 **CD3 22** Listen to the first part of the story. Are these statements true or false? Correct the false ones.

1. Simon made the journey alone.
2. He was attracted to the idea of traveling on a new railway line in such a remote area.
3. They stopped in a desert town called Urunchi.
4. The engine driver spoke impeccable English.
5. He met an exquisitely lovely, rather serious Chinese woman.

What do you think happens next?

3 **CD3 23** Listen to the second part. Were any of your predictions correct? Answer the questions.

1. Why did the woman check her watch?
2. How do Anthony Trollope and his book *The Eustace Diamonds* figure in the story?
3. Who struggled and scribbled? Why?
4. Who scrambled? Why?
5. Why did the woman say, "Don't be silly!"?
6. Complete these excerpts with the next three words.
   a. I could just about remember _____ ...
   b. The last vision I have of her was her scrambling on her _____ ...

How do you think the story ends? What do you think was in the letter? The pictures may help you predict.

4 **CD3 24** Listen to the last part. How close were your predictions? Are these statements true or false? Correct the false ones.

1. The woman wrote to Simon to ask if she could meet him again soon.
2. She and her husband had to move to Kwi Tun as a punishment.
3. She called Kwi Tun "this lovely little town."
4. She regularly bikes thirteen miles across the desert to meet the train.
5. Her main motivation is to find somebody to talk to in English.
6. She once had a conversation with a migrant worker about Trollope.
7. She talked to Simon about religion.
8. Simon and the woman have unfortunately lost touch with each other.

5 Work with your partner to retell the story in your own words, using the pictures to help.

Simon and his friend decided to . . .
After about 150 miles . . .

LANGUAGE FOCUS
Relatives and participles
Defining and nondefining relative clauses

> Underline the relative clauses in these sentences. Then answer the questions.
> a. Here's somebody who speaks English.
> b. The Chinese lady, who speaks impeccable English, lives in the desert.
> c. She works for a company that organizes adventure vacations.
> d. They took a train trip across the desert to Kazakhstan, which sounded fascinating.
> e. The friend who he traveled with is a doctor.
> f. The islanders were taken to what was referred to as "civilization."
>
> 1. Which sentences still make complete sense if the relative clauses are removed? Which are defining relative clauses? Which are nondefining?
> 2. In which sentences can *who* be replaced by *that*? Why?
> 3. In which sentence can the relative pronoun (*who*) be omitted? Why?
> 4. In which sentence can *whom* replace *who*? Transform this sentence. What effect does this have?
> 5. Read the sentences aloud. What is the role of the commas?
>
> ▶▶ **Grammar Reference p. 153–154**

1 Work with a partner and discuss any differences in meaning and/or form between the sentences in each pair.

1. The sailors whose cabins were below deck all drowned.
   The sailors, whose cabins were below deck, all drowned.
2. My sister, who's a travel agent, is terrified of flying.
   My sister who's a travel agent is terrified of flying.
3. The explorer Tristao da Cunha, after whom the island was named, never actually landed there.
   The explorer Tristao da Cunha, who they named the island after, never actually landed there.
4. I'm appalled at everything that happened.
   I'm appalled at what happened.
5. The map showed the place in which the treasure was buried.
   The map showed where the treasure was buried.
6. People seeking adventure meet all kinds of danger.
   People who seek adventure meet all kinds of danger.
7. There are white coral sands fringed by coconut palms.
   There are white coral sands, which are fringed by coconut palms.

2 Read these incomplete sentences and discuss whether they should be completed with a defining or nondefining relative clause, or whether both are possible.

1. I don't like children …
2. The trip from work to home … took over two hours yesterday.
3. Politicians … aren't worth listening to.
4. The Taj Mahal … is built from exquisitely carved white marble.
5. These are the photographs …
6. We docked at the small port on the coast of East Africa …
7. My cousin … went hang-gliding last weekend.
8. We went on a biking trip in Mexico …

CD3 25 Complete the phrases with your ideas, then listen and compare.

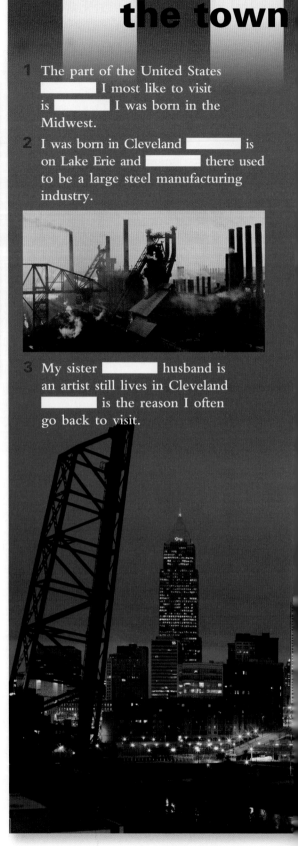

the town

1 The part of the United States [＿＿＿] I most like to visit is [＿＿＿] I was born in the Midwest.

2 I was born in Cleveland [＿＿＿] is on Lake Erie and [＿＿＿] there used to be a large steel manufacturing industry.

3 My sister [＿＿＿] husband is an artist still lives in Cleveland [＿＿＿] is the reason I often go back to visit.

3 Complete the text above with relative pronouns and commas where necessary. If it is possible to omit the pronoun, add nothing.

4 My grandfather ▢▢▢▢ worked in the steelyards left Cleveland only once in his life and that was ▢▢▢▢ the Cleveland Indians baseball team won the World Series in 1948.

5 The Hope Memorial Bridge, ▢▢▢▢ beautiful statues symbolize progress in transportation, spans the Cuyahoga River and ▢▢▢▢ industrial warehouses once stood there are now trendy restaurants and apartment buildings.

6 My brother-in-law ▢▢▢▢ has traveled widely and ▢▢▢▢ paintings depict many exotic places, still prefers to paint ▢▢▢▢ is most familiar to him – the gray, wintry Lake Erie coastline.

7 ▢▢▢▢ I like most ▢▢▢▢ I visit my hometown is all the memories ▢▢▢▢ come flooding back.

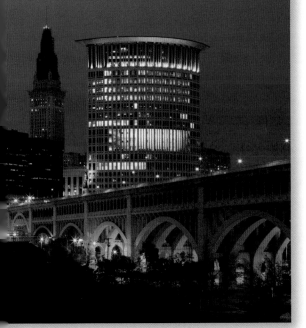

4 Write some notes about the town where you were born. Give it to a partner to read and ask questions.

Participles

> Participle clauses can express these ideas.
> • at the same time • so that/with the result that
> • because • after • if
>
> ▶▶ **Grammar Reference p. 154**

5 Which ideas do the participles in these sentences express?
1. Living in Boston, I appreciate the pros and cons of city life.
2. I cut myself opening a can.
3. Having read the minutes of the meeting, I wrote a report.
4. Having read the minutes of the meeting, I understood the problems.
5. Cooked in a rich sauce, ostrich meat can be delicious.
6. Knowing my love of chocolate, she hid it away in a drawer.
7. Taken from his mother as a child, he's always had problems establishing relationships.
8. Browsing in our local bookstore, I came across this great book on computing skills.

6 Complete the pairs of sentences with the same verb, once as a present participle and once as a past participle.
1. Tomatoes _grown___ under polythene ripen more quickly.
   _Growing___ up in the countryside is really healthy for young kids.

2. We took a shortcut, _____ an hour of driving time.
   With the money _____ from not eating out we've bought a new computer.

3. _____ all things into account, we've decided to offer you the job.
   _____ three times a day, these pills can really help hay fever.

4. Flights _____ one month in advance have a 10 percent discount.
   _____ your flight in advance gives you a better deal.

5. I fell on the ice, _____ my wrist.
   The two boys _____ in the car accident are doing well in the hospital.

6. _____ promises leads to lack of trust.
   _____ promises lead to lack of trust.

7. _____ away secrets won't win you any friends.
   I don't believe a word he says, _____ that he never tells the truth.

8. The new uniforms _____ by the flight attendants looked very sharp.
   Students _____ earrings will be asked to remove them immediately.

EVERYDAY ENGLISH
What on earth!

1 Complete the sentences with a noun from the box.

earth	ground	floor	land	soil	world

1. The sailors didn't see _____ again until the ship reached Australia.
2. Communication satellites orbit the _____ once every 24 hours.
3. This rich, black _____ looks extremely fertile.
4. He fell off the wall and hit his head on the _____.
5. We are all striving for _____ peace.
6. In American English we say, "the first _____," but in British English they say, "the ground _____."
7. What on _____ are you doing down there on your hands and knees?
8. He lives in a _____ of his own, you just can't get through to him.
9. I like her because she's such a down-to-_____ kind of person.

2 Here are some idiomatic expressions using the words in Exercise 1. Match a line in **A** with a line in **B**. Use a dictionary if necessary.

A	B
1. Believe me. That guy's really on the ball.	a. I almost didn't. I had to move heaven and earth to get here.
2. The vacation's over. It's back to the real world.	b. I can't. I failed my chemistry exam, and I've been grounded for a week.
3. What? You're not coming out on Saturday night?!	c. No kidding! He landed that consultancy job that we all applied for.
4. Hey! Great to see you! I thought you weren't going to be able to make it.	d. In your dreams. Not if he were the last man on earth!
5. Come on, you know you really want to go out with him.	e. Don't ask me. I have no idea!
6. Do you understand these instructions? Where in the world do all these screws go?	f. You can say that again. Back to earth with a crash!

3 **CD3 26** Listen and check. Practice the conversations with a partner.

4 Write some similar conversations with your partner, using some of the expressions from Exercise 2. Read them to another pair.

▶▶ **Writing** Describing a trip **p. 126**

12 Life goes on

Grammar: Linking devices
Vocabulary: Synonyms and antonyms 2
Everyday English: Euphemisms

STARTER

1 Describe Pieter Bruegel's picture, *Landscape with the Fall of Icarus*. Where is Icarus?

2 Ask your teacher questions.

When was it painted?

Who was Icarus?

Which one is he in the picture?

3 **CD3 27** Listen to a description of the picture by an art historian. What does she say about . . . ?

• the three men
• the central event
• direction and movement
• an interpretation of the picture

4 Do you agree with Bruegel's message on life? Isn't it good to be ambitious? Is it true that "life goes on"?

Unit 12 · Life goes on   105

READING AND SPEAKING
A sideways look at time

1 What activities do you do at exactly the same time each day? Are you the kind of person who arrives early, exactly on time, or fashionably late? Are you annoyed by people who are not punctual?

2 Why do people often say that the older you are, the faster time seems to go by? When does time seem to fly by? When does it drag?

3 Check these action verbs. Demonstrate some of them.

look sideways	blink
winkle something out	spin
sigh	slip

4 What do you think these mean?

- clock-time
- chronological time
- universal time
- kairological time

Read the article to find out.
Explain the title.

5 Answer the questions.

1. What is meant by "Urban modernity lives under an assault of clocks"? Give some examples of the way our lives are governed by the clock.

2. Give examples of fast food. What is fast knowledge?

3. What is UT?

4. In what way is the earth inaccurate?

5. How is the forest a clock for the Karen tribe?

6. Explain how "sunset" can be described as "one mile away."

7. What is a "scent calendar"? What would you name the "scent months" where you live?

8. How are adults and children different in their attitudes to time?

9. What is the difference between the two Greek gods of time?

10. How is the passage of time different in the town and in the country?

Of course you know what the time is. You can look at your brand new DIGITAL watch, can't you? **But do you really know?** JAY GRIFFITHS invites you to think again and take:

A *sideways* look at TIME

MEASURING TIME

Time's measurement is everywhere. Leaving London, Berlin, New York, Washington, or Paris: at the airport every transaction, each ticket and money exchange is timed. Around Heathrow, as at any other major airport, there are clocks, blinking the date and time, down to tenths of seconds. Urban modernity lives under an assault of clocks. Alarm clocks put the frighteners on sleep: the first thought in so many people's minds, every single waking day is "What's the time? Am I late?" Digital clocks with their digital seconds seem to speed time, relentlessly tightening deadlines. People speak of the frenetic pace of modern society, everything is speeded up, from fast food to fast clothes and fast knowledge.

There are 86,400 seconds in a day and every one is artificially ticked off, day in, day out, by the MSF service of broadcast standard frequency and time on wavelength 60kHz in the LF band. This is the time, since on the first of January 1972 the second was defined as the atomic second, and Coordinated Universal Time (abbreviated to UT) was set by international agreement. Roughly every year a leap-second is added to realign the time with that of the earth – it is added to "accommodate" the earth's unreliable time. For the earth, you see, is too inaccurate for modernity's time measurement, because its spin changes by up to a thousandth of a second in some years. A thousandth of a second, indeed, tut tut, how unpunctual the earth is!

So the timekeepers of today must tell the time from outside the earth itself, insisting that there is one time, abstract and universal, mono-time: the time. There is no such thing.

NOT JUST ONE TIME

The Karen, a hill-tribe in the forests of Northern Thailand, always know the time. Living with them for six months it became clear to me that the only person with a watch and the only person who could never tell the time was, well, myself. To the Karen, the whole forest was a clock. The morning held simplicity in its damp air, unlike the evening's denser wet when steam and smoke thickened the air. The Karen always know where they are and when they are, how far they are from sunset or home: for time and distance are connected in the Karen language: díyi ba – soon – means, literally, "not far away." Sunset, therefore, could be expressed as "one mile away," because the only way of traveling is to walk, which takes a known length of time.

Across the world the nature of each moon-month is characterized and, through each people's names for the months, you can see the specific landscape they inhabit. The Natchez tribes of the lower Mississippi River Valley have months that include the Deer month and the Strawberries month, the Turkey, Bison, Bear, and Chestnut months. In India's Andaman forests, people have a scent-calendar, using the smells of flowers and trees to describe the time of the year. Other peoples characterize time by starscapes. So, see how false is the ideology of Western imperialist time, declaring itself the time. There are thousands of times, not one.

CHILDREN AND *TIME*

Adults, generally, have learned clock-time. While old people sigh over how fast it goes, children are incapable of patience. How long is an hour to a child? Far, far longer than to an adult; asking a small child to wait a few hours for ice cream is like asking yourself to wait till next Wednesday for their morning coffee. Children live in the heart of the ocean of time, in an everlasting now. A child's eternal present is present-absorbed, present-spontaneous, present-elastic. Children have a dogged, delicious disrespect for punctuality.

GODS OF *TIME*

The ancient Greeks had different gods for time's different aspects. One of the most important was Chronos, who gives his name to absolute time, linear, chronological, and quantifiable. But the Greeks had another, far more slippery and colorful, god of time, Kairos. Kairos was the god of timing, of opportunity, of chance and mischance, of different aspects of time. Time qualitative. If you sleep because the clock tells you it's way past your bedtime, that is chronological time: whereas if you sleep because you're tired, that is kairological time. If you eat cookies when you're hungry, that is kairological: whereas if you eat by the clock, that is chronological time. Children, needless to say, live kairologically until winkled out of it.

KAIROLOGICAL *TIME*

Kairological time has a different sense of movement compared to chronological time. For a rough comparison, contrast an urban with a rural day. In cities, where time is most chronological, your progress through the day is like an arrow, while the day of itself "stays still," for time is not given by the day but is man-made, and defined by the working day or rush-hours. In a rural place, time moves towards you and is nature-given, defined by sun or stars or rainstorms. In this more kairological time, the future comes towards you and recedes behind you while you may well stay still, standing in the present, the only place that is ever really anyone's to stand in.

What do you think?

1. "There is no such thing as a time-saving device. They should be renamed time-slaving devices."

   Do you agree? Think of some devices that are supposed to save us time. Do they, in fact? In what ways are we obsessed with speed in our lives?

2. Think of some examples of nature's clocks at work.

   sunrise   hibernation

3. Rename the months of the year according to where you are and what nature is doing in that month.

4. **CD3 28** Read and listen to the poem. What does it say about how time can appear to go quickly or slowly?

Time is too slow for those who wait,

too swift for those who fear,

too long for those who grieve,

too short for those who rejoice,

but for those who love, time is eternity.

LANGUAGE FOCUS
Linking devices

There are many ways of making links between parts of a sentence or between sentences.

1 With conjunctions:
... the future comes towards you **and** recedes behind you ...
This is the time, **since** on the first of January 1972 the second was defined as the atomic second ...

2 With adverbs:
However, roughly every year a leap second is added ...
So the timekeepers of today must tell the time ...

3 With infinitives:
... it is added to **accommodate** the earth's unreliable time ...

4 With relative pronouns:
In cities, **where** time is most chronological ...

5 With participles:
... there are clocks on corporate buildings and hotels, **blinking** the date and time ...

Find more examples in the article on page 106.

▶▶ **Grammar Reference p. 155**

1 Choose the correct linker. Sometimes two are possible.

A day in the life of
Benjamin Ellis

" I always wake up at six o'clock on the dot in the morning, (1) *unless / wherever / no matter where* I am in the world. I'm a morning person, (2) *so / therefore / since* I like to make the best of my creative period. (3) *As soon as / Whenever / After* I've taken a shower, I take the dog out, and (4) *then / at last / finally* it's time for tea and e-mails. (5) *Since / As / Even though* I work at home, I get a lot of e-mails, and (6) *providing / if / unless* I go through them daily, they build up and up.

I work downstairs (7) *to not / in order not to / so as not to* wake up the rest of the family.

(8) *Since / In case / Once* everyone is up, we have breakfast, and (9) *after / afterwards / after that* it's the mad rush for school. (10) *Even though / Even so / Although* we ask the children every evening if they have everything for school the next day, there is always something they have forgotten. "Where's my ...?" is the cry in our house (11) *however / as long as / whenever* a child has lost something. This is followed by the fatuous question from a parent, usually me, "Where did you last have it?" (12) *Provided / Supposing / If* the child knew that, there wouldn't be a problem.

(13) *When / While / Whenever* everyone's ready, we all pile into the car. I like to leave early (14) *in case / unless / although* the traffic is bad. We take back roads (15) *to avoid / so as to avoid / because we avoid* rush-hour traffic, but (16) *even so / all the same / yet* the trip takes half an hour.

(17) *Immediately / Since / As soon as* I get home, it's back to the computer. (18) *Working / As I work / So that I work* at home, I know how easy it is to be distracted. (19) *As long as / Provided / Except when* I do about eight hours' work a day, I manage to stay on top of it. In the evening we all eat together (20) *so that / in order to / since* we can catch up with each other's news from the day. "

2 Write a paragraph about a typical day in your life, using linking devices.

3 Rewrite each sentence in different ways, using the words in the box.

1. The bank robber wore a mask. No one recognized him.

so that	so as not to

The bank robber wore a mask so that no one recognized him.

The bank robber wore a mask so as not to be recognized.

2. I saw the movie. Then I read the book.

having	after

3. Take care of this. It will last a lifetime.

as long as	provided

4. The curry was hot. We couldn't eat it.

so	such	too

5. It doesn't matter what you do, but don't press this button.

no matter	whatever

6. Do I like her or not? I'm not sure.

whether

7. I'm on a strict diet. I still haven't lost any weight.

even though	however	even so

8. I took an umbrella. I thought it might rain.

in case	as

9. He was penniless and starving, but he still shouldn't have stolen the food.

nevertheless	although	despite

10. I went to the party. I met Jenny. We got married and had three children.

Supposing I hadn't . . .

4 Rewrite the biography of Salvador Dalí, using linkers to change each group of sentences into one sentence.

> Salvador Dalí was born in 1904.
> He was born in a small town, Figueres, in Catalunya, northeast Spain.
> His father was a prestigious notary in the town.

Salvador Dalí was born in 1904 in a small town, Figueres, in Catalunya, northeast Spain, where his father was a prestigious notary.

> Dalí wanted to study art.
> He went to the Royal Academy of Art in Madrid.
> He was expelled from the Academy twice.
> He never took his final examinations.

> In 1928 he went to Paris.
> He met the Spanish painters Pablo Picasso and Joan Miró in Paris.
> He established himself as the principal figure of a group of surrealist artists.
> The leader of the group was André Breton.

> By 1929 Dalí found his style.
> This style would make him famous.
> It consisted of the world of the unconscious.
> This world is recalled during our dreams.

> In 1927 he met Gala.
> She was a Russian immigrant.
> She was ten years older than Dalí.

> In 1940 they went to the United States.
> They stayed there for eight years.
> In 1948 Dalí and Gala returned to Europe.
> They spent most of their time in Spain or Paris.

> Gala died in 1982.
> Dalí became deeply depressed.
> He moved to Púbol.
> Púbol was a castle.
> He had bought it for Gala.

> He lived in his castle for the rest of his life.
> He died there in 1989.
> He died of heart failure.

CD3 29 Listen and compare your answers.

LISTENING AND SPEAKING
Do you believe in miracles?

1 What stories of miracles do you know? Do you believe miracles can happen? Are there any rational explanations for these phenomena?

2 Look at the pictures of pilgrims. Where are they? Which religion do they belong to?

3 Dr. Raj Persaud, a consultant psychiatrist at a London hospital, visited Lourdes to make a radio program.

- Where is Lourdes?
- What is it famous for?
- Who goes there? Why?
- Why do you think the doctor wanted to go there?

4 These words are in the program. What do you think they refer to?

- reverential
- introspective atmosphere
- in wheelchairs or carried on stretchers
- sanctuary
- 1858
- six million people . . . every year
- paralyzed
- multiple sclerosis

CD3 30 Listen and check your ideas.

5 **CD3 30** Listen again and answer the questions.

Part one

1. What strikes Dr. Persaud most? Why is this surprising?
2. What are some of the statistics he quotes?
3. What does the sanctuary consist of?
4. What did Bernadette see?

Part two

5. What is special about the spring that Bernadette discovered?
6. Why is Dr. Persaud puzzled?
7. Why, according to Andrew Walker, are Christians divided?
8. What is the miracle that he quotes?

Part three

9. What were Jean-Pierre's early symptoms?
10. What happened in 1984? What were the stages of his cure?

Part four

11. What, for Dr. Persaud, is the danger of modern medicine?
12. What is his explanation of the attraction of Lourdes?

What do you think?

- The program began with the question, "Can miracles exist in the age of science?" What is your opinion? Can miracles only have existed in the past?

VOCABULARY
Synonyms and antonyms 2

1 We often use synonyms for reasons of style. Look at these sentences from the article.

> ...the earth's **unreliable** time...
> ...how **unpunctual** the earth is...

Complete the sentences with a word that has a similar meaning to the words in *italics*. Sometimes the part of speech changes. Use a thesaurus if necessary.

1. It was an *immense* task, but its _____ only became apparent when we started working on it.
2. Progress will be *slow*, but if we persist, things will _____ improve.
3. You *can't count on* her. She's totally _____.
4. You want an *approximate* figure? At a _____ guess, I'd say there were about fifty.
5. "Did he *say* how his job's going?"
   "No. He didn't _____ it."
6. Massage *eased* the pain in my back, and _____ the tension I've felt for so long.
7. He's a very *cunning* opponent. He plays some _____ tricks.
8. He made a *miraculous* recovery, due to his _____ strength.
9. Soldiers *attacked* the enemy headquarters. The _____ took place before dawn.
10. Drugs can treat most *illnesses*, but there are some _____ that are incurable.

IMPENDING DOOM...
annihilation, calamity, catastrophe, condemnation, danger, disaster, downfall, end, fore ordination, Judgment Day, predestination, ruin, tragedy.

©2002

Ironically, a well-developed brain actually contributed to the early extinction of the Thesaurus Rex.

2 Divide the adjectives in the box into four groups, with three synonyms and three antonyms for each head word.

ancient	essential	impeccable	petty
antiquated	faultless	irrelevant	prejudiced
antique	faulty	liberal	second-rate
biased	flawed	novel	up-to-date
bigoted	immaculate	trivial	urgent
current	impartial	open-minded	vital

	synonyms	antonyms
old	ancient	novel
fair		
perfect		
unimportant		

3 Match adjectives from Exercise 2 with nouns from the box that they collocate with.

machinery	crime	organs	Greece
idea	media	vase	manners
racist	performance	mail	affairs

EVERYDAY ENGLISH
Euphemisms

1 A euphemism is a polite way of expressing something thought to have negative connotations.
For example, a blind person is *visually challenged*, a fat person is *full-figured*, and politicians don't lie, they are *economical with the truth*.

2 Complete the newspaper article with euphemisms from the box.

pass away	low IQ	Department of Defense
companion animal	disadvantaged senior citizen	garden plot
disabled	under the weather	retirement pension
lower income bracket	taking industrial action	have a dialog

"I've never been fired, but I've been dehired a few times."

Letters

Stop being coy

I will die – not pass away

I AM an old cripple, drawing an old-age pension, working hard to raise vast quantities of vegetables on an allotment, and well aware that, one of these days, I will die. All this is fact.

If, however, I listen to the voice of officialdom, it turns out that I am a (1)_____, registered as (2)_____, drawing a (3)_____, renting a (4)_____, and presumably immortal, because I will never die – I will merely (5)_____.

And let us please do away with the following euphemisms:
(6)_____ (poor)
(7)_____ (ill)
(8)_____ (stupid)
(9)_____ (Department of War)
(10)_____ (talk)
(11)_____ (pet)

All this effort to avoid unpleasantness is certain to fail, because the euphemism quickly acquires the stigma of the word it replaced. I, and probably others, do not feel younger because I am called a senior citizen.

Bryan Heath
Retired vet

"I need some short-term economic stimulus."

3 What do you think these political euphemisms mean?
1. The rebel fighters were *neutralized*.
2. With all due respect, I think your figures are *misleading*.
3. Could you please *regularize* your bank account?
4. We had a *frank, open exchange of views*.
5. This is not a *non-risk policy*.
6. The company is in a *non-profit situation*.

4 Can you translate any euphemisms from your language?

▶▶ **Writing** Bringing a biography to life **p. 127**

Writing

UNIT 1 FORMAL AND INFORMAL LETTERS

1 You are going to write a formal and an informal letter. Before you begin, think about these things.

- Layout: Where to put the address / date.
- Register and style: Who are you writing to? Should you use formal or informal language?
- Greeting / Opening: Do you know the person's name? Do you know him or her well?
- Planning: Are you asking for / giving information, thanking, or complaining? Always include your reason for writing in the first paragraph.

2 You are planning to work in the U.S. this summer, and wrote to your friends asking them about jobs for students. Read their reply and write back to your friends thanking them, explaining what you have decided to do, and asking them for more information on Florida about these things:

- possible to stay with them for a couple of weeks?
- Miami expensive?
- travel cheap to other states?

Great news that you're thinking of coming over this summer. Miami is a fantastic place to live. The weather is wonderful, the beaches are great, and people are really friendly. It's only been four months since we arrived, but we've made lots of new friends. I already feel at home and Mario does, too.

I'm not sure exactly how you can get a work permit, but I do know that there are organizations, like Go America!, that help foreign students find summer work. There are certainly lots of jobs in the amusement parks and restaurants, so I'm sure you'd have no trouble getting something. Anyway, let us know what you decide.

Lots of love,

Samuela

3 Now read this ad and write a letter to the employment agency, giving them details of your qualifications and asking for further information about these things:

- types of jobs in Florida?
- accommodation?
- cost of flight included?
- work permit?

Go America!

offers students exciting summer jobs on the world's most exciting continent

Work anywhere in the U.S. – the choice of location is yours! Experience the wide open spaces out west, the bright lights of the city, or beach life at east coast resorts. Then take time out and travel.

For more information contact:

Go America!
1065 Center Main Avenue
New York, NY 10003

1 Read these opening paragraphs from three different stories and answer the questions below.

A

Christmas again. Joyce looked out of the frosted window at the bare, winter garden. A pair of sparrows were hopping through the frozen grass, searching for food. It'd been three long years and she still hadn't gotten over it. She sighed and pushed a wisp of white hair back behind her ear. The pictures on the mantlepiece were her only companions now, and she treasured them like nothing else. A few Christmas cards kept them company, but as the years went by there were fewer and fewer. No, she'd never get used to it … but she didn't want to go into a retirement home, not yet. This house was her home, she thought fiercely as she walked unsteadily toward an old threadbare armchair and sat down next to the fire.

B

Hannah glanced anxiously at her watch. It was 11:54 p.m. and the night train for Bangalore was leaving in 6 minutes. She peered along the dimly-lit platform, searching for a familiar figure in faded jeans, carrying a well-worn backpack. But the station was deserted, apart from a tired-looking porter shuffling around aimlessly. She thought back to their conversation earlier that day, perhaps she'd been serious after all? They'd argued many times during their 3-month trip and she'd often gone off on her own to "cool off." But then she'd always turn up later and they'd sort out their differences. Hannah fingered her ticket nervously. She didn't want to leave without her roommate …

C

"What was that!" whispered Jes, his eyes wide with fear. "Shhh," said Luis, slowly edging his way up the creaking stairs. "Probably just a rat." It had been Luis's great idea to explore "Fletcher's place" as it was known, named after the eccentric old man who last lived there. It was the archetypal haunted house and had been deserted for years – nobody brave enough to buy it, or even break into it, Luis had said. They'd been laughing about it just that afternoon, and had speculated wildly about the supposed murder that happened years before. School was out and they were both in high spirits so when Luis suggested a midnight raid, he'd readily agreed. Now, faced with the grim reality of a creepy, damp house, Jes was having second thoughts. "Was there really a murder here?" he thought desperately.

1. How do the opening sentences attract the reader's attention?
   What atmosphere do they create? How do the characters feel?
2. Which tenses are used in the story? Is direct speech used?
   What effect does it have?
3. Who are the main characters in the story? What is their relationship?
4. How old are the main characters? How do you know this?

Brainstorming ideas

2 Discuss what happens next in the stories. Ask yourself these questions:

- In each story, someone is facing a choice. What is that choice and what decision do you think each person will make?
- What could be the consequences of that decision? How will it affect other people?
- What do you think will happen in the end?

3 Now read the rest of story A. Make it more interesting by adding the adverbs below. There may be more than one possible answer.

> carefully   instinctively   softly   encouragingly   slowly   gently   strangely

It was his favorite chair and as she sat there (1) _carefully_ warming her hands, she smiled to herself. She could almost see him at the table, browsing through the Sunday papers. After a while, she fell into a deep sleep.

"Joyce, Joyce," a voice whispered (2)_____ in her ear. Joyce opened her eyes. At first she didn't know him – he looked younger and slightly different than she remembered – but she recognized his voice. "What's the matter, dear?" she asked almost (3)_____. "Come on old girl," he said. "Let's go for a walk." He helped her up and (4)_____ took her arm. She felt calm and (5)_____ light as they walked (6)_____ out of the room. "Almost there," he said (7)_____, as he pulled at the latch on the front door. The door creaked open and warm sunlight streamed into the hall. Joyce smiled and stepped outside – it was a beautiful spring day.

4 In what ways were your ideas for story A similar or different? What happens in the end? Which ending do you prefer and why?

5 Choose excerpt B or C on page 114 and complete the story in 200–300 words. Use the ideas you brainstormed in Exercise 2, and follow the advice below.

- Plan your story carefully. Decide what happens next, the order of events, and how the story ends.
- Decide how the main characters will react to the events in your story, and which verbs, adjectives, and adverbs will best describe their feelings and actions.

- Use linking words to order the events in your story.
- Use direct speech to vary the pace and focus.
- When you have finished check your grammar carefully – make sure you have used past tenses and time adverbs correctly.

1 What features are typical of report writing? Choose from these alternatives.

    1. a. state your goals in the introduction
        b. state your recommendations in the introduction

    2. a. use headings for each section
        b. have one general heading

    3. a. give mostly opinions rather than facts
        b. give mostly facts rather than opinions

    4. a. use mostly active tenses
        b. use mostly passive tenses

    5. a. give recommendations based on your personal experience
        b. give recommendations based on facts

2 Read the report and check your answers.

3 Read the report again. Underline words or expressions the writer uses to introduce recommendations.
e.g., *should introduce*

4 Circle six different ways that customers' opinions are reported.
e.g., *commented that*

WORLDNET
24HR INTERNET CAFÉ

WORLDNET REPORT

INTRODUCTION

The purpose of this report is to evaluate Internet services provided by *Worldnet*, a chain of 24-hour Internet cafes in Chicago. There has been a steady decrease in the number of customers over the past six months. This report will attempt to analyze and explain this trend based on findings from a series of customer questionnaires. It will evaluate the current services in relation to client needs, and will conclude with recommendations for improvements.

MAIN AREAS FOR IMPROVEMENT

Worldnet caters to a wide range of customers with different backgrounds and ages. However, nearly all customers (65 percent) commented that the cost of the Internet service at $15 per hour was too high and suggested half-hourly rates. The speed of the Internet connection was also criticized. At peak times the service was said to be extremely slow and unstable.

OTHER AREAS FOR IMPROVEMENT

In terms of the hardware, the computer terminals were generally thought to be out-of-date and badly maintained. The screens were felt to be too small and the seating uncomfortable. On a more positive note, the cafe was considered to be good value. The prices compared favorably with other cafes, and customers were satisfied with the quality of the food provided. However, although the cafe was popular, there were some complaints about the lack of variety.

RECOMMENDATIONS

In order to become more competitive, *Worldnet* should introduce new half-hourly rates immediately. Special student rates should also be considered as this would attract 16–25-year-old customers, who represent the majority of Internet users outside an office environment. In addition, I would strongly recommend a faster and more reliable Internet Service Provider. The computer terminals and chairs also need upgrading and maintaining more regularly. Finally, the cafe could be improved by introducing a wider variety of food and drinks. If these recommendations are put into practice, the number of *Worldnet* customers should start to increase substantially.

5 Report these opinions about a new cell phone, using the prompts in parentheses.

"I've used the built-in digital camera – the photos are really good."
(considered /good quality)

The built-in digital camera was considered very good quality.

1. *"It makes no difference to me if there's a touch screen."*
(commented /made no difference)

2. *"I don't use the voice recorder – to be honest I don't know how to!"*
(said / too complicated)

3. *"I prefer sending text messages rather than making a call. They're a lot cheaper."*
(thought / better value for money)

4. *"I don't care about the gadgets. I just want a phone that's reliable."*
(felt / unimportant)

5. *"The battery doesn't last very long. It's a real pain having to recharge it all the time!"*
(complaints / recharging inconvenient)

6. *"I never use the Web surfing feature. There's nothing worth accessing apart from sports scores."*
(commented / limited value)

6 Read this introduction to a report on cell phones. Rewrite it in a more suitable way.

> Trident wanted me to write a report telling them what I thought about their new range of hi-tech cell phones. People haven't been buying the phones, although they have lots of great new gadgets. Trident gave me about 50 questionnaires, asked me to look at them, explain why sales were dropping, and give advice on how to improve things.

The aim of this report is to ...

7 Look at the chart containing the results of Trident's survey.

Trident 550–750 cell phones
survey overview

	Good	Satisfactory	Poor	General comments
Price / quality ratio			✓	too expensive
Web service			✓	
Voicemail	✓			clear and reliable
Battery life			✓	
Touch screen		✓		not important
Digital camera	✓			good quality
Voice recorder			✓	
Text messaging	✓			cheap and effective

Write a report evaluating Trident's new generation of cell phones, based on the survey and the opinions in Exercise 5. Use the paragraph plan below to help you.

Paragraph 1: Introduction. State the goals of the report.

Paragraph 2: Summarize the problems and report customer opinions. Select three or four main points you want to address.

Paragraph 3: Summarize areas that are satisfactory and report customer opinions.

Paragraph 4: Conclusion. Give your recommendations for improving the service and/or ways of lowering the cost of the phone.

1 Read the essay title and the essay below. Check the ideas a–g that appear in the essay. Are any of the ideas not relevant to the question?

a. We're intrigued by people who do anything to become famous.
b. Personally, I'd say that the conversations are pretty boring.
c. I think that many people would love to be on television.
d. Unlike soap operas, I don't think they're based on interesting stories.
e. I think they are totally unpredictable, which is very exciting.
f. Generally speaking, I'd say detective series are pretty boring.
g. I can't imagine life without soap operas.

"TV reality shows are third-rate entertainment and not worth watching." What do you think?

There is nothing new about reality TV. Confessional shows, where ordinary people make their private life public, have been around for a long time. However, over the last five years TV reality shows such as *Big Brother* and *Survivor* have become more and more popular. (1) *In fact / Obviously*, some of these programs have been the most successful shows in television history. (2) *After all / Surely* it's unfair to say they are third-rate entertainment?

In order to evaluate reality TV, we need to define (3) *ideally / exactly* what a TV reality show is. Reality shows have several things in common with soap operas. (4) *Generally speaking / Actually*, they both involve a group of people who have to live together and get along with each other while solving various problems. The difference is that reality shows aren't scripted, so the dialogs are often fairly tedious. In addition, the problems contestants deal with are artificial and don't arise naturally from a "story." (5) *Apparently / Clearly*, in this sense, they could be seen as third-rate entertainment.

Why, then, do people watch them? (6) *After all / Presumably*, what holds the audience's attention is the "reality" or spontaneity of the shows. You never know what is going to happen next, and we are fascinated by people who will stop at nothing in their pursuit of fame. (7) *Naturally / At least* we're also fascinated by how the contestants cope in different situations, and to some extent measure their reactions against our own.

To conclude, it's (8) *probably / exactly* true to say that reality shows are third-rate entertainment when compared with classic films or award-winning documentaries. However, as audience figures prove, they are strangely compelling because (9) *incidentally / basically*, we are able to empathize with ordinary people in extraordinary situations. This (10) *ultimately / ideally* is what makes TV reality shows worth watching.

Adverbs and expressions of opinion

2 Read the essay again. Choose the most appropriate adverb or expression of opinion.

3 Writers often use adverbs to express or intensify their opinions. Match sentences 1–6 with follow-up sentences a–f, adding an adverb or phrase from the box below. There may be more than one possible answer.

Admittedly	Presumably	Obviously
Naturally	Frankly	As a matter of fact

1. [f] Some people say that the price of fame is too high.
2. ☐ Famous people complain if there is a sensational story in the newspapers.
3. ☐ Celebrities claim it's difficult to make new friends.
4. ☐ People think celebrities have an easy life.
5. ☐ Stalkers pose a very real threat to many celebrities.
6. ☐ Why are we obsessed with fame?

a. _____, they shouldn't because they exploit newspapers to get famous.
b. _____, most celebrities have to work very hard.
c. _____, it must be difficult to know why people are "friends."
d. _____ it's because it's "the new religion."
e. _____, they have to spend a lot of money on security.
f. **Admittedly**, life is difficult if your private life is public.

4 Write a 250-word essay on the subject below. Use the ideas from Exercise 3 and the paragraph plan to help you.

"Most people think that being famous is heaven, but in fact it's more like hell." What do you think?

Paragraph 1: Summarize why people might want to be famous and paraphrase the question.
Paragraph 2: Why might people think being famous is "heaven"? Do you agree?
Paragraph 3: Why might it be "hell"? What's your opinion?
Paragraph 4: Conclusion: summarize the main points and restate your opinion.

1 Read this excerpt from a magazine article and the essay that follows. Put the paragraphs of the essay in the correct order.

> **Up to the early twentieth century, marriage was considered a necessity. People chose partners who provided them with economic support and stability. Since then attitudes have changed and fewer people are tying the knot. Marriage is not always necessary in modern society.**
>
> Do you agree with this view of marriage? What are the arguments for and against marriage today? *PBS Student* magazine invites readers to write in with their opinions.

A [ ] Secondly, it has been suggested that marriage provides more stability for children. Certain surveys of children in divorced, single-parent families claim they are more likely to commit a serious crime than children from two-parent, married households. But in spite of this, having married parents isn't necessarily the best thing. It's obvious that a stable single-parent environment is a lot healthier for children than an unhappy or abusive marriage.

B [ ] First of all, it could be argued that marriage brings emotional and financial security to a relationship. This is partly true as married people are still legally bound to support their spouses. On the other hand, getting married and divorced is becoming increasingly easy. As a result, fewer people are prepared to work at their relationship, marriage vows are broken, and many couples are left emotionally scarred.

C [ ] Finally, some people claim that marriage is becoming more flexible, with personalized vows and contracts enabling couples to define their relationship themselves. Nevertheless, precisely because the ceremony is flexible and easy to adapt, many people are abusing it. In the U.S. there have been TV game shows where people can win and marry spouses, and in Australia one man actually married his television set.

D [ ] To conclude, it's clear that marriage is not always necessary to a successful, modern relationship. Nowadays, a growing number of people prefer to wait before they get married. This continuing trend means there is greater freedom for individuals to choose their own partners and decide how they wish to live, which is ultimately a good thing.

E [ ] Marriage used to be considered a necessity for anyone of a certain age who wanted to start a family. But over the past two decades fewer and fewer couples have felt the need to tie the knot right away. What then are the advantages and disadvantages of marriage?

2 Read the essay again and look at the highlighted words. How does the writer introduce …

- arguments he agrees with?   • arguments he disagrees with?

What examples does the writer use to illustrate different arguments? Which arguments do you agree with?

Linking words: contrast, reason, and result

3 Find phrases in the essay that introduce …
- a contrasting point of view
- a reason
- a result

4 Rewrite these sentences, using the words in parentheses.
1. It's common for young adults to live at home in some countries, but not in others. (whereas)
2. Many young adults live at home because of the money they save. (on account of)
3. Some people prefer to leave home, even if they don't have much money. (despite)
4. Some people stay at home because of economic circumstances. (due to)
5. Many young adults save money for their own home by living at home. (so that)
6. Some people want more independence so they move out as soon as they can. (in order to)
7. One mother evicted her sons because of their selfish behavior. (owing to)

5 Choose a subject and write a 250-word essay.

   a. What are the arguments for and against young adults living at home?

   b. What are the arguments for and against dating agencies?

   c. What are the arguments for and against living alone?

- First, brainstorm arguments for and against.
- Then organize your arguments into a plan:
   introduction
   first argument
   second argument
   third argument
   conclusion
- Make sure you write a general introduction to the issue and paraphrase the essay question.
- Use phrases you found in Exercise 3 to introduce arguments, and the linking words in Exercise 4.
- Try to illustrate your arguments with examples.
- State the arguments you agree with last.
- Make sure you summarize the main ideas and give a clear opinion in your conclusion.

1 Look at this excerpt from a newspaper editorial, and read the letter to the editor.

Nearly one out of every four children under the age of 18 is obese in our city. This is why the government is considering putting a hefty tax on sugared beverages like soda and fruit drinks that are less than 70 percent juice. It would seem that this is no more than an attempt at grabbing money. To single out one food as the cause for obesity is simply flawed logic. There is no science or logic that justifies it. We need to focus on promoting healthy eating habits and more exercise. Until our kids are exercising more, the scales will be tipped against our next generation.

Tax sugary drinks? We want to hear from YOU. Write a letter to the editor with your opinions at: *In the News*, P.O. Box 33A, Los Angeles, California, 90028

William Himmler
55 Hessel Road
Los Angeles, CA 90101

March 7

The Editor
In the News
P.O. Box 33A
Los Angeles, CA 90028

A _____ There has been much debate about childhood obesity in the papers recently, and I am very concerned about the arguments you have put forward against taxing sodas and fruit drinks. I feel that taxing sugary drinks would be a step in the right direction toward fighting childhood obesity, and voting against this legislation would be the wrong decision to make.

B _____ According to your article, consuming soft drinks plays a minor role in childhood obesity. It is also claimed that soft drinks play an even lesser role in the obesity of adults. Finally, the article insists that a tax on sugary drinks would not lead to a significant reduction in their consumption.

C _____ Studies have indicated that in many high-poverty areas, the rate of childhood obesity is closer to one out of three. Research has shown that soft-drink consumption is one of the main drivers of childhood obesity. One study found that for each soft drink consumed per day, the risk of a child becoming obese increases by 60 percent. For adults, the association is similar. If we are to succeed in reducing childhood obesity, we must reduce consumption of sugared beverages. Experts estimate that an 18 percenet tax will reduce consumption by 5 percent. Moreover, the $400 million this tax would raise next year is expected to go toward funding public health programs, including obesity prevention programs, across the state.

D _____ These types of taxes may be unpopular, but their benefits are undeniable. Our children need more than just a surcharge on soda, but this tax is a step in the right direction. Certainly, people won't like paying more for their favorite drinks. But it's a small price to pay for our children's health

Sincerely,

William Himmler

2 Now match paragraphs A–D to the descriptions below. Which paragraph …

- ☐ summarizes arguments in the article that the writer disagrees with?
- ☐ concludes and restates the writer's point of view?
- ☐ puts forward arguments the writer agrees with?
- ☐ introduces the reason for writing and states the writer's point of view?

How many arguments does the letter put forward? Which ones do you agree with?

3 Choose the best introductory sentence for each paragraph.

Paragraph A
1. Here's my reply to your article about voting down the beverage tax.
2. I am writing in response to your article on the beverage tax.

Paragraph B
1. One of the main arguments against the tax is its potential effectiveness.
2. In your article you say that taxing sodas won't really reduce childhood obesity.

Paragraph C
1. Taking each of your arguments in turn, first of all it has been scientifically proven that soft-drink consumption is higher in high-poverty areas.
2. Looking at your arguments one by one, it really is true that poor children consume more soft drinks.

Paragraph D
1. To be honest, I can think of lots of reasons why unhealthy drinks should be unaffordable.
2. To conclude, there are many reasons why unhealthy beverages should be made less available to children.

4 Rewrite these sentences in the passive, using phrases from the box. There may be more than one possible answer.

It could be argued that …	It is believed that …
It is assumed that …	It would seem that …
It would appear that …	It has been proved that …

1. If we tax sodas, hamburgers should be taxed, too.
   It could be argued that if sodas were taxed, hamburgers should be taxed too.
2. Young people's social activities often revolve around eating junk food and drinking soda.
3. Lack of exercise and an unhealthy diet causes most health problems.
4. People know about the risks of childhood obesity.
5. Companies have increased the sugar content in most packaged foods.
6. You can't make people give up sugary foods and drinks.

5 Read the newspaper excerpt below. Write a letter to the editor in 200–300 words. Make sure the layout is correct and that you use an appropriate tone and register. Use the paragraph plan to help you.

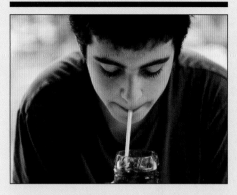

IT IS ESTIMATED that obesity is associated with more than 110,000 deaths in the United States every year. In our state, we spend almost $6.1 billion on health care related to adult obesity — the second-highest level of spending in the nation.

Last year, several critics banned the use of trans fats in restaurant food. To fully address the obesity crisis, we need to ban junk food in our schools, ban all fast-food advertising, and force fast food companies to contribute to this crippling healthcare bill.

Do you agree with this editorial? We'd like to hear your point of view. Write a letter to the editor at:

YOU AND YOUR HEALTH
56 Toole Place, Chicago, IL 60622

Paragraph 1: Introduction: State your reason for writing and your point of view.

Paragraph 2: Summarize the arguments you disagree with.

Paragraph 3: Discredit the arguments you disagree with and put forward the arguments you agree with.

Paragraph 4: Conclusion: Restate your opinion.

1 Read these two versions of the opening paragraph from a personal account, then answer the question below.

> **A** **Two years ago** I was in Dover, a small town in New Hampshire. I'd just been to Mt. Washington and had gone to Dover so I could catch a train there the next morning. I arrived at 11 at night and most places were closed. I guess I should have booked somewhere before I arrived. I was walking around the streets looking for a place to stay, but everywhere was closed. Then I met an old man who offered me a room for the night.

> **B** **It was a** freezing November night and the stars shone coldly as I trudged through the deserted town of Dover with my heavy overnight bag. It was the third time I'd walked around the wintry streets looking for somewhere – anywhere – to stay. But there was no sign of life, even the restaurants were closed. A bitter wind blew in from the north as the church clock struck midnight. I paused to wrap my scarf around my neck. "Five more hours before the next train to Boston," I thought miserably, resigning myself to a bleak night on the streets. Then suddenly I heard a voice behind me, "What's wrong, young man? Need some help?"

Which opening paragraph …

- describes emotions, the surroundings, and the weather?
- gives a mostly factual narrative?
- uses a variety of vocabulary?
- uses similar sentence structures throughout?
- has more impact on the reader?

2 Choose the best title.

a. The weather in New Hampshire   c. An interesting journey
b. The kindness of strangers

3 Now read the rest of the account and answer the questions below.

> **The voice belonged** to a sprightly old man named Robert Douglas. He was walking home after a meal at a friend's when he noticed me huddled in the street. When I explained my predicament he immediately offered shelter for the night. At first I was suspicious. I'd learned from experience not to trust strangers, having been robbed once in Boston. That incident had left its mark, but it soon became clear that what motivated Robert was a genuine desire to help. Dover was a small town and it was obvious I wasn't a local. It was also obvious that I needed a place to sleep.
>
> I followed Robert back to a small cottage on the edge of town where he offered me some tea. As we sat in front of a warm fire we talked for a while about Dover. Robert was a widower and had lived there all his life. He had three children and several grandchildren, although most of them had moved away. I began to understand why Robert was glad to have some company.
>
> After a peaceful night on an old sofa, I got up at 4:30 a.m. to catch my train, leaving behind a crumpled note of thanks. Today I sometimes think about Dover, and wonder if Robert is still there. I'll always remember his simple act of kindness with gratitude.

1. What was the writer's first reaction to Robert's offer?
2. Why did Robert offer to help?
3. Why was the writer suspicious at first?
4. What did he learn about Robert?
5. Why won't he forget him?

Ways of creating emphasis

4 Look at this example from the account.

Robert was motivated by a genuine desire to help. (*What …*)

What motivated Robert was a genuine desire to help.

Now rewrite these sentences in a more emphatic way.

1. People rarely help a stranger in trouble. (*Rarely …*)
2. The problem is mistrust. (*It's …*)
3. People worry about being robbed. (*What …*)
4. We should try to help in some way. (*The thing …*)
5. I won't forget the first time a stranger helped me. (*Never …*)

5 Write about a small or great kindness that happened in your life. Write 200–300 words. Use the paragraph plan below to help you.

Paragraph 1:	Set the scene for the story. Remember to grab the reader's attention at the beginning. Describe the surroundings or the situation, but don't give them all the facts at once.
Paragraph 2–3:	Describe what happened. What were you doing? Were you alone? Why did you need help? How did you feel? Who did you meet? How did they help you?
Paragraph 4:	What happened in the end? Did you learn anything from the experience?

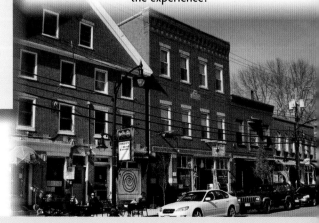

1 Quickly read the movie review.

- What's the purpose of the review?
- Who is likely to read it?
- Is the language mostly formal or informal?

2 Divide the review into paragraphs, then match the paragraphs to these headings.

a. Recommendation
b. Positive points
c. Negative points
d. Subject of the review
e. Summary of the plot

3 Read the review again and answer the questions.

1. What type of movie is it?
2. What does the writer compare the story to?
3. What does the writer compare some scenes to?
4. Which words are used to describe …

- the visual imagery?
- the acting?
- the atmosphere?
- the plot and the ending?

5. What tense does the writer use to describe the story?

4 Complete the sentences with a verb from the box in the correct form.

create	strike	adapt	suspend	reveal	set	tell	see

1. The story _____ in Washington, D.C., in 2054.
2. It _____ from a book by Philip K. Dick.
3. The film _____ the story of a man accused of a future crime.
4. When the truth _____ he goes on the run.
5. The soundtrack and special effects help _____ an atmosphere of suspense.
6. The plot is sometimes unconvincing. You have to _____ your disbelief.
7. What _____ you most is Tom Cruise's impressive performance.
8. I highly recommend it. I'd say it's well worth _____.

5 Write a 250-word review of a film, play, or book. Follow this advice.

- Choose a film, play, or book that you know well.
- Brainstorm your opinions about the characters, the plot, the acting, and the special effects.
- Use intensifiers to reinforce your opinions.
- Summarize the story, but don't give too much away.
- Organize your review into logical paragraphs with logical linkers.
- End the review with a personal recommendation – try to give a balanced opinion.

Reviews movies

The Road
rating ★ ★ ★ ★ ☆

The Road is is the latest film by the fairly unknown director John Hillcoat. Adapted from the Pulitzer Prize-winning novel by Cormac McCarthy, *The Road* is extremely dark and atmospheric. Like a Greek tragedy, the film follows the suffering of the main characters on their quest for survival after an unnamed disaster wipes most animal and plant life off the face of the earth. The film is set in a dismal, dying landscape and tells the story of a father (Viggo Mortensen) and son (Kodi Smit-McPhee) on their agonizing journey to the coast, where it is presumed they will somehow be rescued from this post-apocalyptic wasteland. Visually, the film is depressingly devoid of color, and the bleak monochrome is deliberately crafted to drain you of the last reserves of hope for these people. The acting is first-rate, with both Mortensen and McPhee giving convincing and fearless performances. However, although it is wonderfully directed and acted, *The Road* falls victim to an overwrought score by Nick Cave and Warren Ellis. Instead of playing off of the excessiveness of tragedy, the score reinforces it, going over the top with screeching strings and dramatic piano interludes at the moments when subtlety would have better served the script. What the film really lacks is restraint in this regard, and you leave the theater feeling bludgeoned by the music rather than having been supported by it. To sum up, *The Road* is a devastating drama, a thriller that leaves even the strongest among us numb and in shock. It's well worth seeing, but it's not for the faint of heart.

1 Many people need to write a personal profile as part of an application for admission to a university or for a new job.

Quickly read this personal profile and match paragraphs A–D to the descriptions below.

- ☐ Summary of main skills and qualities
- ☐ Leisure activities
- ☐ Present responsibilities and skills
- ☐ Experience and achievements

A I am currently a student at Duke University, finishing a degree in History. As a member of the Student Union Executive Committee, I am actively involved in the day-to-day running of student life. The Committee is responsible for improvements to student facilities, coordinating student events such as concerts and sports days, as well as fund-raising activities such as Rag Week. I play a large part in organizing these events, my role specifically being to oversee publicity and manage the budgets. These responsibilities test my leadership as well as my organizational and negotiating skills.

B For many years I have been interested in journalism. While I was in high school, I helped to run the school magazine, and in my first year of college I often contributed articles to the student magazine. Running and writing a magazine requires the ability to produce interesting, topical articles while working under pressure and meeting tight deadlines. The success of the school magazine shows that I managed to develop these abilities to a high standard.

C In my free time I enjoy watching movies. I am a member of a local community film club and helped organize a short film festival last year. I contributed my own short film about student life to the festival, which was very well received. My involvement with this local community project has given me experience in organizing off-campus events as well as working with young people in the community.

D I believe I have made a positive contribution to both high school and university life, as well as to the local community. I am confident and competitive, but also a good team worker. My natural enthusiasm has often helped me motivate others and achieve excellent results.

2 Read the profile again and answer these questions.

1. How does the writer contribute to university life? What skills has he developed?
2. What did the writer do in high school?
3. What type of challenges did he experience?
4. Which hobby does he mention? What experience has he gained from it?
5. What qualities help the writer do a good job?

3 Complete the sentences with a verb from the box in the correct form.

take	manage	work	play
coordinate	meet	run	

1. Matt didn't want to _____ responsibility for the project. It was too much work.
2. Your education and experience _____ a large part in the skills you have to offer.
3. It's not easy to _____ a newspaper. You often have to _____ very tight deadlines.
4. People are sometimes most creative when they _____ under pressure.
5. Lin-Na had to _____ a lot of people for the fundraising event.
6. He's no good at _____ budgets. He's terrible at math!

4 Write your own personal profile in 250–300 words. Use the plan below and the phrases in Exercise 3 to help you.

Paragraph 1: Introduce yourself and what you do. Talk about your current responsibilities and skills.

Paragraph 2: Talk about your past experiences and achievements. Highlight the personal qualities you developed as a result of them.

Paragraph 3: Talk about your leisure activities. Describe how they contribute to the skills and experience you already have.

Paragraph 4: Point out the main contributions you have made to your school / university / workplace. Summarize your main skills and qualities.

1 Read this ad for a competition. What do people have to do?

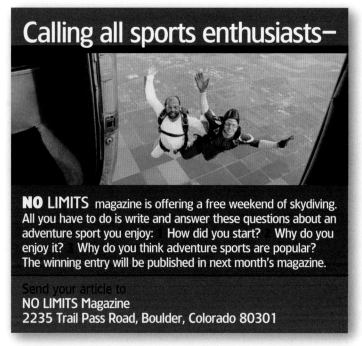

Calling all sports enthusiasts–

NO LIMITS magazine is offering a free weekend of skydiving. All you have to do is write and answer these questions about an adventure sport you enjoy: How did you start? Why do you enjoy it? Why do you think adventure sports are popular? The winning entry will be published in next month's magazine.

Send your article to
NO LIMITS Magazine
2235 Trail Pass Road, Boulder, Colorado 80301

2 Now read the competition entry and answer the questions below.

There comes a time in everyone's life when you want to try something completely new. I'd been a wife and a mother for some years when I started climbing – I knew I was ready for a change. Most winters the family would go to Zermatt in Switzerland. We would rent a chalet there and go skiing. But three years ago it wasn't skiing that interested me. It was climbing. The idea of climbing had always appealed to me, but I'd never really tried it. That year was different and I decided to take a guided climb up Mount Matterhorn. It was a difficult experience, but when I reached the top the feeling of excitement and achievement was overwhelming. I knew then that this was what I wanted to do.

When friends find out that I climb, they often want to know what motivates me. It's difficult to put into words because I'm not the stereotypical adrenaline addict and I'm not terribly competitive. For me climbing is more about personal achievement. It provides a challenge, a change of scene, and a bit of escapism. My friends might relax by watching a movie or reading a book. Well, I prefer to climb. It transports me out of my everyday life and into a world where anything is possible.

1. Is the style of writing mostly formal or informal?
2. How does the opening paragraph engage the reader's interest?
3. How does the writer explain her hobby to her friends?

Answering the question

3 Look at these two versions of the final paragraph. Which do you think is the best at answering the question? Why?

A Some people argue that sports like climbing are dangerous and that the sportsmen and -women who do them are totally irresponsible. Others say that adventure sports are no longer interesting, as there's nothing new to do. But whatever people say, the fact remains that for many of us these sports satisfy a very real need – the need to explore, to push ourselves to the limits, or simply to feel "alive."

B Why are more and more people doing adventure sports? First, it's probably a result of the whole modern-day obsession with sports. Adventure sports especially have a very positive image. They're seen as exciting, daring, and different. Second, many people are attracted to the challenge or are curious to see what they are capable of achieving. But whatever the reason, the fact remains that for many of us adventure sports fill a very real need – the need to explore, to push ourselves to the limits, or simply to feel "alive."

4 Read this ad for another competition.

*free gym membership for one year

SportingLife is offering a free gym membership for one year for the best article about sports.

Simply write 200–300 words about what sports mean today.
1 – Is it about teamwork or individual achievement?
2 – How are we influenced by sports and sports athletes?
3 – Why are sports and fitness centers so popular?

Send your article to:
SportingLife, 2264 Glendale Falls, White Plains, NY 10601.
Closing date: August 30

5 Write your competition entry in 200–300 words. Use the paragraph plan to help you.

Paragraph 1: Begin with a personal anecdote that illustrates what sports mean today. It could describe an experience in which you were watching a sport, or taking part in a sport.

Paragraphs 2–3: Answer the questions in the competition entry one by one. State your opinions clearly and give examples where relevant.

Paragraph 4: Sum up your ideas and give your opinion.

1 Read three excerpts from a travel diary and answer the questions.

1. Which countries did the writer visit?
2. How did he travel? Where did he sleep?
3. In which excerpts does he ...
   - get along with the local people?
   - experience bad weather?
   - comment on the changing scenery?
   - feel anxious about his trip?

A After picking up the Honda in Buenos Aires, I carefully packed my camping equipment and left the city. I was soon making my way south along the storm-tossed Atlantic coast, passing glorious, golden beaches and small bustling resorts. I decided to stop in Bahia Blanca to enjoy the hospitality of the friendly locals, before heading out west. A few days later I set off inland, and was soon riding through bleak wasteland. The days were getting shorter now and the night temperatures were definitely cooler. It was exciting, but also a little troubling to see the next stage of my trip loom ahead – the barren, snow-clad Andes.

B Chile's lush green vegetation was a welcome change after the desolate landscape of the Andes. But then it started raining. Unfortunately, this was no ordinary shower – it was a real downpour and it went on for days, which was pretty depressing. I passed several rain-drenched, dreary towns, which were about as welcoming as the gloomy-looking people. In fact, the rain continued until I reached the capital, Santiago.

C After Santiago, the weather picked up. It was great riding along the wild Pacific coast in the bright sunshine. But as I approached the Atacama desert, the scenery started to change again. Instead of grassland, there was cactus, then sand. Soon I found myself on the edge of the driest desert in the world, where temperatures ranged from a sizzling 104°F in the day to a freezing 23°F at night.

Adding interest

2 Read another excerpt by the same writer. Add adjectives from the box to make it more interesting.

windswept	desolate	spectacular	derelict	shimmering	blazing

In the Atacama desert, the road ahead was my only link with civilization. The sun beat down on the sand dunes and ghost towns that lined the route. In the distance I could see volcanoes, which marked the edge of the desert and the border with Bolivia.

3 Find adjectives in excerpts A–C that describe ...
- beaches • towns and cities • the coastline • people • the mountains

4 Match these sentence halves describing different trips.

1. It was a beautiful sunny day when we headed
2. They crossed the swamp, then slowly made
3. After traveling for several hours on the highway we stopped
4. The road was flooded, so we had to turn
5. If you follow this road for 9 miles, you'll find
6. It was hard work hiking through the snow, but we hung
7. The express train sped
8. We were crossing a bridge when the bus broke

a. off at a service area for lunch.
b. their way to the crocodile farm.
c. out toward the mountains.
d. through the countryside without stopping. / toward the gloomy city.
e. in there until we got to the cabin.
f. back and look for an alternate route.
g. yourself on the coast.
h. down and blocked the road.

5 Write a 250-word description of a memorable journey you have taken. Use the paragraph plan and the questions to help you.

Paragraph 1: Describe the beginning of your trip. Where were you going? Who were you traveling with? How did you get there?

Paragraph 2–3: Describe what happened during the trip. What was the weather like? What were your impressions of people and places? How did you feel? Did anything unusual happen?

Paragraph 4: Describe the end of your trip. What was your final destination? When did you arrive? How did you feel about the trip? Was it a good or a bad experience?

1 Look at these facts taken from a biography. Combine the sentences to make one sentence, using the words given.

1. Robert Capa was a famous photojournalist. **Robert Capa, the ...**
He was also the founder of Magnum Photos.
He was born in Budapest in 1913.

2. He was a very talented photographer. **A talented, ...**
He was self-taught.
He started working for a publishing house when he was just 18.
At the same time, he studied journalism at a Berlin university.

3. There was much political upheaval in the 1930s. **During the 1930s ...**
Many of his fellow students became involved.
Capa was also very much involved.

4. Capa had to leave Hungary as a result. **Consequently ...**
Later he had to leave Berlin, too.
He went to live in Paris.

2 Quickly read the rest of the biography. Match paragraphs A–D to the descriptions.

- [ ] an evaluation of his achievements
- [ ] the end of his career
- [ ] his continuing success
- [ ] how he built his reputation

Robert Capa
photographer

A DURING HIS FIRST years in Paris, Capa worked mainly on local photo stories. It was not until 1936 that he got his big break. He was sent to cover the Spanish Civil War and, as a result, his work started to appear regularly in top magazines and newspapers. It was his picture of a Loyalist soldier falling to his death that brought him international repute and became a powerful symbol of war.

B In 1939, shortly after the Spanish Civil War, Capa worked in New York for a while. However, he quickly returned to Europe at the outbreak of World War II and stayed there for six years. His photographs of the Normandy invasion became some of the most memorable war photographs in history, and he received the Medal of Freedom Citation for his work.

C Capa's job as a war photographer often put him in great personal danger, but despite the risks his motto was always, "If your pictures aren't good enough, you aren't close enough." However, on May 25, 1954, Capa's luck ran out. He was working on an assignment in French Indochina when he stepped on a land mine. He was killed instantly.

D Today, Robert Capa is considered one of the finest war photographers of all time. He was an exceptional photojournalist who used his camera to express and record the horror of the events around him. Not surprisingly, Capa hated war, especially his often passive role in it. "It's not always easy to stand aside and be unable to do anything except record the sufferings around one," he said.

3 Read the biography again and answer the questions.

1. How did Robert Capa get his "big break"?
2. What do you think he was trying to achieve through his pictures? How did he feel about his work?
3. Did any of the facts about his life surprise you? What do you think was the most interesting fact?
4. How does the writer use direct quotes? What effect do they have?
5. Do you think Robert Capa was a brave man? Would you describe him as a "hero"?

4 Write your own biography. Either write about someone who interests you, or use the notes about Isabel Allende below. Use the paragraph plan to help you.

ISABEL ALLENDE

Paragraph 1: The early years
- 1942: born in Lima, Peru – moved to Chile when she was three
- worked as a secretary, then a journalist
- 1973: military coup – her uncle, President Salvador Allende, was assassinated
- went with her husband and children to Venezuela

Paragraph 2: How she built her reputation
- 1975–1984: worked as a journalist in Venezuela
- 1981: wrote letter to her dying grandfather – became her first novel *The House of the Spirits* – critically acclaimed

Paragraph 3: Her continuing success
- 1984–1994: wrote *Of Love and Shadows* and *Eva Luna* – bestsellers and made into films; wrote *Paula* – inspired by the illness of her 28-year-old daughter
- 1995–present: wrote more than 10 books, many bestsellers

Paragraph 4: An evaluation of her achievements
- now lives in San Francisco with her second husband
- continues to write novels – also teaches literature
- one of most talented writers of her generation

Audio Scripts

UNIT 1

CD1 2

1. I tried to fix my car, but I couldn't. I didn't have the right tools.
2. "You look awful. Why don't you see a doctor?" "I have. He just told me to take it easy."
3. "It's a long trip. Be careful driving." "Don't worry. We will."
4. I met your sister last night. She thought we'd met before, but we hadn't.
5. "Have you read this report?" "No, I haven't, but I will."
6. The weather forecast said that it might rain this afternoon. If it does, we'll have to cancel our tennis match.
7. My car's being repaired at the moment. If it wasn't, I'd give you a ride. Sorry.
8. I'm so glad you told Sue exactly what you thought of her, because if you hadn't, I certainly would have!
9. I got that job I applied for, so I was thrilled. I really didn't think I would.
10. "Come on, John! It's time to get up!" "I am! I'll be down in a second."
11. "I think I'll give Bob a phone call." "You should. You haven't been in touch with him for ages."
12. I went to a party last night, but I wish I hadn't. It was awful.
13. My husband insists on doing all the cooking, but I wish he wouldn't – it's inedible!
14. "Aren't you going to Colorado for your vacation?" "Well, we might, but we're still not sure."
15. "Andy got upset at the baseball game and started insulting everyone." "He would! That's so typical. He's always doing that."

CD1 3

1. A Can you come over for dinner tonight?
   B Thanks very much. I'd love to.
2. A Did you mail my letter?
   B Oh, I'm really sorry. I forgot to.
3. A I can't take you to the airport after all. Sorry.
   B But you agreed to!
4. A Was John surprised when he won?
   B He certainly was. He didn't expect to.
5. A Why did you slam the door in my face?
   B It was an accident. I really didn't mean to.
6. A You'll be able to enjoy yourself when you're finished with your exams.
   B Don't worry. I intend to!

CD1 4 I = Interviewer, JK = Jeong Kim
Part one
Jeong talks about his early years
I What were your early years in the States like?
JK I was 14 when we came. We had very little money, and life was tough. No clothes, no food, nothing. I never spoke English until I came here. That was probably one of the most stressful times in my life, because I was a teenager, and I couldn't take it as well.
I How did you adapt to your new surroundings?
JK Some people adapt much quicker, and I'm one of those guys who really didn't. But I did eventually. I have one older brother and two younger sisters, and out of the four of us I'm the only one who speaks with an accent.
I Were you close to your siblings when you were growing up?

JK Not as close as I wish we had been. Our life was very difficult. We came from a broken home, and my brother took his aggression out on me, so we had a lot of difficulties growing up together.
I Were your parents separated?
JK Right. They were divorced when I was very little, and we have a stepmother.
I Did you stay with your mother or your father?
JK My father, which is typical in Korea. Here, when people divorce, the mother normally gets custody of the children. In Korea, back then it was usually the father. Now, it's different, but divorce was so unusual in those days, it was something you didn't want anybody to find out about.
I And you didn't have contact with your mother after the divorce?
JK That's right. I haven't seen her since I was five years old.
I Did you find that hard to take?
JK Sure. I felt that my parents had let me down. Then, when I was 16, my father kicked me out of the house. I'm not quite sure why. I wasn't a bad kid. I was never into drugs or did anything bad. In fact, I was a good student, but for some reason he wasn't interested in me.
I How did this difficult childhood affect you?
JK There was a moment in my life when I hit rock bottom. I just couldn't think of anybody who was more miserable than me. I didn't have enough food. I had no one to turn to for help. And I said to myself, "You've hit rock bottom. From now on life has to get better." After that, everything was extra. Anything was better than nothing. I decided that I was going to make something out of my life and be happy.
I You were 16 years old. You were on your own. What did you do?
JK I had a math teacher who I liked a lot . . . and he lent me his basement room. I paid for the room. He and his wife were kind enough to take me under their wing.
I How did you earn money to pay rent?
JK I worked nights at a convenience store. That was 11 in the evening until 7 in the morning. I went to school during the day, and then on weekends I'd mow the lawn, deliver newspapers, work in restaurants, and that kind of thing. But, working the night shift was hard because . . . you know, you still need sleep.
I When did you sleep?
JK I slept after school, from six to nine or ten – about three or four hours a day.

CD1 5 **Part two**
Jeong talks about his career
I How did you become interested in science and engineering?
JK When you have difficulty with English, you have to concentrate on the things where you don't have a handicap, which for me was math and science. I was very good at analyzing things. So I said to myself, "OK, you can't be a doctor or a lawyer because they have to talk. So what can you do? Why not a physicist or an engineer?"
I Where did you go to college?
JK Johns Hopkins University. I spent all my time designing and building my own computer. I learned that there was this new start-up company, and I became a partner because at that time computers were all new, and the fact that I was young didn't really matter. So I worked as a design engineer. That company did extremely well.

I You've said you weren't the smartest, but you worked hard. Is that true?
JK Yes. I wasn't number one in my class. But the important thing is to get results, and there are different ways of doing this: being strong, being smart, or being lucky. I never felt I was lucky. I never felt that I was the smartest, but working hard is something that I've always been able to do.
I How did you come up with your big idea?
JK It became very obvious to me that the communications revolution was going to be even bigger than the computer revolution. People use a computer to make their lives a little easier, but then they need to talk and work together, and that's where my idea came in. Computers and telecommunications were merging, and I thought there's got to be some smarter way of making it all work together.
I What made you venture into starting your own business?
JK I tried to team up with a couple of people to raise capital. But I couldn't do it. Because I had no track record of running a business, I couldn't get other people to come with me. So I had to borrow the money myself.
I You're a big risk taker!
JK A major, major risk taker! What was it I said earlier? Once you have food to eat and clothes to wear, everything else is extra. There's no need to worry. This is the United States we're talking about! If you're healthy, you can always work. That way you won't go hungry. So why not push yourself to the limit and realize your potential? That's the way I see it, anyway.
I Were you looking to sell your business?
JK No. You cannot build a business thinking that somebody's going to buy it. You have to think in terms of creating value. Like I said, you've got to take one step at a time, especially if you are a small company. You know, you can think too far long-term and you can starve to death. So no, we weren't looking for it. They approached us first.
I Is it true that you're going to personally see $510 million from this sale?
JK I don't know the exact numbers, but it is something substantial, yes.
I Could you have even dreamed of such a figure when you were working at a convenience store?
JK No. It's astronomical. That was kind of difficult to imagine, but I had my dreams. I always wanted to be a major player, even when I was just starting to think about computers. I thought if Steve Jobs from Apple could do it, then so could I. You can put together a good group of people – it's not just one person – and you can create a world-class organization.

CD1 6 **Part three**
Jeong reflects on his life
I You said that people who are successful are often those who feel they have something to prove.
JK That's certainly true for me. I've always had an inferiority complex. I thought I wasn't as good as the guy next to me, so I had to work extra hard. People who are the smartest or the most talented, sometimes they don't realize their full potential because things come too easily for them. They don't have to push themselves to the limit.
I Many successful people have supportive families, but you didn't. It sounds like your drive really came from within.

JK It's true. I never asked anyone to hold my hand. All I ever wanted was the chance to prove myself, to show people what I was capable of.

I What now? You're at a point financially where you could retire comfortably. Why don't you?

JK What's really important to me now is that I add value to society. I want to give back to this country. I think I still have a lot of creative energy in me. I want to do something like social work or teaching at universities. I don't need to prove anything now, so I can just lead my life and set an example.

I Do you think things were possible for you in the United States that wouldn't have been possible elsewhere?

JK Absolutely. I guess nothing's impossible, but I don't think it's probable that it could have happened in other countries. One of the biggest reasons is people's attitude. In America, failure is seen as a learning experience. In other countries, when you try and fail, that's it. People basically look at you as a failure. Here, people look at failure as an excellent experience. And even if you fail, most people will walk away saying, "Well, at least I tried." Taking risks is all part of the game.

I So the American Dream is alive and well?

JK Yes! We are a nation of immigrants and the American Dream is still possible. You don't have to be the smartest to make that happen. I think that's a good thing for all of us.

CD1 7

1. Eric
Many people think of my country as a great big, frozen land of ice, up north, with Eskimos and red-coated policemen, but it's obviously a very different country from that, eh. It's a bilingual country, 40 percent of the population has French as a mother tongue, and it has a very dispersed population, but 90 percent of it lives in a small ribbon of land just 55 miles from the U.S. border, eh. In fact, probably one of the biggest concerns we have is the effect of U.S. domination on our unique culture, because of TV, sports and such like. I think many of us have an inferiority complex relative to the U.S. When we travel, a lot of the time people think we're American, it's annoying.

2. Mary
So our stereotype is that we're miserable, mean and dour and unhappy with our lot and that we're a proud people, maybe quite nationalistic, especially in sport – we'll support *any* team that's playing against England. Maybe there's an element of truth in all of this. I mean you do meet people who are mean but far more you meet people who are generous. I saw a guy collapse in the street and folk were running out the shops and bringing him a chair, and a glass of water and things and d'you know if somebody collapses in London, folk'll step over them. Oh, and as for whether people are miserable, well I remember standing at a bus stop and it was a gorgeous sunny day, real blue sky, you know you don't see many days like that here, not very often. And I said to the woman next to me, "Isn't it a gorgeous day?" And she said, "Aye, but we'll pay for it!" And I thought how can you be so pessimistic when it's such a gorgeous day.

3. Julia
Ah, well, I think we have a very, um, well-deserved reputation for being loud, we are certainly very loud, um, everywhere, it doesn't matter where we are, we just talk all at the same time and quite loud. And we're also very disorganized, um, people believe that we are, and another thing that is well-deserved. Um, what else, we're very lazy, um, I don't think that is true, um, we used to sleep our siestas, but I think we're a bit more European now, and we all have the same sort of timetables. Um, and then well,

we're sociable and outgoing, we're always with other people, we're rarely on our own, um, we tend to do lots of things at the same time, and, that's also because, there are so many places and they open until late.

4. Sook
Most foreigners seem to think that we really don't have any sense of humor. It's just not true. My family and friends are always laughing and joking around. Not everybody is funny, but we're not all serious all the time, either. People also think that we are musical prodigies—that we're amazing musicians, especially with the violin. Well, I've never touched a violin in my life! No one in my family has either. I play tennis for fun, and my sister swims. One more thing is that foreigners think that we're all extremely smart. Well … they may be right about that one. Ha-ha!

5. Rosemary
Um … I think that there is a stereotype in the eyes of a lot of British. I think they consider us loud, they consider us in many cases arrogant. Remember they lost the Revolutionary War, and they still have this attitude of being, "We once ruled you." And although that was two hundred years ago, I think there is still this attitude that we are the rebellious children, or the rebellious offspring of Great Britain. And uh, I think it's, it's very silly as an attitude because I think there are, yes there are a lot, who are extremely narrow, they don't see beyond their border, they are very arrogant, but there are also an incredible amount who are very aware of what goes on in the rest of the world.

6. Tristan
We're generally perceived as being quite cold and … uh … really quite uptight as well, and I know this from my own experience … um … that we're perceived also as being somewhat hypocritical – two-faced, now I don't think that was in relation to me, I hope not anyway, and I think now we also come across as incredibly yobbish, potentially violent, which is … um, not entirely my experience.

CD1 8

1. **A** Where do you live?
   B We've got a small flat. It's on the ground floor of a block of flats in the centre of town.
   A Have you got a garden?
   B No, we haven't, just a car park at the back.
2. **A** Where do you live?
   B We have a small apartment. It's on the first floor of an apartment building downtown.
   A Do you have a yard?
   B No, we don't, just a parking lot in the back.

CD1 9

1. **A** Have you got the time?
   B Yeah, it's five to four.
   A Did you say five past?
   B No, five *to* four.
2. **A** What are you going to do at the weekend?
   B The usual. Play football with my kids, and do a bit of gardening.
3. **A** Did you enjoy the match?
   B Yeah, it was great, but we had to queue for half an hour to get tickets.
4. **A** Did you have a good holiday?
   B Yeah, really good.
   A How long were you away?
   B Five days altogether. From Monday to Friday.
5. **A** Can you post this letter and parcel for me?
   B Of course.
   A And can you call at the supermarket and buy some crisps?
   B Is that all?
6. **A** Did you watch *The Birds* on telly last night?
   B I did, even though I've seen it twice before.
   A My third time. Isn't it just a terrific film?
   B It certainly is. One of my favourites.
7. **A** Have they brought the bill yet?
   B Yeah. They just have. But I can't read a thing.

The lighting is so bad in here.
8. **A** Do we need to stop for petrol?
   B Yes, why not? I need to go to the loo, anyway.

CD1 10

1. **A** Do you have the time?
   B Yeah, it's five till four.
   A Did you say five after?
   B No, five *till* four.
2. **A** What are you gonna do this weekend?
   B The usual stuff. Play soccer with the kids, and rake the yard.
3. **A** Did you enjoy the game?
   B Yeah, it was great, but we had to stand in line for half an hour to get tickets.
4. **A** Did you have a good vacation?
   B Yeah, really good.
   A How long were you away?
   B Five days in all. Monday through Friday.
5. **A** Can you mail this letter and package for me?
   B Sure thing.
   A And can you stop by the grocery store and buy some potato chips?
   B Is that all?
6. **A** Did you see *The Birds* on TV last night?
   B Yeah, even though I've seen it two times before.
   A My third time. Isn't it just an awesome movie?
   B Sure is. One of my favorites.
7. **A** Did they bring the check yet?
   B Yeah. They just did. But I can't read a thing. This place is so badly lit.
8. **A** Do we need to stop for gas?
   B Yeah, why not? I need to use the bathroom, anyway.

UNIT 2

CD1 11

1. What did you think of your brother's new girlfriend?
2. You've lost weight! What have you been doing?
3. When do we have to do that homework by?
4. Did you finish that crossword?
5. I don't have anywhere to stay tonight.
6. What's wrong? You don't look so well.
7. The children look very guilty, don't they?
8. OK, that's it for today. Don't forget! The next meeting's Friday the 6th at 2:30.

CD1 12

1. What did you think of your brother's new girlfriend?
   I liked her. I hope it works out.
2. You've lost weight! What have you been doing?
   I've started working out every morning at the gym.
3. When do we have to do that homework by?
   We have to hand it in on Friday.
4. Did you finish that crossword?
   No, I gave up. It was too difficult.
5. I don't have anywhere to stay tonight.
   Don't worry. We'll put you up.
6. What's wrong? You don't look so well.
   Stay away. I think I'm getting a cold.
7. The children look very guilty, don't they?
   I know. Makes it difficult to come down on them, doesn't it?
8. OK, that's it for today. Don't forget! The next meeting's Friday the 6th at 2:30.
   I'll put that down in my calendar right away.

CD1 13 LB = Lady Bracknell, J = Jack

LB Do you smoke?
J Well, yes, I must admit I smoke.

LB I am glad to hear it. A man should always have an occupation of some kind. There are far too many idle men in London as it is. How old are you?

J Twenty-nine.

LB A very good age to be married at. I have always been of the opinion that a man who desires to get married should know either everything or nothing. Which do you know?

J I know nothing, Lady Bracknell.

LB I am pleased to hear it. I do not approve of anything that tampers with natural ignorance. Ignorance is like a delicate exotic fruit; touch it and thc bloom is gonc. What is your income?

J Between seven and eight thousand a year.

LB In land, or in investments?

J In investments, chiefly.

LB That is satisfactory.

J I have a country house with some land, of course, attached to it, about fifteen hundred acres, I believe; but I don't depend on that for my real income. In fact, as far as I can make out, the poachers are the only people who make anything out of it.

LB A country house! You have a town house, I hope? A girl with a simple, unspoiled nature like Gwendolen could hardly be expected to reside in the country.

J Well, I own a house in Belgrave Square.

LB What number in Belgrave Square?

J 149.

LB The unfashionable side. Now to minor matters. Are your parents living?

J I have lost both my parents.

LB To lose one parent, Mr. Worthing, may be regarded as a misfortune; to lose both looks like carelessness. Who was your father? He was evidently a man of some wealth.

J I am afraid I really don't know. The fact is, Lady Bracknell, I said I had lost my parents. It would be nearer the truth to say that my parents seem to have lost me. I don't actually know who I am by birth. I was …, well, I was *found*.

LB Found!

J The late Mr. Thomas Cardew, an old gentleman of a very charitable and kindly disposition, found me, and gave me the name of Worthing, because he happened to have a first-class ticket for Worthing in his pocket at the time. Worthing is a place in Sussex. It is a seaside resort.

LB Where did the charitable gentleman who had a first-class ticket for this seaside resort find you?

J In a handbag.

LB A handbag?

J Yes, Lady Bracknell. I was in a handbag – a somewhat large, black leather handbag, with handles to it – an ordinary handbag, in fact.

LB In what locality did this Mr. James, or Thomas, Cardew come across this ordinary handbag?

J In the cloakroom at Victoria Station. It was given to him in mistake for his own.

LB The cloakroom at Victoria Station?

J Yes. The Brighton line.

LB The line is immaterial. Mr. Worthing, I confess I feel somewhat bewildered by what you have just told me. To be born, or at any rate, bred in a handbag, whether it had handles or not, seems to me to display a contempt for the ordinary decencies of family life. As for the particular locality in which the handbag was found, a cloakroom at a railway station might serve to conceal a social indiscretion – has probably, indeed, been used for that purpose before now but it could hardly be regarded as an assured basis for a recognized position in good society.

J May I ask you then what you would advise me to do? I need hardly say I will do anything in the world to ensure Gwendolen's happiness.

LB I would strongly advise you, Mr. Worthing, to try and acquire some relations as soon as possible, and to make a definite effort to produce at any rate one parent, of either sex.

J I don't see how I could possibly manage to do that. I can produce the handbag at any moment. It is in my dressing-room at home. I really think that should satisfy you, Lady Bracknell.

LB Me, sir! What has it to do with me? You can hardly imagine that I and Lord Bracknell would dream of allowing our only daughter – a girl brought up with the utmost care – to marry into a cloakroom, and form an alliance with a parcel! Good morning, Mr. Worthing!

CD1 14

I never set out to swipe anyone's boyfriend, much less Nina's. The day it all started, picking up a guy was the last thing on my mind. Even I don't go out on the prowl in grubby old boots and a sweater that's seen better days. All I was thinking of, on that drizzly afternoon, was finding a cab home. Having started off in mist-like fashion, the drizzle had taken it up a notch, as if it were thinking about turning into actual rain. At this point I was in the Village, with damp hair and a sweater starting to smell like a wet sheep. That was when I saw Nina coming out of a chic little restaurant with a guy on her arm.

If I can misquote Jane Austen here, it is a truth universally acknowledged that if you are fated to bump into someone like Nina when you haven't seen her for four years, you will be looking like death warmed over. While she will be looking like a *Vogue* spread in silk and cashmere. Only a few steps away, she was talking and laughing in her silver-tinkle way to the guy, who was holding her umbrella up to stop her from getting wet. The last time I'd seen her (at a wedding four years back) she'd had some tall, dark specimen in tow. Although everything about him was theoretically perfect, I hadn't been particularly impressed – to me he'd seemed just a bit plastic, somehow. I don't quite know what it was with this one – he wasn't good-looking, exactly, but the spark hit me at once!

CD1 15 See p. 22

CD1 16

1. She threw the ring into the wastebasket with the garbage.
2. Sorry we're late. We got behind a farmer with a herd of cattle in the road.
3. We'll meet you outside the theater at six o'clock.
4. Oh, how sweet of you to remember my birthday!
5. Speak up! I can't hear a word you're saying.
6. We saw some deer when we were walking in the mountains.
7. The cupboards are bare. We'll have to go shopping.
8. Those two are a pair of troublemakers.
9. The children sat in orderly rows in the school auditorium.
10. Uncle Bill chews every mouthful of food twenty times.

UNIT 3

CD1 17

Halico enjoyed a steady rise in profits in January. Unfortunately, they fell dramatically in February, then picked up in March and April when they went up gradually. May saw profits shooting up, but then the company suffered a substantial decrease in June. In July and August profits increased slightly, then went up steadily in the early fall months of September and October, before tumbling sharply in November. They then evened out in December.

CD1 18

Becom's sales began the year healthily, with January figures in the mid-5,000 units a month. They dropped dramatically in February and March, plummeting to 1,000. Sales picked up slightly in April, then shot up in the early summer months of May and June, at the end of which period sales were peaking at 6,500 a month. There was a bit of a downturn in July, when sales dropped by 800, but then they remained stable in August and September. October saw a substantial decrease, down to 3,000, before sales picked up in the build-up to the holidays, rising steadily to end the year at 4,500.

CD1 19 I = Interviewer, M = Mayor

I We are very pleased to have with us in the studio tonight the mayor. Mr. Mayor, we've been …

M Good evening, Jeremy.

I Good evening, Mr. Mayor. Uh … Mr. Mayor, we've been hearing endlessly in the media about the latest crisis that is facing your government.

M May I just say right away that this is *not* a crisis.

I Well, many people say …

M No, Jeremy, I don't think so… polls distinctly show that the vast majority of the population strongly support us.

I With all due respect, Mr. Mayor, the poll I read only this morning in the *Post* …

M But surely you don't believe a word you read in the tabloids. No – my government fully deserves every penny of their pay raise.

I Mr. Mayor, you can hardly argue the case for your cabinet voting themselves, … yes, voting themselves, a 40 percent pay raise when your government has offered nurses just 2.6 percent, teachers merely 1.7 percent and firefighters …

M Let me say that I greatly respect our public sector workers. They work hard and have a lot of responsibility. However, my cabinet members also work very diligently and carry burdens that are just as heavy. Also …

I But, Mr. Mayor, how can you justify …

M If I can just finish, Jeremy. The fact is that this pay raise is much closer to 20 percent when you take into account the many expenses that all politicians regularly incur.

I Such as?

M Well, you know, … uh … travel – air and rail fares, an entertainment allowance, their personal secretaries, all of these highly necessary for any cabinet member. You can't expect them to travel second class, eat in third-rate restaurants *and* do a first-class job. You know, Jeremy, the fact of the matter is …

I The fact of the matter is, Mr. Mayor, that this pay raise is five times the rate of inflation, and lately you and your advisers have repeatedly urged workers to accept increases in line with inflation. It seems perfectly clear to me and many people that …

M Jeremy, Jeremy, let me explain. We set up an independent review body to look into …

I As I understand it, Mr. Mayor, this so-called independent review body was made up mainly of members of your cabinet, who, with all due respect, can hardly be called independent.

M Ah, but only politicians can appreciate the particular workload of a politician. And I have to tell you that the review concluded that the effectiveness of our city's caretakers is being severely hampered by lack of funds, and that their salaries are pathetically low compared to those people working in industry, banking, and the like.

I And what about your own pay raise, Mr. Mayor? Is there any truth in the rumor that you will be getting a 50 percent raise?

M Now, Jeremy, I came on your program to talk

about my cabinet's salaries, my own salary is being reviewed separately *and* it will be reviewed fairly. And, as you know, I believe passionately in fair and just compensation for all working people and I include myself in that, Jeremy.

I Of course you do, Mr. Mayor. Mr. Mayor, thank you very much.

M Thank *you*, Jeremy.

CD1 20 I = Interviewer, AR = Anita Roddick

Part one

I I wonder what it was in you that … that enabled you to have that kind of feeling about what business should be.

AR I think it's what, … gave this, um, … whole edge is that I was saved by not going to business school, by not doing the traditional route.

I That's a terrible condemnation of business school.

AR It is because I don't believe … I believe they do an incredibly good job of developing people to understand financial science. You can't expect to raise an entrepreneur in a business school. Entrepreneurs are usually, um … outsiders. That's why immigrants, refugees, make the best, um … entrepreneurs. My parents were economic immigrants. Whether you had the … you know … the Jewish immigrants in the beginning of the century, the Italian immigrants in the midcentury, or the Pakistani and the Bangladeshi, and the Indian … or the Caribbean … they all had … they all dance to a different drumbeat. They're not part of the system. They're outside the system. And when you're a young person, and you feel as an outsider … 'cause we were the first Italians in this town. You were just braver because you didn't know any different. Business school … would have polished my thinking into a much more disciplined way. Market, product development, finance, instead of saying "Hey!" having a great idea, and thinking, "My God! If I make this idea really good, people will buy it from me, hopefully give me a profit." It was a notion of trading, which … entrepreneurs are manic traders. We're buyers and sellers … you know. And all we want to do is go into the marketplace for feedback on our ideas. And all the money we make is of no interest to us. This is what upsets the financial journalists, because we don't give a darn about money. We just want the money to oil the wheels, to see how far this idea could go. And many of us feel fraudulent, because ideas just come out of our head like, uh … you know … like a genie in the bottle. We vomit ideas. But we are terribly, terribly bad at managing.

I But as you … but … business needs, of course, all those other things …

AR Of course it does.

I … the structure, the management.

AR Yeah, but that … it should be subservient. It's like … you need to breathe to stay alive, but if you keep on concentrating, breathing in … out, in, out … What a life you're going to have if you concentrate only on profits. You're going to have a business that's going to die within a nanosecond because it's more than the profit. It's just the avenue, the engine for making you develop other ideas, or to invest in other things. So, you know, for me business school has never been … you know … has never been the sacred ground for it. It's always, "Have an idea. Learn." And the best businesspeople, entrepreneurs are people who ask questions. You know, I don't want to be the biggest retailer in the world. I have no interest in that. I just want to be the most idiosyncratic, the wildest, the bravest.

Part two

Anita Roddick is asked what she sees as the big dilemmas in business these days.

AR You know, for me the big dilemma now in business is businesses rule. That's the fact. Any institution …

I Rule our lives?

AR Rule our lives.

I Rule the world?

AR Rule the world. I mean, you can forget politics, and you can forget religion, as being the two most foremost institutions. Business institution now has, because it's so wealthy, because it's so creative in many ways, it controls government thinking, it controls political thinking. And it controls our health, our safety, it controls what we eat, controls what we think. And it's because this whole growth in the global economy, and which really means corporate global economy. So this growth in corporations, multinational corporations which are … just bow down to nothing, no local laws, no national laws. They stop any environmental standards, any human rights standards if they deem it gets in the way of trade. So they for me are the big enemy. So my message now is, "Look for businesses that support local communities, because you keep the money in the local arena. Support local economic initiatives, support local farming, support local, anything local. And if we're working and trading internationally, let us trade with the grassroots. And let's trade in a way that is honorable. Let us pay living wages, and not slave … slave wages. Let us be penalized if we have human rights abusers within the products that we make or sell." People are standing up and challenging those big brand names because they don't like their business practices.

Part three

Anita Roddick has announced that she has no intention of leaving her children any money when she dies.

I You won't give your wealth, will you?

AR To them?

I To your children.

AR No. No.

I But in that mother role, shouldn't you be doing that?

AR No. One of the biggest criticisms from the media is that my wealth is not going to go to them. And "Oh!" they say, "Oh! What do your kids think about it?" My kids say, "I don't want to even talk about this, 'cause it means that my mum's going to be dead." And number two, well, "What do we have already? We have great homes, we've got our work." And they're not poor. I mean, but they also know that if there's … if the wealth comes out at fifty or a hundred and fifty million bucks, or whatever it is, what better thing to do than to give it away? What a great legacy, just you know, with the building of the schools in Africa, the support of the community organizers, the human rights, this whole campaign I'm putting money into at the moment on the elimination of sweatshops and child labor and slave labor. I can't think of a better legacy. If all you're recognized for is the ability to accumulate money, then I think that is the next thing from being obscene. You know, the thing about wealth, it allows you to be generous. The sadness, one of the sadnesses about poverty, it doesn't allow you to be that.

CD1 21

1. We're in class learning English.
2. It's eight o'clock and time for a break.
3. I'm dying for a cup of coffee.
4. We've been in here for over an hour.
5. As a matter of fact, I think our teacher's asleep.
6. She doesn't understand that her English students are about to sneak out.

CD1 22 See p. 32

CD1 23 See p. 32

CD1 24

1. **A** Could I have your first name, please?
   B It's Marc. That's M – A – R, and then C as in Charlie, not K as in Kilo.
   A And your last name?
   B Delgado.
   A Could you spell that for me?
   B Yes. It's D – …
   A Is that T as in Tango?
   B No, D as in Delta, E as in Echo, L as in Lima, G as in Golf, A as in Alpha, D as in Delta, and O as in Oscar.
2. **C** And your name, please?
   D It's Sou-Chen Lin.
   C Could you spell the first name for me?
   D It's S –
   C F as in Foxtrot?
   D No, S as in Sierra, O – U. Then there's a hyphen. Then C – H – E – N as in November.
   C OK … Sou-Chen. And your last name, please?
   D Lin. That's L – I – N.
   C M as in Mike?
   D No, N as in November.
3. **E** … And could I have the name of the other person who'll be driving the car?
   F Yes, it's Ginny Dummet.
   E Jimmy. You mean, J as in Juliet – I – …
   F No, it's G as in Golf – I – double N – …
   E Double M as in Mike?
   F No, double N as in November, and Y.
   E Was that I as in India or Y as in Yankee?
   F Y as in Yankee. And the last name is Dummet … D – …
   E D as in Delta?
   F That's right. D as in Delta – U – double M as in Mike – E – T.

UNIT 4

CD1 25

1. A celebrity is a person who works hard all his life to become well known, and then wears dark glasses to avoid being recognized.
2. I don't want to achieve immortality through my work. I want to achieve it through not dying.
3. There is only one thing worse than being talked about, and that is not being talked about.
4. What goes up, must come down.
5. Whenever a friend succeeds, a little something in me dies.
6. Genius is one percent inspiration, ninety-nine percent perspiration.
7. If at first you don't succeed, try, try again.
8. Nothing succeeds like success.
9. Let me tell you about the rich. They are different from you and me.

CD1 26

All the A-list stars were there. That model, Angeline, I think it was Angeline, was there with her new boyfriend. They've been secretly going out for months. It was a glittering occasion. Stars everywhere and the crowds outside just begging for autographs. I couldn't believe my eyes. And the dresses! I don't know how much they would have cost – a fortune, I imagine. All designer labels. The photographers were having a field day, and there were reporters everywhere, falling over each other to interview the biggest names. We didn't have the best seats – we were in the back row. We could still see everything. I was so busy star-watching that I didn't pay attention to the plot. You would've done the same. I'm not too keen on thrillers, but it must have been good because at the end the whole audience stood up and clapped. I'm not sure what the story was about, but you really should go and see it when it comes out. It was an amazing evening and to top it all off we went to Quaglino's for dinner afterwards and Sarah Jane Fox and Brad Brat were at the next table. How cool is that? Sarah Jane Fox has terrible skin problems. Who cares about that when you have that much money?

CD1 27

All the A-list stars were there. That model, Angeline, at least I think it was Angeline, was there with her boyfriend. Apparently they've been going out for months. Anyway, it was a glittering occasion. Stars everywhere and the crowds outside just begging for autographs. Quite honestly, I couldn't believe my eyes. And the dresses! I mean, I don't know how much they would cost – a fortune, I imagine. All designer labels, naturally. The photographers were obviously having a field day, and of course there were reporters everywhere, falling over each other, so to speak, to interview the biggest names. Admittedly, we didn't have the best seats – as a matter of fact we were in the back row. Mind you, we could still see everything. Actually, I was so busy star-watching that I didn't pay attention to the plot. No doubt you would've done the same. To tell you the truth, I'm not too keen on thrillers, but it must have been good because at the end the whole audience stood up and clapped. As I was saying, I'm not so sure what the story was about, but you really should go and see it when it comes out.
All in all, though, it was an amazing evening and to top it off we went to Quaglino's for dinner afterwards, and guess what? Sarah Jane Fox and Brad Brat were at the next table. How cool is that? By the way, Sarah Jane Fox has terrible skin problems. Still, who cares about that when you have that much money!

CD1 28 A = Ana, B = Ben

A Have you heard that Jan is thinking of marrying Paul?
B Really? I don't know what she sees in him.
A I know what you mean. Mind you, he is a millionaire.
B Yes, I suppose having all that money does help.
A Where did he get his money from?
B Apparently, he made a fortune in I.T.
A He's been married three times before. Did you know that?
B Actually, it's just once, I think.
A They'll have a big wedding.
B Of course they will. It'll be massive.
A Oh, well. Good luck to them.
B Absolutely. By the way, did you hear that Jenny and Mario had a car accident?
A Oh no! What happened?
B It wasn't serious. They skidded into a tree, but fortunately they weren't going fast. The car's destroyed, but at least no one was injured.
A Thank goodness for that. I should get in touch with them, but I don't have their number.
B As a matter of fact, it's in my phone. I'll give it to you.
A Great. Thanks a lot. Anyway, I have to get going. I'm meeting Jan for lunch.
B OK. See you later. Bye.

CD1 29 G = Gross, DB = Drew Barrymore
Part one

G My guest is Drew Barrymore, who we've been watching in movies since she was about six playing one of the children in "E.T."
How did you know that you liked acting when you were a child? I mean, you obviously were good at it right from the start.
DB Thank you.

G And we could certainly see that in "E.T.," even if we didn't see the things that you did before that. But did you like it? Did you know as a child, yeah, this is for me?
DB Well, there were two things. One is I cosmically and magnetically, with all of the blood running through my veins, felt this connection to this family that I was born into, the Barrymores. I felt a real honest-to-goodness desire to act. I felt it because they instilled it in my soul, and I never wanted to deny myself of that. In fact, I was very proud and excited of the fact that at such a young age that I was in tune and in touch with that connection with them and wanted to honor them and play in their field and keep their name going and be like them. I admired them.
G Your father, John Barrymore, Jr., left – I mean, he wasn't part of the picture when you were growing up, and you never really spent a lot of time with him. How close were you with other members of the Barrymore family?
DB Not close at all, because they mostly were deceased before I was born, and – but I would read their books, and I would watch their movies, and I saw my face in their faces. Unlike other families who aren't close, I have a wealth – trunks and trunks and trunks of research material.
And the reason that I love acting is because of them and because I feel it in my blood that this is what I need to do. This is my creative, cathartic outlet, and if I didn't have it, I'd go – I'd be in a straightjacket, I'm pretty sure. And on the other level, there's another kind of tribe, which is that when you don't have a family, such as I did not have a family growing up, when I went on film sets, there are these amazing, eclectic, interesting groups of people who are like the Island of Lost Toys, a band of misfits, and they're little families in themselves. And when I did "E.T.," that really changed my life because I had really just done TV movies and commercials, so I never really had an experience as profound. And I also met my godfather there, Steven Spielberg, and he was a gift to me, a real father figure, and he showed me and gave me a sense of safety and inspiration and security and someone to look up to like I had never had in my life.

CD1 30 **Part two**

G You're such an interesting mix of – on the one hand, coming from this like, pedigree, this like famous family; and on the other hand, feeling like you didn't have a family, because your father wasn't with you, your mother was – was working a lot and not with you and became your manager for a while. But as you said before, you and she officially parted ways. And I guess it's – it's such a kind of inherent contradiction of your life, that you're part of this like really famous tribe, the most – perhaps the most famous acting family in American history – and at the same time, you feel like you grew up without a family.
DB Yeah. It's – like I said, we're dealt the cards we're dealt with in life and it's up to us on how we want to play them. And I feel anything less than sorry for myself, what I'd really like to do is to keep their name alive and well and honor them. And, you know, when I go to the Chinese Theater in Hollywood, which is where I try to have most of my premieres, they – my grandfather's face is in the cement. He put his profile because he's known as the great profile. And my star is actually, you know, ten feet away from his and here is the place at another time he was and here I am now. And I want to keep that tradition alive.

G Of your family's movies, which made the biggest impression on you?
DB Well, different ones for various reasons, but I loved "Twentieth Century" because I think my grandfather is just funny and genius as that mad director, he's just wonderful in it. But when I watch "A Bill of Divorcement" with Katharine Hepburn, I get so emotional because it's about a father and a daughter reconciling. And I picture myself in her shoes and me getting to have these conversations and moments with him, the way that she got to have them with him in that movie, and so that one is very personal for me.
G Did having them as your family send you back to lots of other early movies, too?
DB Yeah, I – I grew up watching the classics, and I still, I keep Turner Classic Movies on my television at all times. So, I'm always watching old movies, coming home to old movies, and a lot of the time my family is on TV and it just feels… welcoming home – that warm fireplace of good vibes. And I have their pictures all over the wall. And it's not an obsessive thing, it's just like, you know, I'm connected to these people and that connection makes me feel good.

CD1 31 **Part three**

G People who have come from troubled families or, you know, families that broke apart like – like yours. I think a lot of them tend to want to have a family and make it a more, a better family, like – make it the kind of family that they wish they had and didn't, or – or to not have a family because families have like bad – bad memories for them. Where do you fit on that scale if – if you don't mind answering it, if it's not too personal?
DB Not at all. I'm definitely for option A. I believe that I'm going to be a great mother. I cannot wait to have a family. I'm so looking forward to – all the challenges that I've taken on in my life – I can't wait to take on the one that shall be my greatest and most selfless, if I'm so lucky to have the opportunity to have a child. And I know that I will provide the exact family that I would have always wanted. And I do think that you can take damage and pain and dysfunction and use it as the blueprint of what not to do.
G So, I guess one of the things you wouldn't be doing is what your mother did with you, take you to Studio 54, you know.
DB Yeah. It seems irresponsible and I don't want people to hate her for doing that because, you know, it's not the orthodox way of motherhood. On the other hand, selfishly, from my own experience, I can't believe I got to party in that heyday and be a part of a cultural phenomenon. And I'm – I'm glad because she inadvertently gave me the opportunities that I needed, to have the career and the life that I wanted. So, you know, trial by fire – but I – I hope people will forgive her for something like that because I – I don't believe she did them with malcontent intentions.
I think she just, you know, was a bit of a kid herself, and, you know, I got – I got where I was. I got, you know, I got that I was at Studio 54. And I was like, you know what, I'm glad. I'm glad I got to be in this moment and, you know, I saw a lot of amazing things growing up. Maybe they weren't for children to see, but that was my life and I have no regrets. It's what formed me.
G Well, Drew Barrymore, it's been great to talk with you. Thank you so much.

CD1 32

A Cesária Evora is just fantastic! Her concert was amazing!
B It was, wasn't it? And she puts so much energy into her songs, doesn't she?

A Yes, she does. I love that song about missing home. It's so beautiful, isn't it?
B It is. It was her first big hit. She wrote it about Cape Verde, her home country, I think.
A So she can write as well as sing, can she? What a talent!
B Yeah. She writes most of her songs.
A She's playing again tomorrow, isn't she?
B Yes, I think so. Let's go again, shall we?
A Sure, why not?

CD1 33

1. A You haven't seen my car keys, have you?
   B No, I haven't. You had them this morning, didn't you?
   A Yes, I did. If I can't find them, I'll be late for work.
   B Panic over. Here they are!
   A Great. You're the best!
2. A You didn't like that meal, did you? You were pushing it around the plate.
   B No, I didn't. Well, it hadn't been cooked properly, had it? Your steak was OK, was it?
   A Yes. It was fine. Let's get the check and go home.
   B OK. We won't be coming back here anytime soon, will we?
3. A You forgot the map, didn't you?
   B Uh-oh. Yes, I did.
   A But I put it next to the car keys.
   B Well, I didn't see it, did I?
   A You're blind.
   B Oh, and you're perfect, are you?

CD1 34

1. A Jeremy makes an absolute fortune!
   B He does, doesn't he?
   C Does he? I had no idea. How much?
   D So, he's rich, is he? Wow. I didn't know.
2. A Peter's new Brazilian girlfriend, Ana, is very beautiful.
   B Yes, she is.
   C Is she? She's not my type, actually.
   D So she's Brazilian, is she?
3. A Lisa and Kevin are going to Florida on vacation. They're so lucky.
   B They are, aren't they?
   C Are they? I wish I was going.
   D So they're going to Florida, are they?
4. A Zidane played really well in the game on Sunday, didn't he?
   B He did, didn't he?
   C Did he? I didn't think so.
5. A Target is a great store. You can buy everything there.
   B You can, can't you?
   C Can you? I bet you can't buy a camel.
6. A I think our teacher is the best.
   B She is, isn't she?
   C Is she? I don't think she's as good as the one we had last year.
   D So you like her, do you?
7. A Carlos is a very experienced traveler. He's been everywhere.
   B He has, hasn't he?
   C Has he? I didn't realize.
   D He has, has he? I must ask him about it some time.

UNIT 5

CD2 2 J = Joseph, M = Mariela

J Well, it was nearly twenty-five years ago now …
M No, it was twenty-two.
J Yes, twenty-two. And I was traveling in Chile – a hiking trip. I'm from the Midwest – it's so flat – so the mountains here, here in Chile

were irresistible, especially in Patagonia. It has wonderful national parks.
M Yes, you see, I've lived in this village all my life. I was born here. Every day I wake up to the sight of the mountains rising up in front of the village. Every day it's the same, but a little bit different. So beautiful. The way the snowline ebbs and flows in the winter, or how the flowers cover the mountainside in spring. It's entrancing.
J So, I was traveling with a friend of mine, Rob, and we'd hiked a long way. It was a long hike, nearly five hours. We could see a village below us, a little village cascading down the hillside. It took us hours to reach it . . . and by the time we did we were exhausted and very thirsty. So, the first house we came to I knocked on the door to ask for a glass of water, and . . .
M Oh, I remember!
J … and the most beautiful girl opened the door!
M Oh, Joseph!
J And I fell in love. On the spot. That was it! My friend returned to the U.S. alone.
M It's true! Poor Rob.
J But lucky me.
M It was so unexpected. I am an artist, a potter, so my friends always believed I would marry a creative man, another artist or a poet. And in a way I have. You see, Joseph, was a physics teacher when I met him. But I have taught him how to work with the potter's wheel, to throw the clay, work with the kiln. He learned so quickly and became an expert – maybe his science background helped. Friends say my pottery improved the very day I met Joseph, and now we've worked together for over twenty years. He throws the pieces, and I hand-paint them.
J The studio where we work is attached to the house, and we have a small shop next to that. Whether we're working or not, we always have the view of the mountains to inspire us. We never grow bored with that, or each other.

CD2 3

1. I *do* do my homework immediately after class.
2. What it was, was love at first sight.
3. The thing most couples don't realize is how difficult married life can be.
4. It's the parents I blame for badly behaved kids.
5. Not only are the values of society at risk, but also the very survival of our nation is threatened.
6. Only then did I understand what she meant.
7. It was Sam that broke the blue vase!
8. I won't marry *any*body.

CD2 4

A What's your favorite place to travel?
B We like hiking in the Andes.
1. A We like going skiing in Colorado.
   B What *we* like is hiking in the Andes.
2. A What do you like doing for vacation?
   B *One* thing we *like* is *hiking in the Andes*.
3. A You like hiking in the Rockies, don't you?
   B The *Andes* is where we like hiking.
4. A You like driving in the Andes, don't you?
   B It's *hiking* in the Andes we like.
5. A Don't you just hate hiking in the Andes?
   B Hiking in the Andes is something we *like*.
6. A What do you like more than hiking in the Andes?
   B There's *nothing* we like more than hiking in the Andes.

CD2 5

1. What I can't *stand* about the first family is that they're like a soap opera.
2. What surprises me *every* time the president speaks is the way he pronounces his vowels.
3. The thing that annoys me *most* about politicians is that they don't keep their promises.

4. What we did after class yesterday was race home to watch the football game on TV.
5. It's our *teacher* who knows all the answers.
6. Something I've *never* told you is that I've been married before.
7. What the *government* should do is come up with a better health care policy.
8. *Never* in my *life* have I heard such a ridiculous story!

CD2 6

1. A They're back together again, but their relationship's had a bumpy ride.
   B You know what they say – the course of true love never did run smooth.
2. A OK. I'll have one more. But that's the last one.
   B You know what they say – a little of what you fancy does you good.
3. A You? Going to cooking classes? You *must* be in love!
   B You know what they say – the way to a man's heart is through his stomach.
4. A But I don't want you to go off to Mexico for six months. How'll I survive?
   B You know what they say – absence makes the heart grow fonder.
5. A He's always out with his friends, never with her. Can't she see that he's a jerk?
   B You know what they say – love is blind.

CD2 7

Shall I compare thee to a summer's day?
Thou art more lovely and more temperate:
Rough winds do shake the darling buds of May,
And summer's lease hath all too short a date:
Sometime too hot the eye of heaven shines,
And often is his gold complexion dimmed,
And every fair from fair sometime declines,
By chance, or nature's changing course untrimmed;
But thy eternal summer shall not fade,
Nor lose possession of that fair thou ow'st,
Nor shall death brag thou wander'st in his shade,
When in eternal lines to time thou grow'st;
So long as men can breathe, or eyes can see,
So long lives this, and this gives life to thee.

CD2 8 P = Presenter, R = Reporter, O = Olive

P But as a matter of fact, it'll be a rather sad Valentine's Day for Olive Hodges. She's reached the remarkable age of 102 and had been looking forward to her 77th wedding anniversary this year. Sadly her husband Fred died last weekend, but she told our reporter, Bob Walker, about their long relationship. Their first meeting was a brief one during World War I. Their courtship began later after a chance meeting in a park.
O He was seventeen-and-a-half at that time and six months later he was called up into the army. Uh … There were many people who died, were killed by his side, he came through without a scratch. It was a miracle really.
Then just after the war, a friend and I were in the park, and there was a band on Sunday afternoon. This young man walked by and raised his hat, then he went back and raised his hat, and he did this about six times. And I was very amused, but I said to my friend, well, if he goes by again, I'll put him out of his misery. So, the next time he went by I made some small remark to him and he came along and talked to us.
He used to come around and call for me to go for a walk, so we were going for a walk one evening and he said, "I would like to marry you, but I don't have any money." And I said, "Well, we can wait." I didn't see any need for a rush and that was it.
R What is the secret of such a long and happy marriage?

O   Well, we loved one another so intently and our attitude was that we wanted to make the other one happy.

R   Now, you were married almost 77 years. That's right? Was your love for each other as strong right up to the end?

O   I think it was stronger. He didn't want to leave me, and I didn't want to leave him. He wanted me with him all the time. I was happy to be with him for that matter, and he was always asking if I still loved him as much as I used to, and it was quite a job to reassure him that I *did* love him, but *[laughs]* he really loved me so much.

P   Oh – what can you say? That was Olive Hodges.

CD2 9   See p. 50

CD2 10   See p. 50

UNIT 6

CD2 11

And now for the six o'clock news.

Reports are coming in of an earthquake in Japan. Five hundred people are believed to have died, with over two thousand injured. International rescue teams have arrived in the area, and a huge humanitarian operation is under way. The earthquake is reported to have been 6.4 on the Richter scale.
A Monet painting has been stolen from the Louvre Museum in Paris. Thieves are thought to have hidden themselves while the museum was closing, then escaped through a skylight. The painting is said to be worth $50 million.
The crisis over rising housing prices seems to be settling down. Interest rates fell another half percent last month. Government sources say that it is hoped that prices will level out to an overall rise of 5 percent over the last twelve months.

CD2 12   I = Interviewer, SW = Simon Winchester

Part one

I   You've been described as a foreign correspondent of the more adventurous sort. Do you think that does you justice?

SW   I … it's a very flattering thing to say. I think what probably was meant by that is that I really don't like pack journalism. I'm … I'm not in the slightest bit interested in television, or waving a microphone in somebody's face. I'm very much, you know, the man standing in the shadows of a bridge with a notebook in his hand and trying to be inconspicuous, and listening and observing. But going alone to unusual places. I think I find the offbeat more interesting. And although I was a White House correspondent for quite a long time, and so very much was in the thick of things during for instance the Watergate affair, with Nixon's resignation, generally speaking I had a happier time, I think, a more fulfilling time personally when I was based in India, with a patch to cover from Tehran to Bangkok, so wandering really in some of the most exotic countries in the world.

I   Is that something that you relish, that kind of exotic, slightly unknown, almost dangerous side to it?

SW   I've never made a particular virtue out of danger. I mean, I've covered a reasonable number of wars and skirmishes and things. But remote interests me. Remote islands and islands' people are fascinating. So I do … I tend to have been to nearly all the really strange, offbeat places.

Part two

I   Could you talk to me a little bit about how you think the foreign correspondent's role has changed during your career, um … whether they operate differently now from perhaps how they did when you started?

SW   Well, a lot of things have changed … the most notable is the general public's lack of interest in things foreign. It used to be, I think, as a … because of the residual, the sort of echoes of empire … Britain particularly … in British newspapers, always had a very keen interest in the faraway. That's not true anymore, I think. And you look at foreign pages in newspapers and they've shrunk savagely. The *New York Times* is more or less alone in maintaining a really strong collection of foreign correspondents. But even their editors acknowledge that foreign is an expensive luxury. Most readers aren't particularly interested. So it's changed in that degree in that the budgets are smaller, and foreign correspondents are much more constrained by not being able to spend the way they could. Secondly, I think television has taken over, to my way of thinking, in far too … far too obvious a way, and that, uh … the man or woman looking for the … exotic, the faraway, the small story, the little essay that actually does illuminate brilliantly the inner workings of some distant place. There's no time for that, because television leads the charge, television makes the story. … We've lost the ability, the willingness, the interest to paint the subtleties of foreign. We go in … the blazing TV lights … for a short time, and then we go on to the next story. So the subtlety of abroad has disappeared, in terms of newspapers.

I   How did you use to approach that sort of situation?

SW   Well, I worked for *The Guardian* … in those days the foreign editor was keen to … almost encouraged you to … look behind the story, to leave the main story to the agencies. So I used to like doing that sort of thing. Nowadays you can't.

I   So is it the journalists' fault, or is it some sort of editorial control? Is it editors trying to satisfy budgets and political, uh … ?

SW   Yes, I mean it's not the journalists' fault, I don't think. I mean, newspapers have become much more market driven, and less of a public service. Um … the *Guardian* seeks to make money, to increase its circulation, to outdo the *Independent*. And to do that it's got to spend its money, such as it has, in a more focused way. And that might mean more fashion coverage, or more social issues at home. And my friends who remain foreign correspondents now are not the sort of happy bunch that we were then.

I   Do they feel their hands are tied?

SW   Well, yes, I think so. Newspapers particularly in their coverage of foreign have changed mightily, and in my view not for the better.

I   Do you think tabloid journalism has had anything to do with that? That sort of seeking out of sensationalism, and the ephemeral nature of the stories? Has that tarred all journalists with the same brush?

SW   No, I don't think that tabloid journalism has much to do with it. I think the dominant reason for the change is television and budgets.

I   What have you personally gotten out of your career as a journalist?

SW   Enormous excitement, thousands of experiences, the years rushing past. It all does add up to a fascinating life.

CD2 13

1.   **A** Guess what! I won $5 million in the lottery!
     B You're kidding! Really? That's amazing!

2.   **A** My grandfather died last week.
     B Oh, no! I'm so sorry to hear that. You were very close, weren't you?

3.   **A** One of my students told me I was a bad teacher.
     B What a brat! I hope you told him off.

4.   **A** Here we are! Home at last.
     B Thank goodness for that! I thought we'd never make it.

5.   **A** I'm broke since I bought all those designer clothes.
     B Serves you right. It's your own fault.

6.   **A** Did you hear that Jim's leaving to go to another job?
     B Good riddance. He was always useless.

7.   **A** I missed the last bus and had to walk home. I didn't get home till midnight.
     B What a drag! You must have been really annoyed.

8.   **A** When I get a job, I'm going to be a millionaire, and have three houses and ten cars.
     B In your dreams. Fat chance of you being able to afford all of those things.

9.   **A** I'm going on vacation to Bali for two weeks.
     B Nice! Can I come, too?

10. **A** My six-year-old daughter painted me a picture for Father's Day.
     B What a sweetheart!

11. **A** I'm tired of studying. Let's go dancing.
     B Now you're talking! A salsa night would do us some good.

12. **A** Susan says she never wants to see you again.
     B So what? I don't care. I wouldn't be friends with her if she were the last person on earth.

13. **A** My team lost again last weekend.
     B And that surprises you? They lose every weekend.

14. **A** Dad, I'm going to an all-night party. Is that OK?
     B Over my dead body. No way!

CD2 14

1. My sister has twelve kids.
2. My dog died last night.
3. My teenage daughter told me she thought I was boring, stupid, and old-fashioned.
4. When I told little Katie that her grandma had gone to heaven, she asked when we could visit!
5. One day I'm going to be a famous movie star, just you wait.
6. I can't come out tonight. My dad says I have to do my homework and clean up my room.
7. My sister won't speak to me! All because I said girls were stupid.
8. Dad, I know you don't like Johnny, but I love him, and I'm going to marry him.
9. I failed the exam because I overslept and missed half of it.
10. After last week's argument, my roommate has decided to move out.
11. We've been given an extra week to hand in our essays.
12. My parents bought me a new car for my birthday.
13. How would you feel about going to the movies this evening, then out for a pizza?
14. I'm going to tell the teacher what you said.

CD2 15

1. **A** Pete. I wrecked your car. Sorry.
    B Great. That's all I needed. Thank you very much.

2. **A** When you come on Saturday, we're going to have an ice cream.
    B Ooh! How exciting. I can't wait.

3. **A** You know that guy Parker, the millionaire? Apparently he's been sent to prison for tax evasion.
    B Well, ain't that a shame! My heart bleeds for

4. **A** I have finally figured out how this machine works.
    B You're so bright. I don't know how you kept it a secret for so long.

UNIT 7

CD2 16 See p. 60

CD2 17

We have named you Daniel Patrick, but I've been told by my Chinese friends that you should have a Chinese name as well, and this glorious dawn sky makes me think we'll call you Son of the Eastern Star. Your coming has turned me upside down and inside out. So much that seemed essential to me has, in the past few days, taken on a different color. Like many foreign correspondents I know, I have lived a life that, on occasion, has veered close to the edge: war zones, natural disasters, darkness in all its shapes and forms. In a world of insecurity and ambition and ego, it's easy to be drawn in, to take chances with our lives, to gamble with death. Now, looking at your sleeping face, listening to your occasional sigh, I wonder how I could have ever thought glory and prizes were sweeter than life. And it's also true that I am pained, perhaps haunted is a better word, by the memory, suddenly so vivid now, of each suffering child I have come across on my journeys. To tell you the truth, it's nearly too much to bear at this moment to even think of children being hurt and abused. And yet, looking at you, the images come flooding back. Ten-year-old Andi Mikail on a hillside in Eritrea, how his voice cried out, when the wind blew dust onto his wounds. The two brothers, Domingo and Juste, in Menongue, southern Angola. Juste, two years old and dying from malnutrition, being carried on seven-year-old Domingo's back. And Domingo's words to me, "He was nice before, but now he has the hunger."
Last October, in Afghanistan, when you were growing inside your mother, I met Sharja, aged twelve. Motherless, fatherless, guiding me through the gray ruins of her home, everything was gone, she told me. And I knew that, for all her tender years, she had learned more about loss than I would understand in a lifetime. There is one last memory, of Rwanda, where, in a ransacked classroom, I found a mother and her three young children huddled together. The children had died holding onto their mother, that instinct we all learn from birth and in one way or another cling onto until we die.

CD2 18 See p. 61

CD2 19

1. Emily
This is something my father said to me the night before I got married, and I always keep coming back to it. Dad said, "You know, there are only three things in life of real importance – there's love, there's home, and there's work … and as long as two out of the three are OK, you can deal with the third one." But lately I've been thinking that love and home are so intertwined, it's a bit tricky, isn't it?

2. Akemi
Actually, this is something my ex-husband always said – he was quite a nice guy really – whenever we had a friend who irritated or annoyed us in some way, someone who maybe was mean or who never listened and was always full of themselves and their own lives, he, my ex, always said that, before you cast people out of your lives you should allow them

three faults. That way you get to keep most of your friends. I don't know what that says about our relationship – obviously there were a lot more than three faults on both sides!

3. Justin
This is an everyday piece of advice from me to me – something I've learned from bitter experience – never go shopping in the supermarket when you're hungry! Always go shopping on a full stomach. It's absolutely deadly if you don't – you spend a fortune, get fat, and end up with tons of stuff in your cabinets and fridge that goes bad!

4. Juliana
Before I left Mexico to work and travel in the U.S., my grandmother told me that travel is the best education next to books and, well, that was something her mother told her when she was young. She traveled quite a lot for a woman of that time.

5. Young-Il
Oh, my grandfather is a real sourpuss. And if … uh … if me and my brothers ever get excited or happy about anything, like we're really looking forward to going somewhere or watching a soccer game, every time he says the same thing: "Watch it boys – just remember it's better to travel hopefully than arrive." Just how miserable is that? And we say "Well, actually grandpa when our team wins, it's better to have arrived!" You know I think the only thing that makes him happy is being miserable. How sad is that? I'm not going to be like that when I'm old.

6. Victor
Well, I think the words of wisdom I remember most are from my mother who was a hippie in the 1960s, and she said, "Always follow your heart, especially with freedom and love." And there we are.

7. Sunny
I remember my grandmother saying to me – I can't remember what exactly it was about, I was depressed about something, I was just a kid, and she said to me, "This too will pass." I don't know, something had happened at school, whatever, and she was just saying, "Don't worry too much about it, it'll be over soon, it'll be a memory and this too will pass." And I thought that was a really good way of looking at things – you know bad things – they do pass, but I think it's also true of good things. It's important to make the most of good things 'cause they too will pass. It's a good piece of wisdom, don't you think?

8. Chris
Well, these are not really *words* of wisdom, these are *letters* of wisdom, I suppose. The letters are WP, which stand for … uh … willpower, which is something my grandmother repeats at regular intervals, mainly, I should say, to my grandfather. Basically she means that with willpower you can pretty much achieve anything, so if at first you don't succeed, keep persisting and eventually you'll get there. WP, WP!

9. Susana
Well, something my mom used to say a lot when I was younger – it's a little proverb I think and it's … uh … "Love many, trust a few, always paddle your own canoe." And that's something I've remembered all my life, and I suppose in a way I stick to it without really realizing that I am.

10. Rob
It comes from an actor friend of mine. He said this to me, I guess about 15 years ago, he just said, "Robbie, dust it off!" And "dust it off" essentially just means "just DO it."

CD2 20

"You are old, Father William," the young man said,
"And your hair has become very white;
And yet you incessantly stand on your head.
Do you think, at your age, it is right?"

"In my youth," Father William replied to his son,
"I feared it might injure the brain;
But, now that I'm perfectly sure I have none,

Why, I do it again and again."

"You are old," said the youth, "as I mentioned before,
And have grown most uncommonly fat,
Yet you turned a back somersault in at the door –
Pray, what is the reason of that?"

"In my youth," said the sage, as he shook his gray locks,
"I kept all my limbs very supple
By the use of this ointment – one shilling the box –
Allow me to sell you a couple?"

"You are old," said the youth, "and your jaws are too weak
For anything tougher than suet;
Yet you finished the goose, with the bones and the beak
Pray, how did you manage to do it?"

"In my youth," said his father, "I took to the law,
And argued each case with my wife;
And the muscular strength which it gave to my jaw,
Has lasted the rest of my life."

"You are old," said the youth, "one would hardly suppose
That your eye was as steady as ever;
Yet you balanced an eel on the end of your nose –
What made you so awfully clever?"

"I have answered three questions, and that is enough,"
Said his father. "Don't give yourself airs!
Do you think I can listen all day to such stuff?
Be off, or I'll kick you downstairs!"

CD2 21 See p. 64

UNIT 8

CD2 22

1. I suppose it's the eyes, really, that first drew my attention. Not only are they the most extraordinary shade of deep, dark green, they also show how frightened she is. The photo was taken in 1985 by a guy named Steve McCurry, and it was the beginning of yet another war in Afghanistan. This girl had lost her parents and grandparents, she was living in a refugee camp, and the photographer just caught her as she was coming out of her tent. You can see the dust on her face and the torn clothes, and her face is slightly at an angle. It made a real impact on me, that photograph.
2. It was one of the first examples I came across of modern sculpture, and I didn't really expect to like it. I think it's the combination of strength and gentleness that struck me most. All the lines of the mother's body are flowing, curved and soft. But the shoulders and arms surrounding the baby look big and strong, like a protective shield. I think it's a very accurate portrayal of motherhood, especially now that I have children of my own. I know what that fierce protectiveness toward your baby feels like.
3. From a distance it looks like a huge, white, upturned fishing boat and when you get closer that's exactly what it is like – the sides curve upward and seem to be made of white wooden slats. And, at regular intervals, along the sides, are long rectangular portholes, the windows, like long, curved, glassed-in ladders. Inside, despite all the usual departure boards, stores, restaurants and the like, it still feels like a boat – long escalators take you up to the bridge at the top and you walk out onto the platforms. It's visually stunning, and it all seems brilliantly suited to high-speed travel.
4. The first thing that strikes me is the serenity. There's a feeling that this scene has lasted forever

and will continue to last forever. It's very peaceful – Parisians out enjoying themselves on a Sunday afternoon. The people appear to be frozen in time. There is very little movement in the picture. The other thing that greatly interests me is the dappling of light through the leaves. When I first saw this picture, it was a moment of profound delight.

CD2 23 I = Interviewer,
JD = Joe Downing

Part one   The early years

I   Joe, have you always known that you wanted to paint?

JD   No, no, not by any means. I had no knowledge of art until I was twenty-two … uh … twenty-three years old. I grew up in … uh … very rural area, in Kentucky, a village of only a thousand people. The village of Horse Cave … uh …

I   Horse Cave?

JD   Yeah, Horse Cave, Kentucky … and there were no paintings of any kind in Horse Cave. No good paintings, no bad paintings … uh … just no paintings, but what there was, was an immense amount of beauty. We had a farm and there were seven children, but it was beautiful, there was nothing ugly in the house. We slept under the most beautiful patterned quilts, made by my mother and aunts and … uh … cousins.

I   So … so, was your family quite artistic then?

JD   No, no, that word couldn't apply to them – but they knew beautiful things, not just the quilts. I remember my mother calling me when she was shelling the beans that come in the fall, they were veined like marble, … uh … blue, pale purple, you know, very, very beautiful, and I remember her calling me and turning the beans in her hands in the sunlight and saying, "Look, look at the colors!"

I   So, was it … um … an idyllic childhood then?

JD   Well, except that at eighteen years old I was yanked out of my lovely country bumpkin life and thrown into the war – the Second World War and … uh … I landed in France … uh … had my nineteenth birthday in France, in Normandy, then we were sent to the front and I was engaged in the last year of the war in Germany and of course war … uh … that really changes you.

I   Yes, yes, I can imagine. And did you stay in France after the war?

JD   Uh, no, no, I went back to America, to Chicago to study to be an optometrist.

I   An optometrist? How … uh … ?

JD   Well, I had no real desire to be anything, and I had to study something, but I loved Chicago. It's an enormously vital city. It was like a second birth for me to be plunged into city life – *big* city life and I met people – writers, painters, interesting people – and early on, one of them took me to the museum in Chicago, which is just extraordinarily rich and beautiful and there … uh … I was twenty-three – and having never seen a painting in my life, I stood in front of *La Grande Jatte,* by Georges Seurat and …

I   Oh, yes, isn't that Sunday afternoon on the banks of the Seine in Paris?

JD   Yeah, yeah – and to stand in front of *La Grande Jatte,* one of the most extraordinary paintings that ever existed, having never seen a painting before, was for me a remarkable experience. It reshaped my whole life.

I   So without that … uh … you might never have become an artist?

JD   No – I don't think so really, because I would eventually have gone to some museum and seen some painting … I think.

CD2 24 Part two   On being a painter

I   But *your* painting is in an abstract style – *not* like Seurat – have you always painted like that?

JD   Oh, no, no, in the beginning I didn't … uh … I didn't want to be an abstract painter, but you must follow your bent or you're in trouble. You must forever follow where the painting leads you … uh … more than *you* lead the painting. But … um … in the beginning I did … um … landscapes and still life, I love still life, I still love still life – and I did some portraits, perhaps two or three were worth saving! And then it started to become abstract.

I   And your studies? The, um, optometry?

JD   No, no … uh … oh, no … I went back to France, to Paris and for seven years, in order to keep the pot boiling, I worked as a secretary for an American law firm, and I was careful to be a good secretary so that they gave me some free time, and I started doing collages and these were abstract. I did collages obsessively for four or five years, and I think they became the foundation … uh … for my whole painter's life.

I   So when you look back, you can identify different stages in your painting?

JD   I've had, I guess, three, in retrospect. I've had three major exhibitions at different stages, the first in 1968 – and when you look back you can see a very strong thread, what the French call a *fil conducteur,* and that remains the same, but the style changes slowly and constantly and if it doesn't, a painter should be worried, because if it doesn't change, you'll wither.

I   And when you look back, do you have any regrets about the way your work has evolved?

JD   Oh no, no – you must do what your nature tells you to otherwise and … uh … I've been enormously fortunate. Anyone who writes, who paints, who composes, any kind of artist knows how fragile it is – at any moment desire, the desire to do it can go.

I   I've noticed that one of the materials you work with, paint on, is leather, uh, small, small strips of leather. How did this come about?

JD   It's almost too ridiculous to tell. Um … I was having dinner with friends and … uh … an Italian friend from Milan had brought as a gift, a pasta-making machine, and in order to show how the machine worked, she made green lasagne for dinner. And … it was so beautiful coming out of the machine – it was pale green and the … the flour made little valleys and mountains. It was just beautiful, velvety-looking and I said, "I'm sorry it's going to look like I'm showing off, but I really must paint on this." So I made a tiny little landscape, a little rectangular painting on the lasagne, one for everybody at the table, including me, and at the end of dinner we all carefully took them home. And … uh … the next day the phone rang and it was my friend and she was crying and I said, "Why are you crying?" and she said, "Well, haven't you seen your lasagnà this morning?" So I ran to the kitchen and of course it had yellowed and cracked …

I   Ugh!

JD   … it looked awful, sick. So I said to my friend, "Look, quit crying, I'll find something that looks like green lasagnà and I'll make you another painting." So I spent two years looking and finally I came across that pale green leather that they use for making gardeners' gloves, and I made her a little painting, and it was just wonderful!

I   It's a wonderful story – it's a wonderful technique.

JD   Yes, and so the leather work began another stage in my painting. A new door opened.

CD2 25 Part three   On living in the South of France

I   I know you now live most of the time here in the village of Ménerbes, way south of Paris. How long have you lived here?

JD   I've been here thirty-three years.

I   It must have changed a lot in that time.

JD   Um … yes, and for the worse unfortunately … but that's true anywhere there's sunshine and olives and Roman tiles!
This was, still is really, an agricultural village – they grow extraordinary asparagus, beautiful asparagus. It starts now, in March – after that there are cherries, peaches, peppers, and melons … they're famous for the melons so they really didn't need tourism. Of course … uh … I know that's ridiculous and selfish and mean to want to enjoy the extraordinary beauty of this place and want others *not* to come … but it would be terrible to destroy the perfume of this place, a place I've loved.

I   And how did you discover it all those years ago?

JD   Well, every summer when I was living in Paris, and … uh … I can't drive …

I   Really! How do you get around?

JD   Oh, I just don't go anywhere. Anyways … every year, in summer, a friend, she would drive us down south, to the sea to swim … and one time we got down not far from here and she said, "I'm tired of lugging you two around. I do all the driving. This is a beautiful little place, let's stop and spend the night." So there was a charming little hotel, gone now unfortunately, uh … very pleasant. Next morning I got up much earlier than the others and … uh … went out into the village and … uh … there was a little dog, a young hunting dog, and he started up a hill, and I followed him, and he brought me by, what is now, a house, and a farmer was sitting there and he'd written in the top of a shoe box, with a piece of chalk, he'd written "RUINS FOR SALE" and so … uh … I asked him how much he was asking, and it was the only thing that I'd ever come across that we could afford to buy in the sun. So, … uh … on the spot, I asked to buy it and it was very inexpensive 'cause it was total ruins, open to the sky, it'd been empty for thirty years. It took us four years before we could sleep here. So, anyway, I went back to breakfast at the hotel and told them we all had a house! So that's the way it happened.

I   So you're back in a rural setting again?

JD   Yes, in a way it's odd that I should end up in a place that resembles so much where I grew up. Another farming community. Ménerbes has the same number of people as Horse Cave and the people even look the same.

I   A home away from home. And, just finally, and this, this is a big question. If you could live your life again, would you do anything differently?

JD   No, no – oh, well … I think I might skip a war … but otherwise – no.

CD2 26 Conversation B

A   Hi, Annie! I haven't seen you in ages.

B   I know. Time flies, doesn't it?

A   It's true. Work's busy as ever, is it?

B   Yes, I'm slaving away as usual, but we're a bit snowed under at the moment. We're just about keeping our heads above water, but it isn't easy. How about you?

A   OK. Business was bad this time last year, and we really had to tighten our belts, but things have picked up since then. You've moved, haven't you? Where are you living now?

B   We bought an old house in a sleepy little town. You must come and visit us.

A   I'd love to, but we're a bit tied up at the moment. Does it need much work?

B   Everything. I hope we haven't bitten off more than we can chew.

A   You'll be fine. Anyway, I have to scoot. Great to see you again.

B   You, too. Bye!

A I hear Pete's aunt left him everything.
B Absolutely right, he inherited a fortune out of the blue.
A He knew nothing about it? How exciting!
B You bet! When he heard about it, he was over the moon.
A So what's his problem now?
B Well, he's in deep water because he spent the whole shebang in a month, and then his girlfriend walked out on him.
A You're kidding. I thought he'd asked her to marry him?
B He was going to ask her, but then he got cold feet.
A So what next?
B Looks like he'll have to pull himself up by the bootstraps and get a job.
A And a new girlfriend. What about that girl he used to work with? Mm... Miranda, Marilyn – no, that's not it, uh, her name's on the tip of my tongue.
B You mean Melissa. Whatever you do, *don't* mention Melissa! She told him he was a waste of space, money or no money.
A Uh-oh. I'm glad you told me. I might have really put my foot in my mouth.

A Ugh! This hotel is horrible. I wish we hadn't come here. I've never seen such a dirty hotel in my life! It wouldn't be so bad if the bathroom was clean, but it's filthy. I wouldn't even wash my socks in it.
S I know, but it was getting late, and we'd been driving all day, and I wanted to stop. If we hadn't, we might not have found a hotel and we'd still be driving. That would have been awful. This is better than nothing.
A Well, I wish we'd left home earlier. Then we could have arrived in New York today, and we'd have had a whole day to go to galleries and museums. As it is, we won't get there till tomorrow lunchtime, and we'll only have a few hours.
S I'd have liked to spend more time in New York, too, but I had to go to work this morning. If I hadn't, we'd be staying in a nice hotel in New York now instead of this dump.
A I'd love to have seen a show, but we can't, so that's all there is to it. Anyway, it's time we thought about getting something to eat. If it weren't so late, I'd suggest going into town, but if we did, we might not find anything. It's pretty late already.
S I wish you wouldn't complain about everything. I wouldn't mind, but you're so indecisive. If it were left up to you, we'd never do anything or go anywhere.
A OK, OK. I'm sorry. Let's go.

a. 1. Can you help me?
 2. Could you help me?
 3. I wonder if you could help me?
 4. I was wondering if you could possibly help me?
b. 1. Do you mind if I open the window?
 2. Would you mind if I opened the window? It's so stuffy in here.
c. 1. I want to speak to you.
 2. I wanted to have a word with you, if that's all right.
d. 1. Dye it black.
 2. You could dye it black.
 3. If I were you, I'd dye it black.
 4. I'd have thought the best idea would have been to dye it black, but it's up to you.

1. **A** I'd like to reserve a table, please.
 B Certainly. What name, please?

2. **A** How old's Peter?
 B I would think he's about 60.
 C I'd say he's about 65.
 D I'd have thought he was nearer 70.
3. **A** I was wondering if you'd like to go out tonight?
 B Mmm! What were you thinking of?
 A I thought we could try that new pasta place.
4. **A** What time will we be leaving on Monday?
 B I was thinking of leaving about 8:30.
 A Don't you think we should leave a bit earlier to avoid rush hour?
 B That'd be fine.

1. Would you mind if I used your phone?
2. If I were you, I wouldn't paint the wall red.
3. Wouldn't it be better if we went in my car?
4. Would it be possible for you to call back later? Could you possibly call back later?
5. Don't you think we should call to say we'll be late?
6. I was hoping you might give me a ride to the station.
7. I would think she's French.
 I'd have thought she was French.
8. I was wondering if you'd like to come to the movies with me?
9. Would you mind filling out this form?
10. I wouldn't be surprised if it rained this afternoon.
11. I was thinking of going for a walk. Is anyone interested?
12. I just thought I'd pop in to see if you needed anything.
13. I'd say it's a bad idea.
 I'd have said it was a bad idea.
14. I'd have said that apologizing to her would be the best idea.
15. I gave her a present. You'd have thought she could have said thank you.

1. **A** Hi, Jenny. You doing OK?
 J Uh-huh. You?
 A Uh ... yeah. OK. Listen, Jenny. Are you doing anything tonight?
 J Gosh! Uh ... I don't know. Why?
 A Well, I was wondering if you'd maybe ... you know ... if we could go out somewhere ... if you ... if you'd like to.
 J Well, uh ... What did you have in mind?
 A Oh, I don't know. We could have a bite to eat, or we could see a movie. What do you think?
 J Well, that would be really nice. We could meet at the new cafe on High Street and take it from there. What do you think?
 A OK. Good idea. What time ...?
2. **A** Hello. The Bedford Hotel. Karen speaking. How can I help you?
 B I'd like to book a room, please.
 A Certainly, sir. I'll just put you through to reservations.
 B Thank you.
 R Reservations. Robert speaking. I understand you'd like to book a room.
 B That's right. For three nights starting Wednesday the fifteenth of this month.
 R For how many people?
 B Just me. I wonder if it would be possible to have a room at the back of the hotel. I'm afraid I can never get to sleep if I hear the traffic.
 R I'll just see what I can do, sir. Yes ... that's certainly possible. Your name was?
 B Brown. Jonathan.
 R Thank you, sir. Would you mind giving me a credit card number ... ?
3. **A** So what do you think of it?
 B It's fantastic!
 A It needs a lot of work, though. What do you think of the color scheme?

B It's too dark. Browns and blues and reds. You could go with something brighter. If I were you, I'd go for cream or white. You can't beat cream, it goes with everything.
A Mm ... maybe. What about the kitchen?
B Well, this is a bit of a disaster area, isn't it? I'd have thought the best idea would be to rip it all out and start again. I know it would be expensive, but at least you'd end up with a kitchen you love. No?
A Don't you think I should wait a while before I do that?
B Well, you could, but I wouldn't. I was thinking you could go to Ikea and get a whole new kitchen.
A Wow! Would you come with me?
4. **A** Hello.
 B Hi. Can I speak to Amanda, please?
 A She's not here right now. Sorry.
 B Ah, OK. Would you have any idea when she might be back?
 A I'd have thought she'd be back by 8:00. She usually is on a Tuesday.
 B Would you mind giving her a message? Could you tell her that Andy called, and I'll try her again after 8:00?
 A Sure.
 B Thanks a lot. Bye.
 A Bye.

UNIT 9

The day started, uh, much like any other day I got on the subway. We came across the bridge, and I remember noticing what a lovely day it was, uh, with the bright blue sky. I remember coming out of the subway as I normally did, and I saw a – saw a cloud, or what looked like a small cloud, white clouds and I remember thinking "Gosh, that's unusual because this sky is so totally clear" – but I didn't think much more of it, and I started walking to my office – I didn't get far. I got to the first block, and on the corner there were a couple of people, um, looking up, staring up at the tower, um, so I looked up at what they were looking at and, um, noticed that there, what seemed to be, to me, at the time, anyway, a small hole, and you could actually see a few bits of flame around the edge, and I asked these two people what had happened, and one of them said that a plane had flown into it, and I remember thinking, ah, no, can't be true. As I walked, there was more and more smoke coming out, but I made it to my office and went up to the 16th floor. So I went into the office, and there were lots of my colleagues there. Obviously there was a lot of confusion, so I went to one of these offices with the clearest view, and I looked out, and I remember thinking, "Gosh! I don't remember that, there's a hole in the other side." Quite a few people who'd been in the office earlier than me that morning, they'd, um, they'd seen both of them, they started telling me about this second one that went down the river, um, and sort of exploded towards them, um, because it came from the south, um, soon you could start to see – they'd obviously started to evacuate and there were just thousands of people walking straight up towards us, just pouring, pouring up towards us. I tried to phone family and friends, but none of the phones seemed to work, so I sent out an e-mail, that seemed to be the one thing that was still working. I couldn't speak to any of my family. I did speak to my wife once when I first got in, told her to wake up and turn on the television and see what was happening. After that, these sort of surreal goings on, sending these e-mails back and forth about what was happening outside my very window. And it was while I was writing an e-mail I heard some screams, and I ran around just to see sort of this huge, huge cloud of smoke and people just shouting and screaming, "It collapsed! It collapsed!" This huge cloud of dust came, you could see it pouring up the avenues, and it sort of burst out, uh, through Battery Park, right out into the Hudson River – because I remember seeing lots of the ferries were all doing evacuations, taking people from every point they could, and they just got enveloped in this huge cloud of dust. There was so much dust you didn't know, you know whether – how much of it had fallen, whether it was just the top. I suppose we were all expecting to see something still there. We could still see the other one standing because it had the big antenna, the big aerial on top of it. So as we stood there watching it, no idea for how long, and then of course, the other one collapsed. You could clearly see, there's a very particular design, these long, long sort of slightly ornate metal work. I remember seeing that sort of explode out and then you just saw the great big top with this giant aerial on, just drop straight down, and you'd see all this other stuff just peeling away from the sides, um, you could see each corner of it peeling back and this giant top just smashing down through it and obviously there was all the dust and everything and, um, more screaming. We all thought 'cause we'd seen so many, so many thousands of people walking north that maybe everyone had gotten out because there was this, you know, non-stop procession of people. In fact, I think our brains didn't even think about the fact that there were people inside it, you just sort of looked at it as a building, and you just assumed there was no one in it, you just don't actually want to think about that. It was, you know, unlike any feeling you've ever thought, there wasn't really – there was no panic in the office, and also a very clear acknowledgement that, um, something had changed, had – something had changed in the world today, and we were sitting staring at it. It was the most incredible thing, and from what was just a normal lovely New York autumn day, it's just incredible how much changed in that morning.

CD3 | 3

1. After the performance she took five bows.
   She wore five bows in her hair.
2. That was never him singing live. He was lip-synching.
   "Live and let live" is my philosophy.
3. Close that window! There's a draft.
   You're not close to getting the answer.
4. I soon got used to working the late shift.
   I don't trust used-car dealers. I'd never buy a car from one.
5. It's impossible to tear open this packet. Give me a knife.
   A single tear ran silently down her cheek as she waved good-bye.
6. He always looks so content with himself.
   The content of your essay was excellent, but there were a lot of spelling mistakes.
7. The teacher complained to the parents about their son's conduct in class.
   General MacIntyre has been appointed to conduct the next stage of the war.
8. Could you record the next episode for me? I'm going out that night.
   He's broken the Olympic world record for the 100-meter dash.

CD3 | 4 A, B, C, D, F = British soldiers, E = German soldier

A Hey, listen!
B Yeah, they're coppin' it down Railway Wood tonight.
A Nah, nah, not that. Listen. What is it?
C Singin' innit?

B It's those Welsh bastards in the next trench.
C That's Jerry, that is.
B Yeah, it is Jerry. It's comin' from over there.
D Sing up, Jerry! Let's 'ear yer!
C Oh nice, weren't it?
E Tommy? Hello Tommy!
B Eh! 'E 'eard us!
C 'Ello?
E *Fröhliche Weihnacht!*
C Eh?
B What?
E Happy Christmas!
ALL Oh! 'Appy Christmas!
F Hey, yeah, it's Christmas!

CD3 | 5 I = Interviewer, GW = Graham Williams, HS = Harold Startin

Part one

I That scene from the West End musical of the 1960s *Oh What a Lovely War!* is a pretty accurate illustration of the kind of thing that happened in several places on the Western Front on that Christmas Eve of 1914. Listen to the account of someone who was actually there. Graham Williams, a rifleman with the London Rifle Brigade, was on sentry duty that night.
GW On the stroke of 11 o'clock, which by German time was midnight, 'cause they were an hour ahead of us, lights began to appear all along the German trenches, and uh … then people started singing. They started singing *Heilige Nacht, Silent Night*. So I thought, "Well, this is extraordinary!" And I woke up all the other chaps, and all the other sentries must have done the same thing, to come and see what was going on. They sang this carol right through, and we responded with English Christmas carols, and they replied with German again, and when we came to *Come All Ye Faithful*, they joined in singing, with us singing it in Latin, *Adeste Fideles.*
I So by the time you got to that carol, both sides were singing the same carol together?
GW Both singing the same carol together. Then after that, one of the Germans called out, "Come over and see us, Tommy. Come over and see us!" So I could speak German pretty fluently in those days, so I called back … I said, "No, you come over and see us!" I said, "*Nein, kommen … zuerst kommen Sie hier, Fritz!*" And nobody did come that time, and eventually the lights all burned out, and quietened down and went on with the usual routine for the night. Next morning I was asleep, when I woke up I found everyone was walking out into no-man's land, meeting the Germans, talking to them, and … wonderful scene … couldn't believe it!
I Further along the line in the perfect weather, Private Harold Startin of the Old Contemptibles was enjoying that morning, too. He couldn't speak any German, but that didn't stop him from making friends.
HS We were all "Tommy" to them, and they were all "Fritz" to us. They couldn't have been more cordial towards you, all sharing their goodies with you. They were giving us cigars about as big as your arm, and tobacco.
I Were you frightened at first? Were you suspicious at all? Because these were people …
HS No!
I … that you'd been trained to hate, weren't they?
HS No! There was no hatred, we'd got no grudge against them, they'd got no grudge against us. We were … we were the best of pals, although we were there to kill one another, there were no two ways about that at all. They helped us bury our dead, and we buried our dead with their dead. I've seen many a cross with a German name and number on and a British name and number on. "In death not divided."

I Did you do other work during the truce as well? Was it just burying the dead, or were there other things …
HS Oh, there was strengthening the trenches, borrowing their tools …
I You actually borrowed German tools to strengthen your trenches?
HS We borrowed German tools. They … then … they'd come and help you strengthen your defenses against them.

Part two

I Not only was the truce more extensive than anyone has realized before, it also lasted much longer than has been believed until now. In some areas, the war started up again on New Year's Day, but in the part of the line where Harold Startin was, the truce lasted a lot longer than that.
HS Ours, it went on for six weeks. You can read in the history books about Sir John French, when he heard of it, he were all against it. But our truce went on for six weeks. And the Württemberg Regiment, they got relieved before we did, and they told us they thought it were the Prussian Guards goin' to relieve them, and if it was, we should only hear three rifle shots at intervals, and if we only heard three rifle shots we should know that the Prussian Guards were opposite us then, and we'd got to keep down.
I Because they would be fiercer than …
HS Yes!
I … than the Württembergers?
HS Yes!
I Can you remember particular Germans that you spoke to? Over six weeks you must have made friends?
HS I spoke to one, Otto, comes from Stuttgart, 'as … 'as been over to England to see me.
I So you made friends during the truce and kept in touch after the war?
HS Made friends during the truce, and friends after.

CD3 | 6

1. "Oh great! I got the job!"
   "Well done! I knew you would."
2. "My car's making this strange rattling sound."
   "It sounds bad. You should really get it serviced."
3. "Oh no! I've missed the last bus!"
   "Don't worry. We'll give you a ride."
4. "Will you all stop making so much noise!"
   "We're not. We're just talking quietly."
5. "Don't worry, dad. I'll be home by eleven."
   "You'd better be, because if you're not, you're grounded for a week!"
6. "Did you make all this mess?"
   "I'm sorry, really, I am."
7. "I get so nervous when I have to speak in public."
   "Take deep breaths before you start."
8. "We climbed right to the top in record time."
   "Oh yeah? Prove it!"

CD3 | 7 See page 86

CD3 | 8 See page 86

CD3 | 9 See page 86

UNIT 10

CD3 | 10

1. And they're coming into the straight, Cornichon leads from Pegasus who is being closely challenged by River Island. River Island has moved into second place. Cornichon's still going well. They're approaching the winning post. It's

going to be a photo finish … Cornichon has beaten River Island, with Pegasus in third place. What a thrilling finish to this race!
2. Johnson receives the ball in his own half, passes to Mimosa. Mimosa dribbles past two defenders and shoots. Oh! The goalkeeper knocks it behind for a corner kick. The ball comes into the center. The striker, Hughes, is in position and heads the ball into the back of the net! What a goal! Chicago's now up two–nil!
3. It's deuce. Mintoff serves, Everett returns, but Mintoff's at the net, and volleys the ball deep. Everett runs and hits the ball cross-court, but Mintoff's got it covered and punches it down the line. Advantage Mintoff, and match point. She serves to her opponent's backhand, Everett struggles to get the ball back, but it goes into the net. Game, set, and match to Mintoff, 6–4, 6–2.
4. There's the bell for round six and Manson's straight back into the center of the ring. Buckley moves in slowly from his corner. Manson gets in a good punch, he's caught him on the chin and the man from Houston crumples to the canvas. The count starts, Buckley's trying to get up, 8, 9, 10 – he's not up! It's a knockout in Round 6. Manson takes the World Heavyweight title home to Michigan!
5. The Red Sox are two runs down in the ninth inning. They have men on first and second base, a home run now would win it. Jackson swings and misses the first and second pitches. He hits the third pitch cleanly. It looks good. It flies across the field and lands in the stands. A 3-run homer to Jackson and the Red Sox win the game 7–6.
6. The eighteenth hole is a par-three. Mallestro's first shot put him on the green, just two yards from the hole. Spink put his first in the lake, and has taken two shots to get to the green. If Mallestro putts from here he'll win. He strikes it well, the ball trickles to the edge of the hole, and yes, it's in. Mallestro wins the round and the tournament.

CD3 11
1. Annabel is very smart, but Sonia is absolutely brilliant.
2. I thought the book was really stupid, but the movie was absolutely ridiculous.
3. The meal was very pleasant, and the company absolutely delightful.
4. My mother was quite upset, but my father was really devastated.
5. Their house was really unusual, but their garden was quite extraordinary.
6. Her shoes were really expensive, but the dress was absolutely exorbitant.

CD3 12
1. Kate thinks math is hard, and she's absolutely right.
   Kate thinks math is hard, and she's quite right.
2. Personally, I find math totally impossible.
   Personally, I find math quite impossible.
3. She's absolutely terrified of dogs.
   She's completely terrified of dogs.
4. I was very pleased to hear you're getting married.
   I was really pleased to hear you're getting married.
5. I'm sure you'll be extremely happy together.
   I'm sure you'll be really happy together.

CD3 13
1. This cheese is really good. You should try it.
2. I'm absolutely determined to lose weight.
3. The restaurant was pretty nice, but I wouldn't recommend it.
4. The movie was quite interesting. You should see it.
5. If you ask her, I'm pretty sure she'll say yes.

CD3 14   M = Marco, J = James
M Wow, amazing. You know he's back on the circuit this year?
J Sorry, … who's back on what?
M You know, Lance Armstrong … he's the only guy to have won the Tour de France seven times.
J 'Course I know him, he's my all-time sports hero! Ever since I started cycling in my first year at school and …
M I didn't know that you used to …
J Oh yeah, but I gave it up, didn't I – totally, absolutely, completely too lazy to cycle every day! So, how does it say Lance manages it?
M It says here it's all in his secret training routine – he's been in the gym three or four hours a day, five days a week when he's not in a tournament. It says everything he does, from cardiovascular to weight training. A trainer helps him prepare his joints… says here, prepares him for battle…
J Boy, do I remember the battle – Jeez, was I stiff the next day … had joints like an old man.
M Yeah – day in, day out, Lance's down at the gym working out – working on joints, muscles, cardio. Is that man focused or what? Doesn't sound like the kind of lifestyle you'd go for!
J Hey, whoa there … he doesn't have my health problems …
M Oh yeah? And what might those be?
J Uh…well…I … uh… my bad back …
M Oh yeah … only if you're asked to get up and do something like … uh…
J Like what?
M Open a bag of chips! Well, actually… in fact, Lance Armstrong does have health problems .. real ones – not imaginary…
J Like?
M Well you know he's had cancer, and tumors removed…
J You're kidding. I had no idea.
M Yeah, he's had chemotherapy, and he still won the Tour de France. Doesn't sound much like you – you get whiny if you break a fingernail!
J Hey, not fair! You've got nothing to brag about yourself, what about that time you …
M Whatever … but just take a look at Lance's diet, he eats so lean, chicken and broccoli.
J Obviously will never gain a pound… how does he manage, with that kind of workout?
M Says here he's a fitness freak and eats chicken breasts and broccoli, only it's four chicken breasts and a bucket of broccoli!
J And just sooo dedicated to his sport …
M Hey … but you know he also has a charitable foundation. How he keeps up with it all …
J … and keeps winning…
M Yeah. He sounds like a really decent guy – modest – says being a role model is what it's all about, influencing a person's life in a positive light…. you know his foundation raises money for cancer research and support. He's raised millions of dollars.
J Hey, I was thinking of doing that!
M What? Raising millions of dollars?
J Idiot… no, I thought I might start a charity.
M With your laziness!
J OK, maybe next year.

CD3 15   A = Alicia, K = Kate
A C'mon Kate, let's look for stuff about your all-time heroine . .
K So who's that?
A Nastia Lukin, of course. C'mon, she must have a website …
K Hey, you love her, too! Good grief, how many of her posters do you have on your wall?
A I've never counted them - I just think she's the most fantastic gymnast. Hey, look, there's a lot here, some great pics, a bio, an interview – everything.
K Oh, her real name's Anastasia. I didn't know that.
A Look how pretty she is in that picture.

K I just think she's the best gymnast. You know, her parents were Olympic gymnasts, too! Can you believe that?
A Yeah, it says that here. They brought her to the gym where they worked out because they couldn't afford a babysitter!
K Alicia, do you remember when we started?
A Do I! I cried all the way through the first class. I didn't want to go back! But hey, we were only seven.
K This says she was only three years old at the time, playing on the bars at her parents' gym and copying the older children.
A Yeah, and she started competing when she was six! She was really passionate about it.
K Well, I'm passionate about it, you're passionate about it, but it doesn't make us great gymnasts like Nastia!
A Tell me about it. Do you think we're the wrong shape? I mean, look at her. She's so compact and muscular and we're . . .
K Come on, shut up about that, scroll down some more. Look, it says her favorite food is sushi.
A How does she survive on sushi? She must eat a lot of other things. She's got to get her energy from somewhere.
K This says she eats whatever she wants to . . .
A . . . but she prefers to eat healthy food. Oatmeal, eggs, yogurt, salad . . .Oh, look here. She says, "Don't go crazy about dieting! Eat healthy, but if you want to splurge and have a cookie, then have a cookie. Depriving yourself is the worst."
K I'll say. And she says to exercise every day. Well, we exercise every day, and there's no way we'll ever look like her.
A Yeah, but you know it takes a lot more than exercise to become a gymnast like Nastia. I mean, you have to give up your whole life for it. It's not just an hour at the gym every day.
K Of course. Just look at us, we're exhausted after a two-hour lesson!
A That's true. Do you know, she trains seven hours a day?
K It says here that two of those seven hours are warming up and conditioning. I guess she'd have major problems if she didn't.
A It's crazy – I don't think I could be that dedicated about anything. How in the world does she do it?
K I don't know. I think gymnasts just get used to exhaustion and pain.
A And injuries. Says here she had to have surgery on her ankle, that the recovery was really long. All the while, she was getting ready for the Olympics!
K Can you imagine? And then she won the gold. All those people who said she couldn't do it, after her injury . . .
A Yeah, she showed them, all right.

CD3 16   See page 94

CD3 17
1. Mom! Tommy broke the vase!
   It's OK. Accidents happen.
2. I just need to go back in the house and make sure I've turned off the iron.
   Good idea. Better safe than sorry.
3. It's been raining nonstop for weeks! We need some sunshine!
   You can say that again.
4. I got a card from Jeremy a week after my birthday.
   Oh, well. Better late than never.
5. We're going away for two weeks.
   Sounds like just what the doctor ordered.

6. Took me ten years to build this business. Nearly killed me.
   Well, you know what they say. No pain, no gain.
7. Tom failed his exams, Amy has chicken pox. What's next?
   Uh-oh! They say bad luck comes in threes.
8. They have ten kids. Goodness knows what their house is like.
   It boggles the mind.
9. Bob's a strange guy. Did you hear he's going to walk across Europe?
   It takes all kinds.

CD3 18

1. My uncle has never married. He lives in a trailer. He only eats cheese, and he has twenty-five cats.
2. James Herriot had three jobs and wrote nonstop for five years before his book became a bestseller.
3. Isn't it nice when the kids are in bed. The house is quiet, and we can relax!
4. I finally got a date for my knee replacement operation. I've had to wait two months.
5. When I go abroad, I make sure I have life insurance, medical insurance, and traveler's insurance.
6. We had a great vacation. Two weeks sitting around a swimming pool, reading and relaxing.
7. I've spilled coffee on your carpet. I'm really sorry.
8. I've lost the car keys, I've burned the meal, and the washing machine is clogged. How bad is that?
9. My daughter is on a cabbage soup diet. She eats nothing else.

UNIT 11

CD3 19

1. How old is the earth?
   The current scientific estimate for the age of the earth is 4.6 billion years. There are numerous indicators that the earth was in existence billions of years ago, but it is still impossible to prove exactly how many billions.
2. The earth is considered to have a maximum of seven continents. What are they?
   A continent is one of several major land masses on the earth. These are Africa, Antarctica, Asia, Australia, Europe, North America, and South America. Many geographers and scientists now refer to just six continents, where Europe and Asia are combined (since they're one solid land mass).
3. How many countries are there in the world?
   There are 193 countries in the world. Kosovo is the most recent country, having gained independence from Serbia in 2008.
4. Which continent has the most countries?
   Africa is home to 53 independent countries, representing more than 25 percent of the countries of the world. The largest African country is Sudan.
5. What is the population of the world?
   The population of the world is 6.7 billion people, and it is growing all the time. Current research indicates that about five people are born every second, whereas two people die, leaving us with a population increase of three new human beings per second.
6. Which country has the largest population?
   China. It is home to more than 1.3 billion people. India is currently the world's second most populous country with 1.1 billion people,

but by 2040, India is expected to have the largest population.
7. What proportion of the earth is covered by water?
   71 percent of the Earth's surface is covered in water, which maintains the temperature of the planet. Of the 71 percent, 97 percent is salt water, 3 percent is fresh water, of which 1 percent is drinking water.
8. How many oceans are there? What are they?
   Most often the world is divided into four major oceans – the Pacific Ocean, Atlantic Ocean, Arctic Ocean, and Indian Ocean. Some consider there to be five oceans – the fifth being the Antarctic Ocean.
9. How much of the earth's land surface is used to grow food?
   Only 11 percent of the land surface is used to grow food. 31 percent is forest, 27 percent is desert and wilderness, 26 percent is pasture land. 5 percent is urban.
10. Where is the world's largest desert? What is it called?
    The Sahara Desert in northern Africa is the world's largest desert. At more than 3.5 million square miles, it is slightly smaller than the size of the United States.
11. What's the difference between a political and a physical map?
    A political map shows human-created features such as boundaries, cities, roads, and railroads. Physical maps display the natural features of the earth – the location and names of mountains, rivers, valleys, ocean currents, and deserts. Most common maps and globes are combinations of political and physical maps.
12. What is the world's largest island?
    At 840,000 square miles, Greenland is the world's largest island. Australia also meets the definition of an island, but it is large enough to be considered a continent.

CD3 20

1. He gave us some delicious, homemade, whole wheat bread, which was still warm from the oven.
2. A funny little old Irish lady arrived, wearing a big feathered hat.
3. I bought a gorgeous red and white striped silk shirt with gold buttons.
4. She just had a beautiful, fat, bouncing baby boy with lots of brown, curly hair.
5. He showed me into a delightful, light, airy, high-ceilinged living room with all-white furniture and carpets.
6. I met a trendy, young Venezuelan art student who's living in Toronto at the moment.
7. She's wearing shiny, tight-fitting, black leather pants with back pockets.
8. It's an exquisite, sweet-smelling apricot-colored rose bush covering the whole wall.

CD3 21

1. Theo
I think the most unusual and interesting place that I've visited is … um … a place called the *Salar de Uyuni*, which is in the south of Bolivia, and it is … uh … an enormous salt plain and … um … we had to drive out of the nearest town and drive for two days … um … without electricity or running water, those kinds of things . … um … it's about 16,000 feet above sea level most of the time, and most of it is almost completely white because it's covered in salt … um … but because of the mineral content every now and then you get these incredible, strangely colored lakes, like bright red and bright green lakes, and … um … chocolate caramel covered mountains and things like that. I've got photos that when I look at them they look like trick photography of some sort because all the colors are so strange, but that's exactly how I remember it.

2. Lucy
I went to Sydney last, last year in November. I went to, went on a little four-day tour and one of the places I stopped at was a little place called Nundle, and there was a sheep station and it was just out in the sticks and they had … they had a disco at night, and they had the volume up full blast because there was no one, no neighbors, in so many miles, and I just remember dancing and, at the end of the night, the toilets were outside, so I was brushing my teeth and dancing away to the music that was still going on, under the stars, and it was absolutely gorgeous … it was really good. I really enjoyed that.

3. Joe
I think the place that felt most sort of remote from – from normal life was Iceland where I went last year … um … actually on a, on a biking trip … um … which was incredibly empty, I mean really strange landscapes with lots of glaciers and volcanoes and strange volcanic smells … um … and almost no people and constant very high wind, and it really felt like the end of the world.

4. Michi
I once visited a place called Moose Factory, which is a tiny island community in the middle of the Moose River in Canada, and when the river freezes in the winter you can drive a car or a truck across the ice to get to the island, but in the spring and fall, when the ice is thin, the only way to enter or leave the island is by plane, and of course in the summer, people travel across the river by boat.

5 James
The most far-flung or unusual place that I've visited was … is probably … uh … I went to … uh … in Colombia, in the Sierra Nevada Mountains, I went to a place called the Lost City … Lost City, *La Ciudad Perdida* and it was a three-day hike into the jungle, in the tropical rain forest, then a long hike up a basically kind of a hill and into a … um … into this village, which was buried in the jungle up until about fifty years ago, when treasure hunters were out looking for it … um … it was consumed by the jungle … kind of like an Incan thing, but that was a different tribe, but it had all these beautiful rock terraces and … uh … it was an amazing trip..… it was good, it was very kind of Indiana Jones.

6. Linda
The weirdest place that I've ever visited has to be underwater in Sardinia, because I'd never actually snorkeled before, so I put on the mask, looked below, and realized that we only really live on half of the planet, and I just could not believe what I saw, I just felt really small. I was completely out of my depth in every sense, and … um … it kinda put me in my place in a way, because it wasn't man's world and … uh … I was shocked. I was terrified, actually.

CD3 22

Yes, that was a wonderful story. I was … there was a new railway line constructed across far western China, from a place called Urunchi, through a pass called the Zungarian Gate … into what is now Kazakhstan … and I thought it would be nifty to ride on one of the first trains, of course it's an extremely remote part of the world. So I go with a friend of mine named George Robertson, and the two of us go out from Urunchi, crossing the desert and now we're about 150 miles west of Urunchi and it's just sand dunes and nothing. And then suddenly the train stops and I look out and there's this "halt." I mean it's not a station, there's no town, there's just a sort of water tower, and I say to the conductor, "Why have we stopped?" and he said, "Oh, we're taking on water," or something like that, and, "we'll be stopped for half an hour." So I get out and stretch my legs in the blazing sun, the sand dunes, with the camels, until I go and talk to the engine driver and while I'm doing so, I hear a voice from the si.. behind me, saying in pretty impeccable English, "Excuse me, do you speak English?" And I turn around and there is this vision of loveliness, this beautiful Chinese woman and I said, "Yes, I do actually," and she said "Good!" in a very sort of matter-of-fact, slightly unsmiling way.

CD3 23

She looked at her watch and she said, "This train is stopping here for another 27 minutes. Have you ever read the works of Anthony Trollope?" And I'm thinking, wait a minute this is really strange, but, "Yes, I like Trollope a lot." "Good," she said. "Would you be willing to discuss with me *The Eustace Diamonds*, particularly the character of Lady Glencora?" I'm thinking, "this is not happening," but I do my best, struggling, I mean I must have read *The Eustace Diamonds* twenty years before. I could just about remember odds and ends, so I struggle through a conversation with her, and then the guard waved his green flag and blew a whistle and she said, "Quick, quick go back, otherwise you'll miss your train." So I … but I said, "You're beautiful. I love you, I want to live with you for the rest of my life," and she said, "Don't be so silly! Get in the train. Give me your business card." So I didn't have one, but George had one, so I scribbled my name and the train was moving. And the last vision I have of her was her scrambling on her hands and knees to pick up my card while we went around the corner, and I went back into the compartment and I said, "George, I've just had the most really strange experience"… so we then went traveling all over Siberia for the next couple of months, and I arrived back in Hong Kong and there was a letter …

CD3 24

… there was a letter and she said:
"Dear Mr Winchester, I just want you to know that meeting you that day was just one of the most extraordinary events of my life. I … am married to a cadre in the Chinese communist party and we were … he committed some infraction and we were sent to this ghastly little town … it was called Kwi Tun. Nothing happens here. It's 30 miles away from the road and from the railway line. There's no one here that speaks English. I'm the only person, but I'm desperate not to lose my language, so the international train goes through every Tuesday and Thursday, and I bike all the way across the desert, down to the train station, wait for it to come in, knock on every compartment to see if there's anyone there that speaks English. Occasionally there's some sort of migrant worker … but one day I meet this man who not only can speak English, but is English and, my passion is Trollope. He knew all about Trollope. I was able to speak for 25 minutes about Trollope and it was like … you were like an angel from heaven. It was wonderful."Anyway, we're the very best of friends. We have been for years.

CD3 25

1. I don't like children who always have to be the center of attention.
2. The trip from work to home, which usually takes half an hour, took over two hours yesterday.
3. Politicians who make extravagant promises aren't worth listening to.
   Politicians, who make extravagant promises, aren't worth listening to.
4. The Taj Mahal, which took twenty-two years to complete, is built from exquisitely carved white marble.
5. These are the photographs I was telling you about.
6. We docked at the small port on the coast of East Africa where my parents lived twenty years ago.
7. My cousin, who's a real thrill-seeker, went hang-gliding last weekend.
   My cousin who's a real thrill-seeker went hang-gliding last weekend.

8. We went on a biking trip in Mexico, where there are some really steep hills.

CD3 26

1. A Believe me. That guy's really on the ball.
   B No kidding! He landed that consultancy job that we all applied for.
2. A The vacation's over. It's back to the real world.
   B You can say that again. Back to earth with a crash!
3. A What? You're not coming out on Saturday night?!
   B I can't. I failed my chemistry exam, and I've been grounded for a month.
4. A Hey! Great to see you! I thought you weren't going to be able to make it.
   B I almost didn't. I had to move heaven and earth to get here.
5. A Come on, you know you really want to go out with him.
   B In your dreams. Not if he were the last man on earth!
6. A Do you understand these instructions? Where in the world do all these screws go?
   B Don't ask me. I have no idea.

UNIT 12

CD3 27

We are immediately struck by the softness of the sunshine and the activities of the countryside. The everyday pursuits of the three common men pictured – the plowman, the shepherd, and the fisherman – are being carried out with apparent pleasure.
It takes the viewer some time to realize the central event of the painting, the splash of a pair of legs as the fallen Icarus plunges into the sea. They are caught at the precise moment that this symbol of human pride is about to disappear forever. It is ironic that no one is paying attention. All of the movement in the picture is away from the main event. The plowman and shepherd, oblivious, go about their business, as does the fully-rigged boat, also sailing away from the fallen figure.
Landscape with the Fall of Icarus can be interpreted as a warning against pride and ambition. The plowman who labors on, ignoring the hapless Icarus, exemplifies the ideal of the common man, who remains content with his modest lot in life. We should not search for personal gain, nor have ambitions above our station in life. Bruegel will have known the Flemish proverb,"No plow stops for the sake of a dying man."
In the painting we also see life as a process of continuation. No matter what momentous events are happening in the world, near to you or far away, despite wars, death, natural disasters, famine, plagues, or earthquakes, life goes on.

CD3 28 See page 107

CD3 29

Salvador Dalí was born in 1904 in a small town, Figueres, in Catalunya, northeast Spain, where his father was a prestigious notary.
Wanting to study art, Dalí went to the Royal Academy of Art in Madrid, but he was expelled from the Academy twice, as a result of which he never took his final examinations.
In 1928 he went to Paris, where he met the Spanish painters Pablo Picasso and Joan Miró, and established himself as the principal figure of a group of surrealist artists, whose leader was André Breton.
By 1929 Dalí found the style, consisting of the world

of the unconscious recalled during our dreams, that would make him famous.
In 1927 he met Gala, a Russian immigrant ten years older than Dalí.
In 1940 Dalí and Gala went to the United States, where he stayed for eight years until 1948, when they returned to Europe, spending most of their time in Spain or Paris.
When Gala died in 1982, Dalí became deeply depressed and moved to Púbol, a castle he had bought for Gala.
He lived in his castle for the rest of his life, dying there in 1989 of heart failure.

CD3 30 RP = Raj Persaud, FG = Father Griffin, AW = Andrew Walker, JP = Jean-Pierre Bely

Part One

RP We're in the central square of Lourdes, and there's literally thousands of people, most of them fairly elderly, congregating here. A lot of them have brought their own chairs to sit on. It's very quiet, given what a large crowd there is here. And people don't seem to be talking to each other. They seem to be … almost reverential. A lot of them have heads bowed. Very introspective atmosphere. And you feel that when you're talking, you should really be whispering.
Lourdes must be the strangest tourist destination in the world. A hundred thousand seriously ill people come every year, many in wheelchairs or on stretchers, to mingle with millions of able-bodied pilgrims and camera-carrying tourists. There are 30,000 hotel beds in a town of just 15,000 permanent residents. But in the midst of it all lies the sanctuary, several square miles of ring-fenced holy ground, containing three churches, and the famous grotto, where Bernadette Soubirous saw visions of the Virgin Mary, over 140 years ago.
Any pilgrims looking for spiritual guidance amidst a maze of garish souvenir shops can turn to Father Liam Griffin, who's sort of the official tour rep for English speaking visitors … Father Griffin, we're walking in the sanctuary here at the moment. There're thousands of people here today. How important is Lourdes within the Catholic Church?
FG Lourdes is a place of pilgrimage. It is a place where the Blessed Virgin Mary appeared to Bernadette Soubirous back in 1858, and in that way it is an important place of prayer. According to our statistics, about six million people come here every year.

Part Two

RP What is it about this place, this experience, that attracts so many people? Lourdes has long been associated with the miraculous. The spring that Bernadette discovered in 1858 is said to have healing properties, and the place has been linked with sudden dramatic cures of the seriously ill. But in the twenty-first century, I'm puzzled as to why more and more people are coming to Lourdes each year. Are they looking for something that modern science can't offer?
AW We've gone through a much more intellectual, rational age, where science is perhaps the dominant discourse in academic life these days. And it seems to preclude miracles. And modern Christians are divided as to whether they still occur, or whether they only existed in the past.
RP Andrew Walker is Professor of Theology, Religion and Culture at King's College, London.
AW The whole of Christianity, rightly or wrongly, is based on an idea that a man was also God raised from the dead. You can't get anything more miraculous than that. But it doesn't alter

the fact that even if there were no miracles, I think from a sociological point of view, we do need to believe in the impossible, and you find it in Hinduism, and Christianity, and Judaism. There's a certain theatrical joy about the possibility that God can intervene in the world and change things.

Part Three

RP In 1999, Jean-Pierre Bely became the most recent person officially confirmed to have been cured at Lourdes.

JP The illness began in 1971–72, at first very discreetly. There were very minor symptoms, slight manifestations of disease, such as fatigue, a lack of suppleness and mobility in my hands, pins and needles in my fingertips. I work as a nurse in a hospital, so I just chalked it up to stress. Over the years things got worse, but the actual diagnosis wasn't made until 1984, after a particularly violent attack that left me partly paralyzed. It was after this that I went to the hospital, and the doctors carried out a thorough examination. Afterwards the doctor, who I knew from my work as a nurse, said to me, "Jean-Pierre. Prepare yourself for the worst. I think you have multiple sclerosis."

RP By 1987 Jean-Pierre was bedridden, and he even had his house modified structurally to accommodate his extreme disability. Later that year, he was persuaded to go on a pilgrimage to Lourdes, but while taking part in morning mass, he was overcome by a strange experience.

JP At that moment, everything was turned upside down, and I was sucked into a whirlwind of emotion, of joy, of peace, and an extraordinary feeling of serenity that came over me, which remains with me still to this day. The second part of the cure took place later that same day. I was back in the sick room, lying on the bed, and felt terribly cold, like an intense chill in my bones. But slowly it got warmer and warmer, until it felt like a fire burning through the whole of my body. I was overwhelmed by it. I heard this voice, like an order, "Get up and walk!" And then, all of a sudden, I don't know how, I found myself sitting up on the bed, my legs dangling over the edge, and I started to touch the back of my hands. I realized I'd regained mobility and sensitivity in my spine and shoulders, which had been blocked for years. They were normal. In fact, you could say I'd found normality again.

RP By the time Jean-Pierre, now able to walk again, returned home, all signs of his crippling illness had vanished. And remain so today.

Part Four

RP It's perhaps no surprise that scientific research has confirmed what millions of pilgrims have always known, that visiting Lourdes profoundly improves your mental state. But this raises troubling questions for a doctor like myself. After all, I prescribe anti-depressants to my patients. Why not visits to Lourdes? What's stopping me? Well, personally I'm unhappy with the idea that just because something may seem inexplicable at the moment, that it means the only account left is a spiritual solution. Perhaps the key point about a miracle is that it is a mechanism for providing hope when in many circumstances, there is no hope. For me, the danger of modern medicine is that when it runs out of technological answers, as it does for millions of the seriously ill, it turns its back and offers nothing else. Into this chasm of despair steps religion, miracles, and hope. And Lourdes as a concrete place you can visit, it provides an opportunity to renew your belief that something good can still come of catastrophe.

Grammar Reference

UNIT 1

Avoiding repetition

To avoid repetition in many languages, it is common for words to be left out. This is called ellipsis. In English it is common for the main verb to be left out, leaving just the auxiliary, and this can cause problems.

1.1 Using auxiliaries to avoid repetition

In short answers

When a *Yes/No* question is asked, we use the auxiliary on its own when answering rather than repeating the whole verb form.
"Will it rain this afternoon?" "Yes, I think it will (rain this afternoon).*"*
"Should I study for this test?" "Yes, I think you should (study for the test*).*"

Commenting on given information

When we make comments in conversation, we usually avoid repeating information that has just been given.
"Mary's coming." "I know she is."
"Angela can speak Spanish and Chinese." "She can't, can she?"

Note

Where there is no auxiliary verb in Present and Past Simple positive statements, *do/does/did* is used to reply. This is to avoid repeating the full verb.
"I love Mexico." "I do too, and so does James."
"I thought the movie was fantastic." "I didn't. I hated it."

Responding with a different auxiliary

To know which auxiliary verb to use, it is necessary to reconstruct the part of the sentence that is missing, and to consider carefully the meaning and the time of the events in the sentence.
"I didn't see the movie." "Oh, you should have (seen the movie). *It was great."*
"You must see the Renoir exhibition. It's wonderful!" "I have (seen it).*"*
"I wish you'd lock the door when you leave." "But I did (I locked it).*"*

Using more than one auxiliary

When there is more than one auxiliary, we can use one or more when responding.
"He could have been lying." "Yes, he could/could have/could have been."
"Would I have enjoyed it?" "No, I don't think you would/would have."
We always use more than one if there is a change in auxiliary.
"You should be given a raise." "Well, I haven't been."
"She couldn't have told him yet." "She must have."

1.2 Reduced infinitives

We can use *to* instead of the full infinitive in replies.
"Haven't you done the dishes yet?" "No, I'm just about to."
"Are you coming for a walk?" "No, I don't want to."
The verb *to be* is not usually reduced to *to*.
She's less moody than she used to be.
I wasn't as impressed as I had expected to be.

UNIT 2

Phrasal verbs

2.1 Multiple meanings

Phrasal verbs can have multiple meanings.
a. *She worked out the plot of her book.* (= devise, plan)
b. *What you owe me works out to about $150.* (= add up)
c. *It worked out that I was able to come after all.* (= result in a certain outcome)
d. *Their marriage didn't work out.* (= wasn't successful)
e. *I'm sure you'll work out your differences.* (= resolve)
f. *She works out at the gym every day.* (= do exercises, train)

2.2 Degrees of metaphorical use

There can be different degrees of metaphorical use.
a. *Take off your coat.*   Literal
b. *The sick sailor was taken off the ship.*
c. *They're taking $25 off income tax.*
d. *We're taking off two weeks in the summer.*
e. *The plane took off.*
f. *His business is taking off.*
g. *The episode was a hilarious take-off on the original TV show.*   Metaphorical
Sentence f is an example of transference, in that it derives from the meaning of *take off* in sentence e. This is typical of the way in which the meaning and use of phrasal verbs grow and change.

2.3 Transferred or metaphorical meanings

The transferred (or metaphorical) meanings of phrasal verbs are often derived from the literal meaning.
The court stood up when the judge came in. (literal)
You should stand up for what you believe in. (transferred)

She gave away her money. (literal)
Don't give away my secret. (transferred)

2.4 The grammar of phrasal verbs

There are four types of phrasal verbs.
Type 1: verb + adverb (no object)
a. *He went out.* (literal)
b. *I didn't put enough wood on the fire, so it went out.* (metaphorical)
Type 2: verb + adverb + object (separable)
a. *I put up the picture on the wall.* (literal)
b. *I put up my sister for the night.* (metaphorical)
Type 2 phrasal verbs are separable. The object (noun or person) can come between the verb and the adverb.
I put the picture up.   *I put my sister up.*
But if the object is a pronoun, it always comes between the verb and the adverb.
I put it up. (NOT *I put up it.*)   *I put her up.* (NOT *I put up her.*)
If the object is a long noun phrase, a noun with a qualifying clause, or a noun clause, the adverb comes immediately after the verb. This avoids the adverb being too far separated from the verb.
They turned down the majority of the applicants for the job.
She told off the children who had stolen her apples.
You should think over what I've been talking to you about.

Type 3: verb + preposition + object (inseparable)

a *She* **came across** *the street.* (literal)
b *She* **came across** *an old letter while she was cleaning out her drawers.*
   (metaphorical)

Type 3 phrasal verbs are inseparable. The object (noun or pronoun) always comes after the preposition.

She **came across** *a letter.*
She **came across** *it.*   NOT ~~She came it across.~~

Type 4: verb + adverb + preposition + object

Don't just sit there! **Get on with** *your work.* (Continue with it.)
I've got to **cut down on** *my spending.* (reduce)

Type 4 phrasal verbs are nearly all metaphorical. The object cannot change position. It cannot come before the adverb or the preposition.
I'm looking forward to it.   NOT ~~I'm looking forward it to.~~

Tense review

English tenses have two elements of meaning: time and aspect.

Time

Is the action present, past, or future? Does it refer to all time?

It is important to remember that *time* and *tense* are not always the same in English. Present tenses often refer to the present time, but not always; similarly past tenses do not always refer to past time.

Your plane **leaves** *at 10:00 tomorrow morning.* (present tense form referring to the future)
In the book, the heroine **goes** *back to her youth.* (present tense form referring to the past)
I wish I **knew** *the answer, but I don't.* (past tense form referring to the present)
I **could** *come tomorrow, if you like.* (past tense form referring to the future)

Aspect

The three aspects add another layer of meaning to the action of the verb.

Simple   The action is seen as a complete whole.
Continuous   The action is seen as having duration.
Perfect   The action is seen as completed *before* another time.

Choosing the correct tense

The choice of verb form depends on many factors, and not on a set of rigid grammatical rules.

1. **The nature of the action or event**
    Because English can employ its various aspects, events can be viewed with a multiplicity of implications. Look at this sentence:
    I have been asking my husband to fix this door for two years.

    In some languages this verb form is in the present – *I ask my husband …* – which indeed conveys the same basic message. But English has added on two aspects. The perfect aspect emphasizes both past and present, so that the enormity of this lack of attention to the door can be appreciated. The continuous aspect expresses the repetitive nature of the wife's requests. She hasn't asked once but a hundred times, every week for two years. Neither of these ideas are expressed by the present tense.

2. **How the speaker sees the event**
    Look at these sentences:
    a. *He always buys her flowers.*
    b. *He's always buying her flowers.*
    c. *I'll talk to Peter about it this afternoon.*
    d. *I'll be talking to Peter about it this afternoon.*

    In each pair of sentences, the actions are the same, but the speaker looks at them differently.

    In sentence *a*, the Present Simple expresses a simple fact. The Present Continuous in sentence *b* conveys the speaker's attitude, one of mild surprise or irritation.

    In sentence *c*, *will* expresses a promise or a decision made at the

moment of speaking. In sentence *d*, the Future Continuous is interesting for what it *doesn't* express. There is no element of intention, volition, or plan. The speaker is saying that in the natural course of events, as life unfolds, he and Peter will cross paths and talk, independently of the will or intention of anyone concerned. It is a casual way of looking at the future, which is why we can find it in questions such as *Will you be using the computer for long?*, which is much less confrontational than *Are you going to be using the computer for long?*

3. **The meaning of the verb**
    In some cases, the choice of verb form might be suggested by the meaning of the verb. A verb such as *belong* expresses a state or condition that remains unchanged over a period of time. Other such verbs are *mean, understand, believe, adore, remember*, etc. It would therefore be more likely to find them in simple verb forms.
    This house **belonged** *to my grandfather. Now it* **belongs** *to me.*
    Similarly, verbs such as *wait* and *rain* express the idea of an activity over a period of time, and so are often found in continuous verb forms.
    I've **been waiting** *for you for hours!*
    It's **raining** *again.*

2.5 The simple aspect

The simple aspect describes an action that is seen to be complete. The action is viewed as a whole unit.

The sun **rises** *in the east.* (= all time)
I've **read** *the book and* **seen** *the film.* (complete)
My father always **wore** *a suit to work.* (habit)
He **died** *in 1992.* (action completed in the past)
This store **will close** *at 5:30.* (fact)

Because the simple aspect expresses a completed action, we must use it if the sentence contains a number that refers to "things done."

She's **written** *three letters today.*   *I* **drink** *five cups of tea a day.*

2.6 The continuous aspect

Continuous verb forms express activities, or a series of activities, viewed at some point between their beginning and end. The continuous aspect focuses on the duration of an activity: We are aware of the passing of time. The activity is *not* permanent, and its duration is limited.

I'm **staying** *with friends until I find a place of my own.* (temporary)
Why **are** *you* **wearing** *that silly hat?* (in progress)
I've **been learning** *English for years.* (duration)

The activity may not be complete.

I've **been painting** *the kitchen.* (We don't know if it's finished.)
He **was dying***, but the doctors saved him.*
Who's **been drinking** *my soda?* (There's some left.)
Compare: *Who drank my soda?* (It's all gone.)

The action of some verbs, by definition, lasts a long time, for example, *live* and *work*. The continuous aspect gives these actions limited duration and makes them temporary.

Mario **is living** *in Washington while he's learning English.*
I'm **working** *as a waiter until I go off to college.*

The action of some other verbs lasts a short time. These are often found in the simple aspect.

She's **cut** *her finger.*   *He* **hit** *me.*

In the continuous aspect, the action of these verbs becomes longer or repeated.

I've **been cutting** *wood.* (for a long time)
He **was hitting** *me.* (again and again)

2.7 The perfect aspect

The perfect aspect expresses two ideas:

1. **An action completed before another time**
   I've read his latest book. (sometime before now)
   *When I arrived, Mary **had cooked** the meal.* (sometime before I arrived)
   *I **will have learned** my lines before the play starts.* (sometime before then)

2. **An action producing a result or a state of affairs relevant to a later situation**
   I've read his latest book. (I know the story **now**.)
   When I arrived, Mary had cooked the meal. (It was on the table **then**.)
   I will have learned my lines before the play starts. (I'll know them **in time for the play**.)

An important characteristic of perfect verb forms, therefore, is that they explicitly link an earlier action or event with a later situation. If we want to direct attention specifically to the result or state produced by the earlier action without drawing attention to the activity that has produced that state, we don't use a perfect form.

I know the book. It's good. (present)
The meal was ready. I ate it. (past)
I will know my lines. I'll give a good performance. (future)

Another characteristic of perfect verb forms is that the exact time of the action or event is either irrelevant or disregarded. The important elements are not *time when*, but the occurrence of the action itself and the results or state of affairs produced by it.

2.8 Active and passive

The passive is frequently used in English to express ideas that require a reflexive or impersonal construction in other languages, and in many cases is also used where other languages use the active.

*English **is spoken** all over the world.*
*His books **are sold** in Latin America.*

Passive sentences move the focus of attention from the subject of an active sentence to the object.

***Shakespeare** wrote Hamlet in 1599.*
***Hamlet**, one of the great tragedies of all time, was written in 1599.*

In most cases, *by* and the agent are omitted in passive sentences. This is because the agent isn't known, isn't important, or is understood.

*This house **was built** in the seventeenth century.*
*The escaped prisoner **has been recaptured**.*

Sometimes we prefer to end a sentence with what is new.

*"What a lovely painting!" "Yes, it was painted **by Canaletto**."*

In informal language, we often use *you* or *they* to refer to people in general or to no person in particular. In this way we can avoid using the passive.

***You** can buy anything at Target.*
***They**'re building a new airport soon.*

2.9 Future forms

English has several forms that express future events, and which one the user selects depends on how he or she sees the event as much as its certainty or nearness to the present. The main forms are given here in order of frequency of use.

will

Will can function as an auxiliary of the future in simply predicting a future event.

*They **will open** the new hospital next Thursday.*
*Tomorrow **will be** warm and sunny everywhere.*

Will can also function as a modal auxiliary to express ideas of willingness and spontaneous intention.

***Will** you **help** me for a minute?   What a nice shirt! **I'll buy** it.*

going to

Going to expresses a premeditated intention.

***I'm going to decorate** the bathroom this weekend.*
*The government **is going to reorganize** the entire health department.*

Going to is also used to predict a future event for which there is some evidence now.

*Great news! **I'm going to have** a baby!*
*They look very angry. I think they**'re going to start** throwing things.*

The Present Continuous

The Present Continuous is used to express an arrangement, usually for the near future.

*"What **are you doing** tonight?" "**I'm going out** to dinner."*

It is wrong to use the Present Simple in this sense. We cannot say ~~What do you do tonight?~~ or ~~Do you go to the party on Saturday?~~
The Present Continuous cannot be used to express an event that has not been arranged by human beings. We cannot say ~~It is raining tomorrow.~~ or ~~The sun is rising at 5:00 tomorrow morning.~~

The Present Simple

The Present Simple is used to express a future event that is seen as being certain because of a timetable or calendar.

*What time **does the film start**?*
*My train **gets in** at 11:00.*
*The Cup Final **takes place** on April 13.*

The Future Continuous

The Future Continuous expresses an activity that will be in progress around a specific time in the future.

*Don't call at 8:00 – **I'll be having** dinner.*
*This time tomorrow **I'll be flying** to Hong Kong.*

The Future Continuous also expresses an action that will occur in the natural course of events, independently of the will or intention of anyone directly concerned.

*In a few minutes we **will be landing** at Kennedy Airport.* (Of course the pilot has not just decided this!)
*Hurry up! The bus **will be leaving** any minute!*

The Future Continuous is often used to express a casual or polite question about someone's future plans. The speaker is trying not to impose his/her will in any way. This is related to the use of the Future Continuous described above, i.e., that it can express an action that will occur independently of the will or intention of the people concerned. Compare:

Will you bring Kate to the party? (Perhaps a request.)
Will you be bringing Kate to the party? (I'm just asking.)

The Future Perfect

The Future Perfect expresses an action that will have finished before a definite time in the future.

*I **will have finished** my work by the time you get back.*
*Most of the leaves **will have fallen** by the end of November.*

2.10 The future in the past

Sometimes when we are talking about the past, we want to refer to something that was in the future at that time. This is called the "future in the past," and it is expressed by *was going to*, the Past Continuous, or *would*. *Would* is very common in reported speech and thought.

The last time I saw you, you were going to start a new job. Did you?
I was in a hurry because I was catching a plane that afternoon.
He said he'd give me a ride.

The uses of these three forms are exactly parallel to *going to*, the Present Continuous, and *will* to refer to the real future.

I'm going to start a new job. (intention)
I'm catching a plane this afternoon. (arrangement)
I'll give you a ride. (offer)

The future in the past is often found in narratives.

Alice smiled as she thought of the evening to come. She was meeting Peter, and together they were going to see a play at the Adelphi Theater. She was sure the evening would be enjoyable.

UNIT 3

Position of adverbs

3.1 Adverb + adjective

When an adverb qualifies an adjective or past participle, it comes immediately before it.

*The hotel is **completely full**.*
*We were **deeply disappointed** with his performance.*

3.2 Adverb + verb

When an adverb qualifies a verb + object, we do not usually put the adverb between the verb and its object.

I like Mozart very much. (NOT *I ~~like very much~~ Mozart.*)
I usually have lunch at 1:00. (NOT *I ~~have usually~~ lunch at 1:00.*)

3.3 Front, middle, or end position?

There are three normal positions within a sentence for adverbs.

1. Front (at the beginning of the clause)
   Today *we're studying adverbs.* ***Obviously*** *it's difficult.* ***However**, we're having fun.*
2. Middle (before the main verb, but after the verb *to be*)
   *I **sincerely** hope you can come to the party.*   *Pat and Robert are **always** late.*
3. End (at the end of the clause)
   *They told me the news **yesterday**.*   *She speaks three languages **fluently**.*

Different kinds of adverbs go in different positions, and many can go in all three. The rules about this are complicated, and you should consult a good grammar book for details. However, here are their common positions.

Manner (*quickly, sincerely, gently*)	end or middle	*She **quickly** cleaned the room. She cleaned the room **quickly**.*
Place (*here, outside, upstairs*)	end	*They're playing **outside**.*
Point in time (*tomorrow, yesterday, tonight*)	end or front	*We're going to Rio **tomorrow**. **Tomorrow** we're going to Rio.*
Indefinite time (*already, still, just*) Some indefinite time adverbs can go in the end position.	middle	*I've **already** seen the film. I **still** don't understand. I've seen the film **already**. I haven't seen it **yet**.*
Frequency (*always, never, seldom*)	middle	*I **always** drink tea in the morning.*
Comment (*clearly, obviously, naturally*)	front or middle	***Obviously** I got it wrong. I **obviously** got it wrong.*
Linking (*however, so, although*)	front	*It was raining, **so** we went home.*
Degree/intensifier (*very, nearly, really*)	before the word they qualify	*I **really** like you.* (before a verb) *I'm **really** hot.* (before an adjective) *You **very nearly** killed me!* (before another adverb)

Notes

1. Some adverbs can be both comment and manner. The position depends on which use it is.
   *I can see the boat **clearly**.* (manner)
   ***Clearly** you need to curb your spending.* (comment)
   *Many herbs grow **naturally** in hot climates.* (manner)
   ***Naturally**, I'll pay you back the money I owe you.* (comment)

2. Some adverbs express how complete something is. They come in the middle position.
   *I have **completely** forgotten her name.*
   *We have **almost** finished our work.*

3. If there is more than one adverbial in the end position, the normal order is manner, place, time.
   *He played **well yesterday**.*
   *I watched the sun rise **slowly above the horizon**.*
   *I was **at home yesterday**.*

3.4 Adverb collocation

Adverbs can go with certain verbs or adjectives because there is a link in meaning between the two. For example, emotions can be deep, so we often find the adverb *deeply* with words that express feelings.

***deeply** regret*   ***deeply** embarrassing*   ***deeply** hurt*
Here are some more examples.

freely admit	sadly missed
highly recommended	feel strongly
severely damaged	fully insured
walk briskly	easily confused

3.5 Adverbs with two forms

Some adverbs have two forms, one with and one without *-ly*. Sometimes the two meanings are connected:

*We were flying **high** over the ocean.*
*I think very **highly** of Joe and his work.*
*Sit **tight**! The doctor will call you in a minute.*
*We control our budget **tightly**.*
Sometimes the two meanings are not connected:
*We work **hard**.* (a lot)
*I **hardly** recognized her.* (= almost not)

3.6 *just*

Just has several meanings.

exactly	This house is just right for us.
only	He isn't a man. He's just a boy.
a short time before	I just tried calling you.
right now	I'm just getting dressed.
simply, only	I just want you to go. I'd just like an egg for breakfast.
equally, no less	You're just as bad as David.

Just about means *almost*.
*"Are you ready to go?" "**Just about**."*

It can express something that is almost impossible.
*I can **just** reach the top shelf.*

Sometimes it doesn't mean very much. It just emphasizes what you're saying!
***Just** what do you think you're doing?!*
*It's **just** incredible!*

UNIT 4

4.1 Discourse markers

Discourse markers are words and expressions that show how a piece of discourse is constructed. They can:

- show the connection between what is being said now to what was said before.
- show the connection between what is being said now to what is about to be said.
- show the speaker's attitude toward what has been said.
- show the speaker's attitude toward what he/she is saying.
- clarify, direct, correct, persuade, etc.

This list is not exhaustive.

> **Basically**, you're spending too much money.
> (*This is the most important point.*)
>
> You think I'm wrong, but **actually** I'm right
> (*I'm correcting you as gently as possible.*)
>
> **Quite honestly**, you need a better job.
> (*I'm going to speak to you sincerely.*)
>
> **Apparently**, there are good jobs on Wall Street.
> (*I've heard this, but I don't know if it's true.*)
>
> **Admittedly**, you'd have to move.
> (*I know this point weakens what I'm saying.*)
>
> **Surely** you can understand what I'm saying?
> (*I don't know why you don't agree with me.*)
>
> **After all**, I gave you good advice before.
> (*Don't forget this. It explains why I'm right.*)
>
> **As a matter of fact**, I saved your company.
> (*This is a fact that might surprise you.*)
>
> **Mind you/Still**, that was a long time ago.
> (*It occurs to me that this contrasts with what I just said.*)
>
> **Actually**, you didn't thank me then, either.
> (*I'm adding some new information to what I just said.*)
>
> **I mean**, why should I bother to help you?
> (*I'm trying to make things clear to you.*)
>
> **Obviously**, you aren't going to take my advice.
> (*This fact cannot be doubted.*)
>
> **At least**, I doubt you will.
> (*I'm correcting or changing what I just said.*)
>
> **Naturally**, you'll do what you think is best.
> (*This is what I would expect.*)
>
> **Anyway**, it's up to you.
> (*I'm concluding, and not talking about that anymore.*)
>
> **All in all**, finding an interesting job isn't easy.
> (*I'm considering every part of the situation.*)
>
> The ball's in your court, **so to speak**.
> (*I'm using words that don't have their usual meaning.*)
>
> **By the way**, can you lend me some money?
> (*This isn't connected to what we've been talking about.*)

4.2 Question tags

Falling intonation

With a falling intonation on the tag, this is not a real question. It means "Agree with me, talk to me."

It's a lovely day, isn't it?

The film was great, wasn't it?

Note

We can reply to a statement with a question tag.

"Nice day today!" "Yes, it is, isn't it?"
"You're filthy!" "Yes, I am, aren't I?"
"Their kids have good appetites." "Yes, they do, don't they?"

Rising intonation

With a rising intonation on the tag, we really want to know something because we aren't sure of the answer.

You didn't say that to him, did you?

They wouldn't take my car away, would they?

Notes

Notice the auxiliaries in these questions tags.

Let's go, shall we?
Give me a hand, will you?
Don't forget to post my letter, will you?
Nobody called, did they?

These question tags can be used in requests.

You couldn't lend me a twenty, could you?
You haven't seen Marco anywhere, have you?

Same way tags

These occur after affirmative sentences. The tag is positive and the intonation rises. The speaker repeats what he/she has just heard and uses the tag to express interest, surprise, concern, or some other reaction.

So you're Kevin's sister, are you? I've heard a lot about you.

So you like rap music, do you? Well, just listen to this.

4.3 Replies

Short answers

Short answers are used in reply to *Yes/No* questions.
"Did you have a good time?" "Yes, I did. It was great."
"Have you been to Costa Rica?" "No, I haven't, but I'd like to."

Reply questions

We use reply questions to show interest, and to show we're listening.
"I had a terrible day today." "Did you, dear?"
"The boss was in a foul mood." "Was he?"

Avoiding repetition

This was dealt with in Unit 1.
"Who wants an ice cream?" "I do." (I want an ice cream.)
"Who came to the party?" "Everybody did."

UNIT 5

Adding emphasis

5.1 Structures that add emphasis

Sentences can be emphasized by adding certain structures. They are called cleft or divided sentences. Look at this base sentence.

Lucy moved to Toronto.

We can emphasize different parts of the sentence according to which element is the most important:

What *Lucy did was move to Toronto.*   (*What* = the thing that)
Where *Lucy moved to was Toronto.*   (*Where* = the place that)
Why *Lucy moved to Toronto was because …* (*Why* = the reason why)
It was *Lucy* **who/that** *moved to Toronto.*   (*who* = the person who/that)

Or we can emphasize the whole sentence:

What happened was that	
What surprised me was the fact that	*Lucy moved to Toronto.*
What interests me is why	

5.2 Negative inversion

Sentences can be given emphasis by negative inversion, which can take place …

1. after negative adverbials such as *never, nowhere, not for one minute, not since, not until, never again, rarely.* It is mainly used in written English but can also be used to emphasize points in more formal spoken English such as when making speeches.

    Never *had he eaten such a huge meal.*
    Nowhere *will you come across a more hospitable nation.*
    Nothing *do they appreciate more than a trip to the country.*
    Not until *1918 did British women get the vote.*
    Rarely *do you meet a man of such integrity.*

2. in certain established sentence patterns.

    Hardly *had he begun to speak* **when** *the majority of the guests departed.*
    No sooner *had we sat down to dinner* **than** *the doorbell rang.*
    Little *did anyone realize the seriousness of the situation.*

3. after expressions with *only* and *no.*

    Only *when I myself became a parent did I realize the value of my parents' advice.*
    Not only *did she write short stories,* **but** *she was* **also** *a talented painter.*
    At no time *was I ever informed.*
    In no way *can this government deny its guilt.*
    On no account *will I compromise my ideals.*

5.3 Pronunciation

Of course a major way of adding emphasis in spoken English is by stressing individual words. In English a change of word stress changes the meaning of a sentence. Look at this base sentence:

John likes the brown shoes.
John *likes the brown shoes.* (Tom doesn't.)
John **likes** *the brown shoes.* (He doesn't hate them.)
John likes the **brown** *shoes.* (Not the black ones.)
John likes the brown **shoes**. (Not the brown boots.)

Note

It is possible to stress the word *the* (pronounced /ði/) when it means that something is so superior to the alternatives, it can be considered the only real choice.

If John wants brown shoes, those Gucci shoes are **the** *brown shoes to buy.*

5.4 Emphatic *do, does, did*

Do, does, and *did* can be used to give emphasis in positive statements in the Present and Past Simple, and also in the imperative.

John **does** *like the brown shoes.* (You were wrong!)
Do *come with us on vacation. We'd love you to.*
I **do** *love you, really I do.*
He **does** *seem pretty upset.*
They **did** *question him very thoroughly, didn't they?*

UNIT 6

Reporting with passive verbs

We can report words and actions using the passive in various ways.

6.1 *It* + passive verb + *that* clause

It is **said** *that Bet Molam, the writer, earns $1 million a year.*
It is **reported** *that she is living in a rented house in Malibu.*
It has been **alleged** *that she married her third husband last week.*
It is **known** *that she has been working on a new book.*
It is **said** *that the book is based on her experiences in the Far East.*
It is **understood** *that she has been given an advance of $500,000.*

Other verbs that follow this pattern are:

agree	calculate	discover	hope	show
allege	claim	estimate	know	suggest
announce	consider	expect	presume	suppose
assume	decide	fear	propose	think
believe	declare	feel	recommend	

6.2 Subject + passive verb + *to* infinitive

Bet Molam is said **to earn** *$1 million a year.* (Present Simple infinitive)
She is reported **to be living** *in Malibu.* (Present Continuous infinitive)
She is alleged **to have married** *her third husband.* (perfect infinitive)
She is known **to have been working** *on a new book.* (perfect continuous infinitive)
The book is said **to be based** *on her experiences.* (present passive infinitive)
She is understood **to have been given** *an advance.* (perfect passive infinitive)

Other verbs that follow this pattern are:

allege	consider	know	say	think
assume	estimate	presume	suggest	understand
believe	expect	report	suppose	

Notice this transformation with *there* :

It is thought that there has been a plane crash this afternoon.
There is thought to have been *a plane crash this afternoon.*
It is estimated that there are one million unemployed.
There are estimated to be *one million unemployed.*

6.3 *seem* and *appear*

We can use *seem* and *appear* to give information without stating categorically that we know it to be true.
They can be used in two patterns.

1. It + *seem*/*appear* + *that* clause
   It **seems** that she's upset.
   It **appears** that she's crying.
   It **seems** that I made a mistake.
   It **appeared** that his car had been stolen.

2. Subject + *seem*/*appear* + *to* infinitive
   She seems **to be** upset.
   She appears **to be crying**.
   I seem **to have made** a mistake.
   His car appears **to have been stolen**.

We can make the statement more tentative with the use of *would*.
It **would seem** *the problem has been nipped in the bud.*
I **would appear** to have mislaid my wallet.

UNIT 7

Modal auxiliary verbs

Modal verbs are a very rich and subtle area of the English language. They can *all* refer to the certainty, possibility, or probability of an event, and they can all refer to future time. Certain modals can also express other areas of meaning (see below).

7.1 Modals of probability in the present and future

The main modal verbs that express present and future probability are given here in order of degrees of certainty, *will* being the most certain and *might*/*could* being the least certain.

1. ***will***
   Will and *won't* are used to predict a future event that is seen as certain, a future fact.
   *I'll be on vacation next week. I **won't** do any work at all.*
   *The school term **will** end on June 29th.*
   Will and *won't* are also used to express what we strongly believe to be true about the present. They indicate an assumption based on our knowledge of people and things: their routine, character, and qualities.
   *Is that the phone? It**'ll** be John. He said he'd call around now.*
   *"I wonder what Meg's doing now?" "It's 7:00. I suppose she**'ll** be getting ready to go out."*
   *Don't take the bread out of the oven. It **won't** be ready yet.*

2. ***must*** and ***can't***
   Must is used to assert what we infer or conclude to be the most logical or rational interpretation of a situation or events. We have a lot of evidence but it is less certain than *will*.
   *Wow, look over there! That **must** be John's new car.*
   *You **must** be joking! I simply don't believe you.*
   The negative of this use of *must* is *can't*.
   *She **can't** have a ten-year-old daughter! She's only twenty-five herself!*

3. ***should***
   Should expresses what may reasonably be expected to happen. It also carries the meaning that we want whatever is predicted to happen, and is therefore not used to express negative or unpleasant ideas. It can also suggest a conditional: if everything has gone/goes according to plan, then (x) should happen.
   *Our guests **should** be here soon. (if they haven't gotten lost)*
   *This homework **shouldn't** take you too long. (if you understand what you have to do)*
   *We **should** be moving into our new house soon. (as long as all the arrangements go smoothly)*

4. ***may***
   May expresses the possibility that something will happen or is already happening.
   *We **may** go to Florida on vacation. We haven't decided yet.*
   *We **may not** have enough money to go away this year.*

5. ***might***
   Might, like *may*, expresses possibility, but in a more tentative way.
   *It **might** rain. Take your umbrella.*
   *I **might not** be back in time for dinner, so don't wait for me.*

6. ***could***
   Could is used in a similar way to *might*.
   *It **could** rain, but I doubt it.*
   *That French film **could** be worth seeing, but it didn't get very good reviews.*
   The negative, *could not*, is NOT used to express future possibility. **Might not** is the negative of *could* in this use.
   *It looks like it could rain, but it **might not**.*
   *He **might not** come.*
   The negative *couldn't* has a similar meaning to *can't* in 2 above, only slightly weaker.
   *She **couldn't** have a 10-year-old daughter! She's only 25 herself!*

7. ***can***
   We use *can* to express what is generally and all-time true, and logically possible.
   *Biking downtown **can** be dangerous.*
   Can cannot be used to predict future possibility. We must use *will be possible* or *will be able to*.
   *In years to come it**'ll be possible** to have vacations on the moon.*
   *We**'ll be able to** travel by spaceship.*

7.2 Modal auxiliaries in the past

All the modal verbs given above are also used with *have* + past participle (the perfect infinitive) to express varying degrees of certainty about the past. Again, *will*/*would* is the most certain and *might*/*could* the least certain. *Can* is a special case (see below).
*You met a man with a big black moustache? That **would have been** my Uncle Bill.*
*It **won't have been** Peter you met at the party. He wasn't invited.*
*It **must have been** Kevin. He looks a lot like Peter.*
*It **can't have been** a very interesting party. No one seems to have enjoyed it.*
*Where's Henry? He **should have been** here ages ago! He may have gotten lost.*
*He might have decided not to come. He **could have had** an accident.*
*He **can hardly have forgotten** to come.*
Can have is only used in questions or with *hardly*, *only*, or *never*.
*Where **can he have been** all this time?*
*They **can only have known** each other for a few weeks.*

7.3 Other uses of modal auxiliary verbs, present and past

Obligation

Must is used to express strong obligation. The past is expressed by *had to*.
*You **must** try harder!   I **had to** work hard to pass my exams.*
Should is used to express milder obligation. The past is expressed by *should have* (+ past participle).
*You **should** rest.   You **should have** taken it more seriously.*

Permission

Can and *may* are used to ask for permission. *May* sounds more formal than *can*.
***Can** I ask you a question?*
***May** I ask what the purpose of this visit is?*

The past of *may* and *can* is expressed by *was allowed to*. *Could* can only be used to report permission.

*I **was allowed to** do whatever I wanted when I was young.*
*My parents said I **could** stay out until after midnight.*

Ability

Can is used to express general ability; the form in the past is *could*.

*I **can** swim. I **could** swim when I was 6.*

To express a particular ability on one occasion in the past, *could* is not used. Instead, *was able to* or *managed to* is used.

*The prisoner **managed to** escape by climbing onto the roof.*
*I **was able to** give the police a full description.*

Willingness

Won't expresses a refusal, by either people or things. The past is *wouldn't*.

*The car **won't** start.*
*He was angry because she **wouldn't** lend him any money.*

Characteristic behavior/habit

Will is used to express characteristic behavior. The past is expressed by *would*.

He'll sit for hours staring into the fire.
*My grandma **would** always bring me a little present when she came to visit.*

If *will* is stressed, it suggests criticism and irritation.

*David **will** leave his homework until the last minute. It's infuriating.*

Past forms of *need*

Need has two past forms.

Didn't need to (+ infinitive) expresses an action that was not necessary, but we do not know if it was in fact completed or not. The context usually makes this clear.

*I **didn't need to do** any shopping because I was eating out that night.*

Needn't have (+ past participle) expresses an action that was completed but that wasn't necessary. This is chiefly used in British English.

*You **needn't have bought** any butter. We have plenty.*

UNIT 8

8.1 *would*

Would can express past habits.

When I was a kid, we'd go looking for mushrooms.
*My grandfather **would** sit in his armchair and nod off.*

If *would* is stressed, it suggests criticism and irritation.

*My sister **would** borrow my clothes without asking. It really annoyed me.*

Stressed *would* can also be used to criticize a single past action. The meaning is "that's typical of you/him/her."

*Did she say I hit her? She **would** say that. I hate her.*

Would is used to express the future in the past (see page 74). It reports speech and thoughts.

You promised you'd help me.
*I knew you **wouldn't** like it.*

Would can express a refusal on a particular past occasion.

*I asked him if he was going out with anyone, but he **wouldn't** tell me.*
*The printer **wouldn't** stop printing, so I turned it off.*

Real and unreal tense usage

Introduction

English tense usage can be divided into two categories: tenses used to refer to fact, and those used to refer to non-fact. Fact is what is considered to be real or quite possible; non-fact is what is supposed or wished for, which is either unreal or improbable.

Fact	*I work in a restaurant, but I don't earn much.*
	If I find a better job, I'll take it.
Non-fact	*I wish I had a lot of money.*
	If I had a lot of money, I would open my own restaurant.

Tenses used to refer to fact are related to real time. For example, a past verb form refers to the past.

*I **had** a great vacation in New Orleans last year.*

Tenses used to refer to non-fact are not related to real time. Generally speaking, this unreality is expressed by shifting the verb form "backwards," for example, from present to past.

*If I **had** a car, I **could** visit my friends.*

Here the past verb form does not refer to the real past, but to the "wished for" present and future. It has the effect of distancing the meaning from reality.

8.2 Type 1 conditional sentences (real)

It is important to understand this difference between fact and non-fact when discussing conditional sentences.

- Type 1 conditional sentences are based on fact in real time. They express a possible condition and its probable result.
  If it rains, I'll get wet.
  If he doesn't come soon, we'll miss the bus.

- *Will* is not usually used in the condition clause. However, it can appear when *will* expresses willingness (or in the negative, refusal).
  If you'll wash the dishes, I'll put them away. (if you are willing to)
  *If Peter **won't give** you a ride, I will.* (if Peter isn't willing to)

- *Should* and *happen to* can be used in the condition clause to suggest that something may happen by chance, but is unlikely.
  *If you **should come across** Pearl, tell her to give me a ring.*
  *If you **happen to find** my book, pop it in the mail to me.*

- There are several other links with meanings similar to *if* that can introduce Type 1 conditional sentences.
  Provided/Providing I have the time, I'll give you a hand to fix it.
  Supposing you miss the plane, what will you do?
  I'll come tomorrow unless I hear from you before. (if I don't hear from you)

8.3 Type 2 conditional sentences (unreal)

Type 2 conditional sentences are not based on fact. They express a situation that is contrary to reality in the present and future; a hypothetical condition and its probable result. This unreality is shown by a tense shift "backwards":

Present → Past, *will* → *would*

If I were taller, I'd join the police force. (In reality I am not, and never will be, tall enough to join the police force.)
If you saw a ghost, what would you do? (I don't believe in ghosts, so I don't think you will ever see one.)

The difference between Type 1 and Type 2 conditional sentences is not related to time. Both can refer to the present or the future. By using a past verb form in Type 2, the speaker suggests that the situation is less probable, or impossible, or imaginary.

Compare the following.

If it rains this weekend, I'll … (Said in England, where rain is common.)
If it rained in the Sahara, the desert would … (This would be most unusual.)
If there is a nuclear war, we will … (I am a pessimist. Nuclear war is a real possibility.)
If there was a nuclear war, we would … (I am an optimist. I think nuclear war is very unlikely to happen.)
If you come to my country, you'll have a good time. (Possible.)
If you came from my country, you'd understand us better. (Impossible – you don't come from my country.)

Notes

Were is often used instead of *was*, especially when the style is formal. It is also commonly used in the expression *If I were you …* when giving advice.
*If he **were** more honest, he would be a better person.*
*If I **were** you, I'd cook it for a little longer.*
The Type 2 conditional can make a suggestion sound less direct and hence more polite.
Would it be convenient if I called this evening around 8:00?
Would you mind if I opened the window slightly?
Would is not usually used in the condition clause. However, as with *will* in Type 1, it can appear when it expresses willingness. Again, it makes a suggestion sound more polite.
*I would be grateful if you **would** give this matter your serious attention.*
Were to can be used in the condition clause to suggest that something is unlikely to happen.
*If you **were to find** that your neighbors were terrorists, what would you do?*

8.4 Type 3 conditional sentences (unreal)

Type 3 conditional sentences, like Type 2, are not based on fact. They express a situation that is contrary to reality in the past. This unreality is shown by a tense shift "backwards":

Past → Past Perfect, would → would have

If I had known his background, I would never have employed him. (I didn't know his background and I did employ him.)
If I hadn't seen it with my own eyes, I wouldn't have thought it possible. (I did see it with my own eyes, so it must be possible.)

8.5 Type 2 and Type 3 mixed

It is possible for each of the two clauses in a conditional sentence to have a different time reference, and the result is a mixed conditional.
If we had brought a map with us, we would know where we are.
If we had brought … is contrary to past fact (we didn't bring a map).
… we would know … is contrary to present fact (we don't know).
If I didn't love her, I wouldn't have married her.
If I didn't love her … is contrary to present fact (I do love her).
I wouldn't have married her … is contrary to past fact (I did marry her).
Care needs to be taken when the Type 2 conditional refers to the future.
I'd come to the party next Saturday if I hadn't made plans to go to the theater.
This conditional is sometimes "unmixed" to regularize the tense sequence.
I would have come to the party next Saturday if I hadn't made plans to go to the theater.

Hypothesizing

There are certain other constructions that have a hypothetical meaning and, as in conditional sentences, the unreality that they express is again shown by shifting the verb form "backwards."
I wish I knew the answer. (But I don't know.)
If only I hadn't behaved so badly. (But I did behave badly.)

8.6 Hypothesizing about the present and future

The Past Simple tense form is used for present and future time reference. Notice that *were* is used instead of *was*, especially in formal style.
*I wish I **were** taller!   If only he **were** here now!*
*Supposing/suppose you **had** a million dollars? What would you do?*

Present state vs. present action or event

When we hypothesize about a present state, the Past Simple tense form is used.
*I wish you **lived** nearer.   If only I **had** a car!*
When we hypothesize about a present action or event, *would* is used.
*I wish you**'d help** more around the house.*
*If only she **wouldn't wash** her socks in the bathtub!*
Would here expresses willingness in the first sentence, and annoying habit in the second.

I wish/If only

Notice that it is unusual to say *I wish/If only I wouldn't …* because we can control what we want to do. However, we can say *I wish/If only I could …*
*I wish I **could remember** where I put my glasses.*
*If only I **could give up** potato chips.*
We can say *I wish/If only … would* to refer to a definite time in the future, but only if we think that the action will probably not happen.
*I wish she**'d come** with me tomorrow.*
*If only you**'d fix** the car this weekend, we could go for a drive.*
If it is possible that our wish will be realized, then a different structure such as *I hope* is needed.
*I **hope it doesn't rain** tomorrow.*

Fact vs. non-fact

Notice the difference between fact and non-fact in the following pair of sentences.
*He looks **as if he is** French.* (Fact – it is possible that he is.)
*He looks **as if he were** French.* (Non-fact – we know he isn't.)
The same distinction is found with other *as if/as though* structures.
*Why is that girl smiling at me **as though she knew** me?*
*He behaves **as if he owned** the place.*

It's time

It's time can be followed by an infinitive.
*It's time **to go** to bed.   It's time for us **to go**.*
It is also possible to use a past tense.
*It's time we **went** home.   It's time I **was** going.*
When we want to say that it is time for someone else to do something, the past tense is often used.
*It's time you **got** your hair cut.*

would rather

Would rather can be followed by an infinitive (without *to*).
*I'd **rather have** water, please.*
When *would rather* is followed by another person, the construction *would rather* + person + past tense form is used.
*I'd **rather you kept** this a secret.*
*She **would rather you paid** by check.*

8.7 Hypothesizing about the past

The Past Perfect tense form is used for past time reference.
*I wish she **hadn't been** so mean.*
*If only the police **had looked** in the attic, they would have found him!*
*Supposing/Suppose we **had missed** the plane? What would we have done?*

would rather

Would rather + the Past Perfect is possible, but it is more usual to express the same idea using *wish*.
I'd rather you'd left.   I wish you'd left.

Fact vs. non-fact

Notice the difference between fact and non-fact in the following sentences.
*He looked as if he **was** tired.* (Fact – this is probably how he felt.)
*He looked as if he **had seen** a ghost.* (Non-fact – very improbable.)

would like

Would like can be used with a perfect infinitive to talk about things we wish we had done.
*I **would like to have lived** in the eighteenth century.*
This can also be expressed by *would have liked* followed by either an ordinary infinitive or a perfect infinitive.

I would have liked to live I would have liked to have lived	in the eighteenth century.

The same forms can be used to refer to the present and the future if it is contrary to fact.

I would like to have stayed in I would have liked to stay in I would have liked to have stayed in	tonight, instead of going out.

8.8 Softening the message

We can make our message less direct by using certain constructions.

A past tense

*I **wondered** if you were free tonight? I **thought** we could go to a movie.*

The continuous

*I **was hoping** you could tell me the answer. When **will** you **be arriving**?*

would

Would it be possible for you to come back tomorrow?
Wouldn't it be better if you did it my way?
I would say/think she's in her seventies.
I would have said/thought she was about 65.
I wouldn't be surprised if Jack didn't come soon.
I just thought I'd give you a ring to see if you were all right.
You'd have thought she could have remembered my birthday.

UNIT 9

Verb patterns

9.1 Verb patterns with the gerund

The gerund or *-ing* form is used:

1. After certain verbs

admit   deny   regret   suggest

   *He **admitted** stealing the money.*

2. After prepositions, prepositional verbs, and phrasal verbs
   *After **leaving** school he joined the army.*
   *She **apologized for arriving** late.*
   *I've **given up eating** sweets at last.*

Note

The preposition *to* (not *to* as part of the infinitive) can cause problems. This is because *to* + *-ing* seems a strange combination.
*I'm **looking forward to seeing** you.*

---

*I'm **not used to driving** a stick shift.*
*Do you **feel up to going** out this evening?*

9.2 Verb patterns with the infinitive

Verb + infinitive + *to*

The pattern of verb + infinitive + *to* is used:

1. After certain verbs

ask   agree   offer   promise   refuse   want

   *He **asked** to do it.*

2. After certain verbs + object

ask   beg   encourage   order   persuade   tell   want

   *They **asked** him to do it.*

Note

Some verbs can take both of the above patterns.

ask   beg   want   help

*She **wanted** to do it.*
*She **wanted** him to do it.*

Verb + infinitive without *to*

make   let   help

*They **made** me do it.*

Notes

1. All infinitive patterns are possible with *help*.
2. The passive of *make* takes *to*.
   *I was **made to** do it.*
3. The passive of *let* is *allowed to*.
   *I was **allowed to** do it.*

9.3 Verb + *that* + clause

In some (not all) of the above examples, a *that* clause can be used after the main verb in place of a gerund or infinitive. There is no change in meaning. *That* itself can be omitted.
*She **admitted (that) she had made** a mistake.*
*He **promised (that) he would do** it.*
*They **suggested (that) we should have** a long break.*

Notes

1. *Suggest* has special problems. These constructions are also possible.
   *They **suggested (that) we have** a long break.*
   *They **suggested (that) we had** a long break.*
2. *He ~~wanted that I do it~~* is a common mistake.

9.4 Verb + *-ing* or *to* with little or no change of meaning

The verbs *begin*, *start*, and *continue* can take either *-ing* or *to* and mean the same.

It	started began continued	to rain. raining.

Note

The choice may be governed by style or the nature of the following verb.
It's just starting to rain. (NOT ~~starting raining~~)
He slowly began to understand the situation. (NOT ~~began understanding~~)

Many verbs that express feelings and attitudes (*like, love, prefer, can't stand*, etc.) can be followed by either *-ing* or *to*, and the distinction in meaning is small.

*I **like traveling** by train.* (general truth)
*I **like to travel** by train when I go to my grandmother's.* (a little more particular)

Like + -ing can mean *enjoy. Like + infinitive* can express what you think is the right thing to do.

*I like **cooking**.*   *I like **to pay** my bills on time.*

Note
The infinitive is always used with *would like/prefer*, etc.
*I'd **like to travel** by train when I next visit her.* (one particular occasion)

9.5 Verbs + *-ing* or *to* with a change of meaning

1. After the verbs *remember, forget*, and *regret*, the gerund refers to an action earlier in time than the main verb; the infinitive refers to an action at the same time or later.
   *I **remember giving** her the message when I saw her.*
   *Please **remember to give** her the message when you see her.*
   *I **regret saying** that because I upset her.*
   *I **regret to say** we can't offer you the job.*

2. After the verb *stop* and the phrasal verb *go on*, the gerund refers to an existing action; the infinitive refers to a following action.
   *He **went on repeating** the question.*
   *He **went on to say** that he wanted my advice.*

3. After verbs of the senses *see, hear*, etc. + object the gerund signifies an action in progress; the infinitive a completed action.
   *We **saw him cutting** the hedge.* (He was in the middle of doing it.)
   *We **saw him cut** the hedge.* (We saw the whole event from start to finish.)

9.6 Perfect and passive forms

The gerund and infinitive also have perfect and passive forms.
*I **don't remember having said** that.*
*She **suffered from having had** a difficult childhood.*
*He **doesn't like being told** what to do.*

Unit 10

10.1 Intensifying adverbs and verbs

As we saw in Unit 3, certain verbs and intensifying adverbs go together because there is a link in meaning.

deeply regret   *sincerely hope*   *desperately need*

However, in most cases of verb + intensifying adverb, there is no reason at all why some combinations are possible and some are not.

Possible combinations		Impossible combinations
totally absolutely	agree	~~sincerely agree~~
totally	disagree	~~totally remember~~
completely fully perfectly	understand	~~fully think~~ ~~completely adore~~ ~~fully destroy~~ ~~strongly like~~
seriously sincerely	believe	
completely strongly entirely really thoroughly greatly	forget disapprove depend like enjoy appreciate	

10.2 Intensifying adverbs and adjectives

It is important to understand the difference between gradable and extreme (or limit) adjectives. Gradable adjectives express qualities that can exist in different strengths. For example, a person can be more or less intelligent, a room more or less dirty, a film more or less interesting. Limit adjectives express extreme qualities.

a brilliant person   *a filthy room*   *a fascinating film*

Look at these pairs of gradable and limit adjectives.

angry / furious	big / enormous	important / essential
tired / exhausted	long / endless	tasty / delicious
happy / delighted	upset / devastated	surprised / amazed

Different intensifying adverbs go with gradable and limit adjectives.

Intensifying adverbs + gradable adjective			Intensifying adverbs + limit adjective		
very	extremely	really	absolutely	totally	really
awfully	terribly	pretty	completely	entirely	simply
rather	fairly	quite	utterly	pretty	quite

As with verbs, not all combinations are possible. There is no real reason why we can't say ~~totally essential, entirely determined, completely furious~~ – we just can't!

The only combinations that are always possible are *very* + gradable adjective and *absolutely* + limit adjective. *Really* can go with most adjectives, both gradable and limit.

very happy/tired/big
absolutely enormous/delicious/delighted
really angry/surprised/amazed

UNIT 11

11.1 Adjective order

Generally speaking, value adjectives (which indicate personal opinion) come first, followed by size, age, shape, color, origin, and material.
Compound nouns (e.g., *washing machine; coffee pot*) are never separated.
There are several examples below of noun phrases with adjectives in this order.

two lovely black leather riding boots
a priceless nineteenth-century Impressionist painting
their huge circular swimming pool
my Thai wooden salad bowl
the dirty old metal garden chair
one tiny L-shaped utility room
Jane's pretty midcentury writing desk
his charming whitewashed country farmhouse

Relative clauses

Introduction

It is important to distinguish between defining and nondefining relative clauses. Defining relative clauses are an essential part of the meaning of a sentence and therefore they cannot be left out. They define exactly who or what we are talking about.
*There's the woman **you were telling me about**.*
Nondefining relative clauses add extra information of secondary importance, and can be left out of a sentence.
*Mrs. Bottomley, **who was an extremely mean person while she was alive**, has left all her money to a shelter for cats.*
Nondefining relative clauses are mainly found in written English, where sentences are carefully constructed. In spoken English, they sound rather formal, and can easily be expressed by simpler sentences.
Did you know Mrs. Bottomley has left all her money to a shelter for cats? It's incredible, really. She was such a mean person.

11.2 Defining relative clauses

These are the main forms used. The forms in parentheses are possible, but not as common.

	Person	Thing
Subject	who (that)	that (which)
Object	— (that)	— (that)

Notice that English likes to drop the relative pronoun when it defines the object of the clause.

*The doctor **who helped me most** was Dr. Clark.* (subject)
*The doctor **I found most helpful** was Dr. Clark.* (object)
*The treatment **that** helped me most was acupuncture.* (subject)
*The treatment **I liked best** was acupuncture.* (object)

Notice that there are no commas before and after defining relative clauses when written, and no pauses when spoken.

that

That is usually used as subject after the following: superlatives, *all*, *every(thing)*, *some(thing)*, *any(thing)*, *no(thing)*, and *only*.

*He wrote some of the best poetry **that's ever been written**.*
***All that's needed** is a little more time.*
*Don't take **anything that's valuable**.*
*The **only thing that matters** is that you're safe.*

We often omit *that* when it is the object.

She's one of the nicest people I know.
Is there anything I can do to help?

Prepositions

Prepositions can come either before relative pronouns or at the end of the relative clause. In spoken English, it is much more common to put the preposition at the end (and to drop the pronoun).

*This is the book I was talking to you **about**.*
*The people I work **with** are very kind.*

Second relative clause

A second relative, introduced by *and* or *but*, usually takes a *wh-*pronoun, not *that*.

*Someone that I greatly admire, but **who** I've never met, is Professor Keats.*

11.3 Nondefining relative clauses

These are the main forms used. The form in parentheses is possible, but not as common.

	Person	Thing
Subject	… , who … ,	… , which … ,
Object	… , who … (, whom …)	… , which …

*Mr. Jenkins, **who has written several books,** spoke at the meeting last night.* (subject)
*Peter Clark, **who the governor fired from his cabinet,** has become the chairman of Center Bank.* (object)
*My favorite food is a McDonald's hamburger, **which is one of U.S.'s most profitable exports**.* (subject)
*I gave him a sandwich, **which he ate greedily**.* (object)

Notice that there are commas around nondefining relative clauses when written, and pauses before and after them when spoken.

Prepositions

Prepositions can come at the end of nondefining relative clauses, but in a formal style they are usually put before the relative pronoun.

*The lecturer spoke for two hours on the subject of Weingarten's Theory of Market Forces, which none of us had ever heard **of**.*
*The privatization of all industry, **to** which this government is deeply committed, is not universally popular.*

which

Which can be used in nondefining clauses to refer to the whole of the preceding clause.

*He passed the exam, **which** surprised everyone.*
*The elevator isn't working, **which** means we'll have to use the stairs.*

whose

Whose can be used in both defining and nondefining relative clauses to refer to possession.

*There's the woman **whose** son was killed recently.* (defining)
*ABC Airways, **whose** fares across the Atlantic were lower than anybody else's, has just declared bankruptcy.* (non-defining)

what

What is used as a relative pronoun instead of *the thing that* in some sentences.

*Has she told you **what**'s worrying her?*
*I have to do **what** I believe is right.*

when and where

When and *where* can be used to introduce both defining and non-defining relative clauses. In defining relative clauses, *when* can be left out.

*Can you tell me the exact time (**when**) you hope to arrive?*
Where cannot be left out unless we add a preposition.
*That's the hotel **where** we're staying.*
*That's the hotel we're staying **at**.*

In nondefining relative clauses, *when* and *where* cannot be left out.

*We go swimming after 5:00, **when** everyone else has gone home.*
*He shops in Atlanta, **where** his sister lives.*

why

Why can be used to introduce defining relative clauses after the word *reason*. It can be left out.

*Do you remember the reason **why** we are arguing?*
We can also say *Do you remember why we are arguing?* where the clause beginning with *why* is the object of the verb.

Participles

11.4 Participles as adjectives

Present participles describe an action that is still happening.
*He dove into the sea to save the **drowning** child.*
*They watched the **burning** forest.*
Past participles describe the result of an action that has happened.
*She looked at the **broken** chair.*
*The **completed** statue looked very lifelike.*

11.5 Participles as reduced relative clauses

When participles come after a noun, they are like reduced relative clauses.
*I met a woman **riding** a donkey.* (who was riding)
*The cash **stolen** in the raid was never recovered.* (that was stolen)
*The man **being interviewed** by the police is suspected of arson.* (who is being interviewed)

11.6 Participles in adverb clauses

1. Participle clauses can describe actions that are going on simultaneously.

   *She sat by the fire **reading** a book and **sipping** a mug of coffee.*
   *He went to the party **dressed** as a monkey.*

2. Participle clauses can describe actions that happen consecutively.
   Opening the suitcase, he took out his jacket.
   Released from its cage, the lion prowled around.
3. If it is important to show that the first action has finished before the second begins, the perfect participle is used.
   Having finished lunch, we set off.
4. Participle clauses can express the idea of *because*.
   Being a mean person, he never spent more than he had to. (Because he was a mean person …)
   Not knowing what to do, I waited patiently. (Because I didn't know …)
   Weakened by years of bad health, she could hardly sit up in bed. (Because she had been weakened …)
5. Participle clauses can express the idea of result.
   It rained every day for two weeks, completely ***ruining*** our vacation.
6. Participle clauses can express the idea of *if*.
   Taken regularly, aspirin can reduce the risk of a stroke.
7. Participle clauses can be introduced by *while, when, after, by, on,* and *since*.
   While studying at Yale, he met the woman he was to marry.
   When leaving the plane, remember to take your belongings with you.
   After saying goodbye, he ran to catch the train.
   I paid my debts ***by taking*** on another job.
   On entering the room, I noticed that everyone was looking at me.
   Since arriving in San Francisco, I've made a lot of friends.

Note
In all participle clauses, the subject of the clause and the subject of the main verb must be the same.

11.7 Participles after certain verbs

Many verbs can be followed by an *-ing* form.
I ***spent*** the evening ***decorating***.
He ***spends*** his money ***traveling***.
Don't ***waste*** time ***thinking*** about what might have been.
Let's ***go swimming***.

UNIT 12

Linking devices

12.1 Result

so and *such*

It was raining, ***so*** we went home.
The play was ***so*** boring ***that*** I fell asleep.
It was ***such*** a boring movie ***that*** I fell asleep.

as a result, *therefore*, and *consequently*

As a result, therefore, and *consequently* can also express the result of something.
He worked hard all his life. ***As a result***, he amassed a fortune.
The dollar has gone down against the yen. ***Therefore/Consequently***, Japanese goods are more expensive for Americans. (more formal)

Participles

As we saw in Unit 11, participles can also express result.
He fell off his motorcycle, ***breaking*** his leg and ***injuring*** his arm.

too and *enough*

When result involves degree (*heavy, hot*) or quantity (*little, much*), we can express the result with *too* or *enough*.

This table is ***too*** heavy for me to lift.
There are ***too*** many people to fit into this room.
I'm not strong ***enough*** to lift the table.
The room isn't big ***enough*** to fit everyone in.

12.2 Reason

as and *since*

As and *since* are used when the reason is already known to the listener/reader, or when it is not the most important part of the sentence.
As it was getting late, we decided it was time to leave.
Since he had very little money, James decided he should look for work.
Both these clauses are quite formal. In an informal style, we would be more likely to use *so*.
It was getting late, ***so*** we decided it was time to leave.

because

Because puts more emphasis on the reason, and most often introduces new information.
Because she was getting frail in her old age, she went to live with her daughter.
When the reason is the most important part of the sentence, the *because* clause usually comes at the end.
I went to live in Chicago ***because I wanted to learn English***.

because of, *due to*, and *owing to*

Because of, due to, and *owing to* can also express the cause of something.
We had to stop playing tennis ***because of*** the weather.
Due to the economic situation, fewer people are taking vacations this year.
Owing to a lack of funds, the project will discontinue next year.

Participles

As we saw in Unit 11, participles can also express reason.
Being an inquisitive person, I love to start conversations with strangers.
Deprived of water, the plant soon died.

12.3 Purpose

The infinitive

The infinitive on its own is the most common pattern in informal English.

| I went to Spain | to learn
in order to learn
so as to learn | Spanish. |

We cannot use the infinitive in the negative.

| I tiptoed upstairs | so as not to
in order not to | wake anyone up. |

so that

We can use *so that* + *can/could* or *will/would* to express purpose.
I left for work early ***so that*** I could avoid rush hour traffic.
We also use *so that* when there is a change in subject.
Henry called a taxi ***so that*** his daughter would arrive on time.

in case

When we want to prevent something that might happen, we can use *in case*.
I called her ***in case*** she thought I was still angry with her.
This is more common than *so that she wouldn't think I was …*

12.4 Contrast

But is the most common way of expressing contrast. *Even though* is more emphatic than *although*. *Though* is more formal than *although*.

| There was a general strike, ***but*** | most people managed to get to work. |
| ***Although*** there was a general strike, | |

Even though there weren't any trains, I was only an hour late.
The trip back home was all right, **though** it wasn't easy.
Though can be used as a comment adverb.
*"That meal was expensive." "It was good, **though**."*
All the same and *even so* express contrast informally, whereas *however* and *nevertheless* are more formal.

I know he's a difficult person. | **All the same,** **Even so,** | *I really like him.*

Our task became more and more demanding. | **However,** **Nevertheless,** | *we persevered.*

In spite of and *despite* can also express contrast.

We enjoyed our picnic | **despite** *the rain.* **in spite of** *the rain.*

Despite being *over eighty, my grandmother enjoyed the party.*

12.5 Time

Linkers
The following linkers are conjunctions of time.
When *I saw the time, I realized I was late.*
As soon as *I got up, I took a shower.*
After *I took a shower, I got dressed.*

As **While** | *I was getting dressed, I thought about the day to come.*

Before *I went to work, I read the mail.*
Once *I'd seen the bills to pay, I left the house.*

I worked **until** *I had finished my project.*

*I've been working on this project **since** I joined the company.*

Participles
As we saw in Unit 11, participles can also express links of time.
Grabbing *my briefcase, I left to catch my train.*
Having bought *a ticket, I went onto the platform.*

12.6 Condition

The following linkers are used to express a condition.
If *you want time off, let me know.*

Providing **Provided** **As long as** **So long as** | *you look after my dog, you can stay in my apartment.*

Even if *I'm there, I don't mind.*
*I'll presume you're coming **unless** I hear from you.*
Whether *you come **or not**, it would be nice to see you soon.*
*I'll go **wherever** you want.*
*Come **whenever** you want.*
*Bring **whoever** you want.*

However *late it is,* **No matter how** *late it is,* | *just call me.*
(no matter who/what/when …)
Supposing *you ever ran out of cash, I could help.*